LIVING
BY THE
BOOK

HOWARD G. HENDRICKS
WILLIAM D. HENDRICKS

MOODY PRESS
CHICAGO

ISBN 0-8024-0743-9

Table of Contents

PREFACE

Teaching others how to study the Bible for themselves is like leading a tour through mountain grandeur. Every feature is virtually indescribable. One can only feel the greatness. Though we climb the hills and breathe the air, we struggle for words to describe the adventure. Yet whereas the awesome magnitude of the biblical terrain belittles our security blanket of pride, its attraction never pales. Exposure to that powerful message never ceases to stir our spirit.

I've been escorting students into those heights for more than four decades. But even I still pant with excitement every time I make the trip, and I still struggle to develop the mental film I've shot into understandable concepts. Fortunately, the probing questions of countless participants in my study groups have helped to crystallize many of the insights I've gained. To them I owe much in helping to make my courses—and this book—more usable.

But how does one translate the pedagogy of the classroom into user-friendly text? Where does one find a literary artist who can reduce my idiom to clear ideas? Who can tailor theological truth for everyday wear? Who can read the pulse of this balding professor from a passing generation? Little did I realize that such a rare talent arrived in my fourth microburst of fatherhood more than thirty-five years ago.

My son Bill was "to the manner born." Not only does he share my gene pool, as one of my former students he has already grabbed my academic hand-off and scored on his own as an writer, editor, and video producer. His communication skills take second place only to his integrity and commitment to the task. My appreciation for his work surges off the graph.

It's with a sense of deep privilege that I share my life's passion on paper—that believers who rest their eternal salvation on Christ will hear and heed His written revelation. The study of the Bible is de rigueur for the Christian. More than a duty, it provides protection for the daily battle, comfort for dashed hopes, and continuing education for a life that is worth living.

HOWARD G. HENDRICKS

Why Study the Bible?

1

WHY PEOPLE DON'T STUDY THE BIBLE

Shortly after I became a Christian, someone wrote in the flyleaf of my Bible these words: "This book will keep you from sin, or sin will keep you from this book." That was true then, and it's still true today. Dusty Bibles always lead to dirty lives. In fact, you are either in the Word and the Word is conforming you to the image of Jesus Christ, or you are in the world and the world is squeezing you into its mold.

And yet the great tragedy among Christians today is that too many of us are under the Word of God, but not in it for ourselves. I met a man once who had driven his entire family all the way across the country to attend a Bible conference.

Amazed, I asked him, "Why did you come so far?"

"Because I wanted to get under the Word of God," he said.

On the face of it, that sounds wonderful. But later it hit me: Here was a man willing to drive twelve hundred miles to get under the Word of God; but was he just as willing to walk across his living room floor, pick up a Bible, and get into it for himself?

You see, there's no question that believers need to sit under the teaching of God's Word. But that ought to be a stimulus—not a substitute—for getting into it for ourselves.

Even though the Bible remains the most sold book in the world, it's also one of the most neglected ones. The Barna Research Group of Glendale, California reports that in a typical week, only 10 percent of Americans read the Bible every day. And even that figure

may be high, states George Barna, president of the research firm. Many people who claimed to read the Bible once a week or more admitted that they had not read it during the week prior to a 1991 nationwide survey.

Gallup polls confirm those findings. One survey found that 82 percent of Americans believe that the Bible is either the literal or "inspired" Word of God. More than half said they read the Bible at least monthly. Yet half couldn't name even one of the four gospels, Matthew, Mark, Luke, and John. And fewer than half knew who delivered the Sermon on the Mount.

How Often Do We Read the Bible?

(NATIONWIDE, In percentages)[1]	1990	1986	1982	1978
Daily or more often	17	11	15	12
Weekly or more often	23	22	18	18
Once a month or more often	13	14	12	11
Less than once a month	25	26	25	28
Rarely or never	20	22	24	24
Can't say	2	5	6	7

BIBLE READING—1986[2]

	Daily	Weekly	Monthly	Less Than Monthly	Never
Nationwide	11	22	14	26	22
Men	8	18	12	30	27
Women	15	25	16	22	17
Whites	11	21	14	26	23
Blacks	17	31	12	21	15
Protestants	18	27	15	23	12
Catholics	4	16	13	32	31
Evangelicals	29	37	15	15	4
Non-evangelicals	4	15	13	31	30

SOURCES: 1. 1990 Gallup Poll of 1,000 adults randomly selected nationally during the period November 1-4, 1990.
2. 1986 Gallup Poll of 1,559 adults, 18 and older, conducted in more than 300 scientifically selected localities across the country during the period of October 24-27, 1986.

Have you ever seen a Bible "parked" in the rear window of someone's car? That's common where I come from. A guy will come out of church, hop into his car, toss his Bible in the back, and leave it there until the next Sunday. That's quite a statement of the value he places on God's Word. In effect, when it comes to Scripture he's functionally illiterate six out of seven days a week.

The Bible is owned, read on occasion, even taken to church—but not studied. Why? Why is it that people do not get into Scripture for themselves, to understand it and see it make a difference in their lives? Let's find out by listening to six Christians describe their experience in this regard.

KEN: "I NEED SOMETHING THAT WORKS."

HGH: Ken, you're an executive with a lot of responsibility. You're well educated. I know you love the Lord. Where does Bible study fit into your life?

Ken: Back when my kids were young, we used to read a verse or two every morning at breakfast, or maybe at dinnertime. But I wouldn't say we ever studied the Bible. And of course it's not the sort of thing you'd do at work.

HGH: Why not?

Ken: Well, work is work. You're there to do a job. At work I think about our payroll, our customers, the bills we've got to pay, what our competitors are doing. The Bible's about the last thing on my mind.

Don't get me wrong. I'm not one of these people who acts one way at church and another way at the office. But let's face it—the business world is no Sunday school class. You're up against things that aren't even mentioned in the Bible. So it doesn't exactly apply to your day-to-day situation.

HGH: Ken, you've put your finger on the problem of relevance. And that may be the number-one reason people are not studying God's Word today. They think it's archaic, out-of-date. It may have had something to say to another generation, but there's a serious question whether it has anything to say to ours. Yet, as we'll see, God's revelation is as alive today as it was when it was first delivered.

WENDY: "I DON'T KNOW HOW."

HGH: Let's move on to Wendy, who is a copywriter for an ad agency. Wendy, you seem to have a lot of energy and initiative. I'd be willing to bet that you'd make an outstanding student of the Bible.

Wendy: Actually, I've tried, but it just didn't work out.

HGH: How so?

Wendy: Well, I went through a phase once where I decided I was really going to study the Bible. I'd heard someone at a seminar say that it's impossible to know God apart from knowing His Word. I knew I wanted to get closer to the Lord, so I made up my mind to really get into Scripture. I bought all these books about the Bible. I came home from work every night and spent about an hour or more reading and trying to understand it.

But I realized that I didn't know Greek or Hebrew. And there were an awful lot of things that people were saying about different passages that made no sense to me. I mean, I'd read what somebody had to say about a text, and then I'd read the text, but I couldn't figure out how they'd come up with it. Finally, it just got so confusing, I quit.

HGH: Oh, so it was a problem of technique. That's common for many people today. They're reluctant to jump in because they know they can't swim. And our culture doesn't help much. With television and computers and so forth, we've become visually oriented, and frankly, we're losing our ability to read. That's why one of the things we're going to do in the next section is recover the skills of how to read something such as the Bible.

ELLIOTT: "I'M JUST A LAYMAN."

HGH: OK, let's hear from Elliott. Elliott's the man you want if you've got a swimming pool on the fritz. He can show you how to keep that water crystal clear. Furthermore, he brings an incredibly strong work ethic to the job, and I think his faith has a lot to do with that. Elliott, something tells me you pay a lot of attention to your Bible.

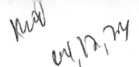

Elliott: Well, let me put it this way—I pay attention to what I understand in the Bible. The Ten Commandments. The Golden Rule. "The Lord is my shepherd." That sort of thing. But the rest of it I pretty much leave up to my pastor. I mean, he understands all that stuff, and if I ever have a problem, I can just go to him. He seems to know what it all means. Me, I just try to live it out the best I can.

HGH: That's encouraging. You're trying to practice the truth you do understand. But Elliott, I hear you saying what thousands of Christian are saying today: "I'm just a layperson." Or, "I'm just a housewife. I'm not a professional. You can't expect me, an individual who has no theological training, who maybe never even finished college, to study a book like this."

That's the way I felt when I started out as a new believer. Somebody said to me, "Howie, you need to spend time in the Word."

I thought, *How in the world do I go about doing that? I've never been to seminary. I'm not a minister. I can't understand this stuff.*

But as we're going to see, you really don't need professional training to understand the Bible. You don't have to know Greek and Hebrew. As long as you can read, you can dig into the Scriptures for yourself. In this book, I want to help you learn how.

And by the way, don't be put off by the word *study*. I wish we had a better term than "Bible *study*," because for most of us, "study" is a bad news item. It has all the appeal of flossing our teeth. We know we're supposed to, but.... Actually, we're going to discover that Bible study can be fascinating beyond words, and even fun. So hold on.

LINDA: "I JUST DON'T HAVE TIME."

HGH: I mentioned homemakers, and I guess that describes you, Linda. You're at home full-time with three small children. How do you feel about Bible study?

Linda: Oh, I'd love to study the Bible. I really would. Like you say, I've got three little ones to keep up with, and sometimes I'd do anything to get a break. My husband works day and night so that I can stay home. But that means I've got the kids all day long, and I'm lucky to get even twenty minutes to myself. You can't study the Bible in twenty minutes. Even if I could, I'm usually just trying to catch my breath. I wouldn't have the energy.

HGH: I understand exactly what you're saying. My wife, Jeanne, and I reared four ourselves. Parenting was an extremely demanding job. For us it was a priority. I guess that's really the issue you're raising—where does Bible study fit on my list of priorities? Unfortunately, for many of us it's number twenty on a list of twenty-seven things. It's nice but certainly not necessary. Hang onto that, because in the next chapter we're going to discover that the study of the Word is not an option—it's an essential.

TONI: "I HAVE MY DOUBTS ABOUT THE BIBLE."

HGH: Toni, I'm eager to hear your comments. You're a student on a university campus. Is there still a place for studying Scripture in that setting?

Toni: Yeah, I suppose people ought to read the Bible. There are some very inspiring passages in it. I don't know about some of the miracles and predictions and stuff. I mean, Jonah and the whale—that sort of thing is really hard to believe. And I know people quote Scripture to say whether something is right or wrong. But it seems like you can make the Bible say just about anything you want it to say.

So I think you should read it once in a while, just to kind of know what's in there, or maybe to help you feel better if you're down. But study it? Gee, I don't know about that.

HGH: All right, you raise some legitimate concerns. Is this Book reliable? Is it authoritative? Can we base our lives on it? Does it have credibility? Or, when we read it, do we have to throw our intelligence out the window and, as one person put it, strain to believe what we know, deep down, is utterly preposterous? We're going to discover that it is completely reliable, and that the more we study it, the more consistent and reasonable it turns out to be.

GEORGE: "I CAN'T SEEM TO MAKE IT INTERESTING."

HGH: Let's take one final comment. George, your interest in the Word has a lot to do with the fact that you teach an adult Sunday school class at your church.

George: Yes, I guess I have more reason than most people to study the Bible. When I read through a passage, I'm always thinking about my class and how I'm going to teach it to them. But I'll be honest—it's hard to get people interested in the Bible. It seems like they'd rather talk about sports or what's going on at work than the great doctrines of the faith.

I don't expect anybody to become a great theologian. But 2 Timothy 3:16 says that the Bible is profitable for doctrine, and it seems to me that a lot of the problems people complain about could be remedied if they paid a little more attention to what the Bible has to say.

HGH: I think you're discovering what anyone who wants to communicate spiritual truth runs into: It's very difficult to get people excited about one's own insights into the Word. Unless they're making their own discoveries on topics that relate directly to their experience, Bible study will just bore them to tears. They won't feel motivated to invest time in it. So that's really your challenge as a teacher—to offer them a process by which they can uncover spiritual truths for themselves. And I hope you'll learn some ways to do that through this book.

By the way, one way not to do it is through guilt. Guilt is a poor motivator. It's very powerful, but it's also poisonous to the learning process. It kills the joy that ought to mark firsthand acquaintance with the Word. Guilt drives more people away from the Scriptures than into them.

HOW ABOUT YOU?

Well, we've seen a number of reasons that people do not study the Bible. Which one(s) applies to you? Do you question the Bible's relevance to real-life issues? Are you locked out of the process by a lack of technique and basic skills? Are you convinced that this Book is just for professionals, not laypeople, that it takes special training to understand it? Is Bible study a low priority (or no priority), especially with so many other demands begging for your time? Do you have doubt about the Bible's reliability, and whether you can ever really determine its meaning? Do you perceive Bible study as dreadfully boring and not worth your attention?

If you identify with any of those reasons, then this book is for you. I'm going to address all of those obstacles and more. Every one of them can be overcome.

But first, having looked at the negative—why people don't study the Bible—let's turn around and ask, Why must we study the Bible? In the next chapter, I'll give you three important reasons Bible study is not an option—it's an essential.

How About You?

The great tragedy among Christians today is that too many of us are under the Word of God, but not in it for ourselves.

What about you? Do you regularly read and study the Bible on your own? Or are you part of the majority of people who rarely if ever open the Bible for themselves? Here's a simple exercise to help you evaluate your Bible reading habits.

How often do you read the Bible? (Circle one)

NEVER	ONCE A MONTH	ONCE A WEEK	TWO OR THREE TIMES A WEEK	EVERY DAY

When you read it, how much time do you spend reading?

5 MIN. OR LESS	15 MIN.	30 MIN.	45 MIN.	1 HR. OR MORE

Here are a few reasons that people give for not reading the Bible. Check the ones that express why you don't read the Bible more than you do.

____ The Bible doesn't seem relevant to my life.

____ The Bible seems confusing and hard to understand. I don't know how to make sense out of it.

____ I used to read the Bible, and it made me feel good. But after a while, it didn't seem to have the same impact, so finally I gave it up.

____ I feel guilty when I read the Bible.

____ The Bible is hopelessly out-of-date. It may have some interesting stories, but it has little significance for life today.

____ I rely on my pastor or minister to explain the Bible to me. If I need to know something, he will tell me about it.

____ I have doubts about the Bible's reliability.

____ I don't have time. I'm just too busy.

____ The Bible seems boring to me.

____ I don't own a Bible.

____ The Bible is full of myths and half-truths. Why study something that lacks credibility?

____ I don't read, period! It's not just the Bible; I don't read anything.

2

WHY STUDY THE BIBLE?

In the last chapter we saw six common reasons that people do not dive into Scripture for themselves. Let me add a seventh: Nobody ever told them what they'd gain by it. What are the benefits of Bible study? What's in it for me? If I invest my time in this manner, what's the payoff? What difference will it make in my life?

I want to suggest three benefits you can expect when you invest in a study of God's Word, which are available nowhere else. And frankly, they're not luxuries, but necessities. Let's look at three passages that conspire to build a convincing case for why we must study the Bible. It's not an option—it's an essential.

BIBLE STUDY IS ESSENTIAL TO GROWTH

The first passage is found in 1 Peter 2:2:

As newborn babes, long for the pure milk of the word, that by it you may grow in respect to salvation.

Let me give you three words to unpack the truth contained here. Write them in the margin of your Bible, next to this verse. The first one is attitude. Peter is describing the attitude of a newborn baby. Just as the baby grabs for the bottle, so you grab for the Book. The baby has to have milk to sustain its life physically; you have to have the Scriptures to sustain your life spiritually.

I had four children, and I learned early that about every three or four hours a timer goes off inside an infant—and you'd better not ignore it. You'd better get a bottle of milk there fast. As soon as you do, there's a great calm. Peter picks up that expressive figure and says that's to be your attitude toward Scripture.

But he also says a word about your appetite for the Word. You should "long" for it. You're to crave the spiritual milk of God's Word.

Now to be honest, that's a cultivated taste. Every now and then somebody will say to me, "You know, Professor Hendricks, I'm really not getting very much out of the Bible." But that's a greater commentary on the person than it is on the Book.

Psalm 19:10 says that Scripture is sweeter than honey, but you'd never know that judging by some believers. You see, there are three basic kinds of Bible students. There are the "castor oil" types. To them the Word is bitter—*Yech!*—but it's good for what ails them. Then there is the "shredded wheat" kind. To them Scripture is nourishing but dry. It's like eating a bail of hay.

But the third kind is what I call the "strawberries-and-cream" folks. They just can't get enough of the stuff. How did they acquire that taste? By feasting on the Word. They've cultivated what Peter describes here—an insatiable appetite for spiritual truth. Which of these three types are you?

There's a purpose to all of this, which brings us to the third word, aim. What is the aim of the Bible? The text tells us: in order that you might grow. Please note, it is not that you may know. Certainly you can't grow without knowing. But you can know and not grow. The Bible was written not to satisfy your curiosity but to help you conform to Christ's image. Not to make you a smarter sinner but to make you like the Savior. Not to fill your head with a collection of biblical facts but to transform your life.

When our kids were small, we set up a growth chart on the back of a closet door. As they grew, they begged us to measure how tall they had gotten and record it on the chart. It didn't matter how small the increments were; they bounced up and down with excitement to see their progress. One time after I measured my daughter, she asked me the sort of question you wish kids wouldn't ask: "Daddy, why do big people stop growing?"

How could I explain that big people don't stop growing—we just grow in a different direction? I don't know what I told her, but to this day the Lord is still asking me, "Hendricks, are you growing old, or are you growing up?"

How about you? How many years have you been a Christian? Nine months? Seven or eight years? Thirty-nine years? The real issue is, how much have you grown? Step up to God's growth chart, and measure your progress. That's what this passage is teaching.

So the first reason for studying Scripture is that it is a means of spiritual growth. There is none apart from the Word. It is God's primary tool to develop you as an individual.

BIBLE STUDY IS ESSENTIAL TO SPIRITUAL MATURITY

The second passage we need to look at is Hebrews 5:11-14:

> Concerning [Christ] we have much to say, and it is hard to explain, since you have become dull of hearing. For though by this time you ought to be teachers, you have need again for some one to teach you the elementary principles of the oracles of God, and you have come to need milk and not solid food. For every one who partakes only of milk is not accustomed to the word of righteousness, for he is a babe. But solid food is for the mature, who because of practice have their senses trained to discern good and evil.

This is an instructive passage in terms of studying Scripture. The writer says he's got a lot to say, but it's "hard to explain." Why? Is it the difficulty of the revelation? No, it's the density of the reception. There's a learning disability: "You have become dull of hearing," meaning "you are slow to learn."

The key word in this passage is *time*. Underline it in your Bible. The writer tells his readers, when by virtue of the passing of time you ought to go on to the college department, you've got to go back to kindergarten and learn your ABCs all over again. When you should be communicating the truth to others, you need to have someone communicate the truth to you.

In fact, he says, you still need milk, not solid food. Solid food is for the mature. Who are the mature? Are they the people who go to seminary? Who can whip anyone in a theological duel? Who know the most Bible verses?

No, the writer says you are mature if you've trained yourself through constant use of Scripture to distinguish good from evil. The mark of spiritual maturity is not how much you understand, but how much you use. In the spiritual realm, the opposite of ignorance is not knowledge but obedience.

So that is a second reason Bible study is essential. The Bible is the divine means of developing spiritual maturity. There is no other way.

BIBLE STUDY IS ESSENTIAL TO SPIRITUAL EFFECTIVENESS

There's a third passage, 2 Timothy 3:16-17. George alluded to in chapter 1:

> All Scripture is inspired by God and profitable for teaching, for reproof, for correction, for training in righteousness; that the man of God may be adequate, equipped for every good work.

"*All* Scripture." That includes 2 Chronicles. I said that once to an audience, and a guy said, "I didn't even know there was a first one."

How about Deuteronomy? Can you even find it? Have you ever had your devotions in it? When Jesus was tempted in the wilderness (Matthew 4:1-11), He defeated the devil three times by saying, "It is written." All three are quotations from the book of Deuteronomy. I've often thought, *If my spiritual life depended on my knowledge of Deuteronomy, how would I make out?*

Paul says all Scripture is profitable. But profitable for what? He mentions four things. First, for doctrine, or teaching. That is, it will structure your thinking. That's crucial, because if you are not thinking correctly, you are not living correctly. What you believe will determine how you behave.

He also says the Bible is profitable for rebuke. That is, it will tell you where you are out-of-bounds. It's like an umpire who cries, "Out!" or, "Safe!" It tells you what is sin. It tells you what God wants for your life. He provides your standards.

Third, it is profitable for correction. Do you have a closet where you put all the junk you can't find room for anywhere else? You cram it in, and then one day you forget and open the door and— *Whoosh!*—it all comes out. "Good night," you say, "I'd better clean this thing up." The Bible is like that. It opens up the doors in your life and provides a purifying dynamic to help you clean out sin and learn to conform to God's will.

A fourth advantage of the Bible is that it is profitable for training in righteous living. God uses it to show you how to live. Having corrected you on the negatives, He gives you positive guidelines to follow in life.

What is the overall purpose? In order that you might be equipped for every good work. Have you ever said, "I wish my life were more effective for Jesus Christ"? If so, what have you done to prepare yourself? Bible study is a primary means to becoming an effective servant of Jesus Christ.

One time I asked a group of businessmen, "If you didn't know any more about your business or profession than you know about Christianity after the same number of years of exposure, what would happen?"

One guy blurted out, "They'd ship me."

He was right, you know. The reason God can't use you more than He wants to may well be that you are not prepared. Maybe you've attended church for five, ten, or even twenty years, but you've never cracked open the Bible to prepare yourself for effectiveness as His instrument. You've been under the Word but not in it for yourself.

Now the ball is in your court. God wants to communicate with you in the twentieth century. He wrote His message in a Book. He asks you to come and study that Book for three compelling reasons: It's essential to growth. It's essential to maturity. It's essential for equipping you, training you, so that you might be an available, clean, sharp instrument in His hands to accomplish His purposes.

So the question facing you now is: How can you afford to stay out of it?

Can We Trust the Bible?

After captivating an audience at Yale University, the late novelist Ayn Rand was asked by a reporter, "What's wrong with the modern world?"

Without a moment's hesitation she replied, "Never before has the world been so desperately asking for answers to crucial questions, and never before has the world been so frantically committed to the idea that no answers are possible. To paraphrase the Bible, the modern attitude is, 'Father, forgive us, for we know not what we are doing—*and please don't tell us!*'"

That's very perceptive for an acknowledged agnostic. Many of us want a word from God, but we don't want *the* Word of God. We know enough to own a Bible but not enough for the Bible to own us. We pay the Bible lip service, but we fail to give it "life service." In a world where the only absolute is that there are no absolutes, there is little room left for the authoritative Word of God as revealed in the Bible.

The question is, can we trust the Bible? Is it credible? Is it reliable? Is it determinative for life in our time? Consider what Scripture says about itself.

THE BIBLE IS A UNIT

If you've ever studied some complex or controversial subject in depth, you know the frustration of trying to find two or three authorities who agree on any and all points. It basically never happens.

The Bible stands in marked contrast. It is unique in that its parts conspire to form a unified whole. You see, the Bible is not only one Book, it is sixty-six books collected in one volume. These sixty-six separate documents were written over a period of more than sixteen hundred years by more than forty human authors who came from a wide variety of backgrounds.

Yet the Bible is a single unit, bound together by the theme of God and His relationship to humankind. Each book, section, paragraph, and verse works together with the others to reveal God's truth. That's why Scripture is best understood by relating its individual parts to the integrated whole.

THE BIBLE IS GOD'S REVELATION

The Bible presents itself as revealed truth from God. The word it uses for "revelation" actually means "unveiling," like pulling back a curtain to show what is behind it. In Scripture, God has revealed things that would otherwise not be known at all. He has unveiled that which is absolutely true—not speculated, not conjectured, not hypothesized. It is truth that is entirely consistent—never controverted, compromised, or contradicted by other parts of the revelation.

THE BIBLE IS INSPIRED BY GOD

The great theologian B. B. Warfield said, "The Bible is the Word of God in such a way that when the Bible speaks, God speaks." That's a good description of inspiration. The reason we call the Bible the Word of God is because it is indeed the very words that God wanted communicated.

Of course, some have a problem with this concept because the Bible was penned by human authors. If they were "inspired" it was only as great artists are "inspired" to produce great art.

But that's not what the Bible means by inspiration. Remember 2 Timothy 3:16-17? "All Scripture is inspired by God." The word translated "inspired" means "God-breathed." It conveys the idea of God "breathing out" the Scriptures. And since the word for "breath" can also be translated "spirit," we can easily see the work of the Holy Spirit as He superintended the writing.

So what part did the human authors play? God supernaturally used them to pen the words, without compromising the perfection, integrity, or purity of the finished product. It's a case of dual authorship. As Charles Ryrie puts it, "God superintended the human authors so that, using their own individual personalities, they composed and recorded, without error, His revelation to man in the words of the original manuscripts."

Peter used a brilliant word picture to describe this arrangement when he wrote that "men moved by the Holy Spirit spoke from God" (2 Peter 1:21). The word *moved* is the same word used to describe a ship moving along under the power of a blowing wind. The biblical writers were guided in their writing to go where God wanted them to go and to produce what God wanted them to produce. Without question, their personalities, writing styles, perspectives, and distinctives are reflected in their words. But their accounts are more than the words of men— they are the Word of God.

Have you heard of the Jesus Project? Certain scholars doubt the reliability of the words of Jesus recorded in the four gospels. So they meet annually to discuss those texts. For each statement ascribed to Christ, they vote on the relative merits of whether Jesus actually said the words or whether the New Testament writers put them in His mouth.

The vote can go one of four ways: The group may decide that Jesus' words are "red," indicating that He definitely spoke them. On the other hand, the scholars may label them "black" if they believe that He definitely did not say them. In the middle are "pink" (Jesus probably spoke them, though there is some question), and "gray" (Jesus probably did not speak them, though it is possible that He might have).

What is the purpose of this exercise? A spokesperson says the group wants to strengthen people's faith by letting them know what is reliable and what is not.

I don't know how such a project strikes you, but it seems ludicrous to me—to say nothing of dangerous. How is it that a committee of doubters living two thousand years after the fact feels qualified to pass judgment on the authority of Scripture? I guess they hold to "inspiration by consensus."

I prefer inspiration by the Holy Spirit. The text of the Bible is not the musings of men but a supernatural product, the very Word of God.

THE BIBLE IS INERRANT

In order to be authoritative, the Bible must be true, that is, without error. As someone has noted, "Either the Bible is without error in all, or it is not without error at all." There's really no middle ground. A "partially inerrant" Bible is an errant Bible.

"Inerrancy" means without error—containing no mistakes or errors in the original writings, and having no errors in any area whatsoever. That's is a tough concept for our generation. We tend to be relativists, for whom nothing can be true in an absolute sense. Furthermore, our culture would have us believe that modern science has left the Bible far behind.

The reality is that Scripture has withstood the test of pure science. Indeed, many of the most eminent, learned scientists of our day are taking a "third" look at Scripture in light of recent developments and discoveries.

Believing in an error-free Bible does not mean that we take every statement in a wooden, rigidly literal way. As we're going to see, Scripture often speaks in figurative language. Furthermore, we accept that there have been errors in transmission of the Bible from copy to copy, over the years (though surprisingly few).

Nevertheless, the Bible bears witness to its own inerrancy. The most powerful witness is the Lord Jesus Himself. In Matthew 4:1-11, He emphasizes that the actual written words of Scripture can be trusted, not just the ideas they contain. In Matthew 5:17-18, He extends the absolute reliability of the text all the way to individual letters, and even the parts of letters.

Throughout the gospels, Jesus referred to portions of Scripture questioned by some "authorities" today. There's no hint that He regarded them as anything other than accurate, reliable, and true. (In Matthew alone, see 8:4; 10:15; 12:17, 40; 19:3-5; and 24:38-39.)

Inerrancy means that we have a Bible that is completely trustworthy, reliable, and without error in its original form. As we study it, we can eagerly anticipate answers to the questions that are essential.

3

HOW THIS BOOK
CAN HELP

B y now, I hope you are sold on the necessity as well as the value of getting into the Bible on a firsthand basis. I've been a believer for five decades, and I can assure you, reading God's Word has made all the difference in my Christian experience.

It will do the same for you. It will revolutionize your life. As we saw in the last chapter, it's the key to spiritual growth, maturity, and effectiveness.

But please note: effective Bible study requires a method. You don't teach a kid to swim by tossing him into the deep end of a pool and saying, "OK, swim."

No, you start out slowly, showing him how to float, how to hold his head under water, how to kick his feet, and how to dog paddle. You give him direction and a process so that he gradually develops the skills required.

The same is true for learning to study the Bible. So in this and the next chapter, I want to introduce a method for approaching the Word of God.

By "method" I mean a strategy, a plan of attack, that will yield maximum results for your investment of time and effort. Lacking a method, you can get very frustrated very quickly, as Wendy found out in chapter 1. You can also go off the deep end in terms of interpretation and application. That was Toni's complaint, you'll recall.

WHAT YOU CAN EXPECT FROM THIS BOOK

This book presents such a method. And I want to tell you up front what the costs and benefits are of using this method. First, let me give you the benefits. Based on more than forty years of teaching this material, I have found at least four major advantages to this approach.

1. You'll find a simple, proved process.

As we saw in chapter 1, one main reason people give for not getting into the Bible is that they think it's too hard. "I'm not trained," they say. "I don't know Greek and Hebrew. I'm just a layperson. I'm not smart enough." All kinds of excuses. Yet the truth of the matter is, they're making Bible study harder than it really needs to be.

The process presented in this book is one that anyone can use, no matter what your level of spiritual maturity or education. It doesn't matter whether you've been in the faith five weeks or five decades— the principles remain the same. As long as you can read, you can study the Bible. I'm not saying you won't have an advantage if you know something about the original languages. But with all of the resources available to us today, you are not seriously *dis*advantaged without them.

Another plus for this process is that it can expand as the ability of the student expands. In other words, as you grow in your knowledge and insight into the Word, this method will keep pace with you. You'll never outgrow it. I'm still using it after all these years. Sure, I've added expertise here and there, and I do many things much better now than when I started. But the basic approach remains the same. It's like a set of tools that increase in their usefulness as the skill of the craftsman increases.

2. You'll gain a valuable sense of self-confidence in your ability to handle Scripture.

There's nothing like the self-assurance that comes from firsthand knowledge of the Bible. It gives you confidence to think for yourself. Most people don't think—they merely rearrange their prejudices. But it's altogether different when you know what the Bible says, where it says it, and what it means. That kind of personal ownership of spiritual truth cuts you free from the leash of popular opinion.

Furthermore, firsthand Bible study enables you to evaluate the thoughts of others. Suppose I run into a problem in a particular passage. So I go to a commentary to find out what it's all about. I read commentary A and come up with an answer. How exciting! But then I decide to compare it with commentary B, only to discover that B is diametrically opposed to A. What in the world do I do? I was confused before; now I'm more confused. Do I take A or B? So I decide to read another one. Then I'm really in trouble. The third one agrees with A in some respects but not in others, and it totally disagrees with B. What do I do? Just flip a coin and make a decision?

Well, it's amazing how much light the Scriptures throw on the commentaries. If I've got a method that helps me work with the biblical text and understand what the text says, then when I go to a commentary I have a basis for evaluating what is being said.

3. You'll experience the joy of personal discovery.

I can assure you, there is no joy comparable to that which comes from firsthand study of Scripture. To discover for yourself what God has revealed there will send you out of your gourd with excitement! Yet most people are not excited by the truth—they're embalmed by it.

I used to teach a class for professional men and women. There was a doctor in that class whom I'll never forget. He'd come up afterward, Bible in hand, and say, "Hendricks, let me show you what I found in this passage." He was beside himself with enthusiasm.

You know what he was saying? "I'll bet John Calvin never saw this. I'll bet Martin Luther never heard of this." And, although he never said it, "Hendricks, I'll bet you haven't seen it either."

I met his wife in the parking lot at church one day, and she said, "What in the world are you doing to my husband?"

"Why, what's the problem?" I asked.

"I've got to set the alarm clock to tell this guy what time to go to bed at night. He won't quit reading his Bible."

Now there's a new wrinkle! But it was a result of that man's making his own discoveries in the Word. I hope you'll catch that disease as you get into the process spelled out in this book.

4. You will deepen your relationship with God.

The ultimate benefit of firsthand Bible study is that you will fall in love with the Author. You see, it's hard to fall in love by proxy. Sermons, books, commentaries, and so on—those can be wonderful resources to spiritual growth. But they are all secondhand. If you want to know God directly, you need to encounter His Word directly.

The Bible — 66 Books

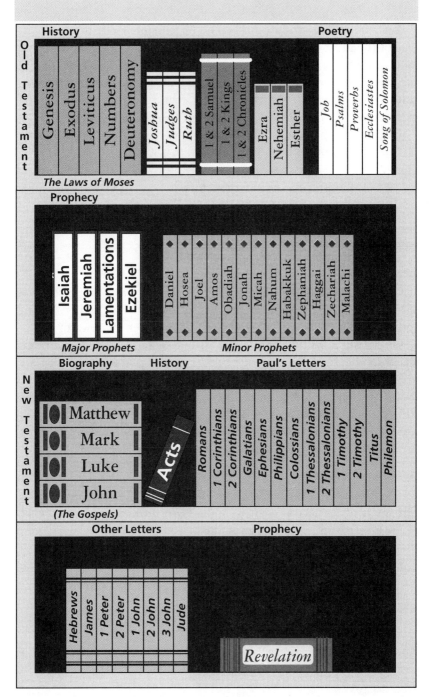

Yet even Bible study can become an end in itself, if you let it. One of the great problems believers have today is that often we know more about the Scriptures than we know about the God of the Scriptures. But my Bible tells me: "Eye hath not seen, nor ear heard, neither have entered into the heart of man, the things which God hath prepared for them that love him" (1 Corinthians 2:9, KJV[*]).

God has prepared incredible things for you. The Scriptures are His appointed means for bringing them to you.

COSTS

But there are costs involved. The riches of God are free, but they are not cheap. Bible study places several expectations on you. Let me mention three.

Effort

Scripture does not yield its fruit to the lazy. Like any other discipline of life, Bible study pays in proportion to how much of an investment you make. The greater the investment, the greater the reward.

Obviously it will take time, the issue that Linda, the homemaker, raised in chapter 1. But if your Bible study is productive, if you are making exciting discoveries that you never knew existed, if the process is making a real difference in your life—you will likely find time for it. Otherwise, you'll always find something else to do. I want this book to help you get started in a productive effort so that time becomes a price you willingly pay in light of the benefits.

Openness to God

As I said earlier, the ultimate aim of Bible study is to know God. The question is, do you want to know Him intimately? Is that what you're after? If so, He promises to honor your diligence in the Word.

> Blessed is the man who listens to me,
>   watching daily at my doors,
>   waiting at my doorway.
> For whoever finds me finds life
>   and receives favor from the Lord.
>
> (Proverbs 8:34-35, NIV[**])

[*]King James Version.
[**]*New International Version.*

Everyone wants the blessings and the life promised here. But are we willing to "watch daily" at the doors of Scripture?

Openness to change

The Bible was written not to be studied but to change our lives. Life-change is the product we are after. The human heart resists nothing more than change, but spiritual growth is a commitment to change.

Romans 8:29, for example, says that God intends to conform you to the image of Jesus Christ—in other words, to make you like Christ. If that's true, how much change do you think you can expect? Are you open to that? Are you willing to allow God to invade your character and conduct with His truth?

Getting Started

We're about to launch into the process. In the next chapter I'm going to give an overview of what method in Bible study is all about. But before we get there, let me make two suggestions.

First, set some goals. What do you want out of this process? What needs in your life must be addressed? Are there relationships that need to be healed, cultivated, or altered? Are there attitudes that need to be changed or reinforced? Are there habits that you need to break or establish? Questions such as these can help you set goals to guide you in your Bible study.

Second, adjust your expectations. Be realistic. You may be a tiger, quivering with anticipation. You can't wait to get started. That's fantastic! But remember, you're not going to master the process overnight. It takes time. On the other hand, you may feel like a tortoise: you'll never get there; it's just too hard. In that case, take heart. The issue in Bible study is not speed, but direction. What matters is not how far you get but whether you keep at it and keep making progress. Diligence is the key.

Are you ready to get started? Then turn with me to the next chapter, and let's begin by getting the big picture of what firsthand Bible study is all about.

How to Select a Bible

The most important tool you need to get into God's Word for yourself is a study Bible. If you don't have one, get one. It will be well worth the investment. Use it to start applying the principles covered in this book.

There are many excellent Bibles around. Some are even called "study Bibles," such as the *Ryrie Study Bible*. When I started out as a Christian, someone gave me a *Scofield Reference Bible*—the one, in fact, with the little statement on the flyleaf that I mentioned in the first chapter: "This book will keep you from sin, or sin will keep you from this book."

However, when I talk about a study Bible, I'm thinking of a Bible that has these ideal characteristics:

Large print
Convenience is the byword of our culture. For Bibles that means small print since small print produces small Bibles that are easier to carry. But small print can be nearly impossible to study. It not only strains the eye, but it makes it difficult to write in and around the text. Choose an edition with print large enough to read and mark easily.

Wide margins
If you can find one with them. That way you'll have plenty of room to record your observations and insights.

No notes
When you're studying the Word, you want to come to the text unbiased, without any extraneous comments competing for your attention. Ideally you want the biblical text and only the biblical text.

No subheadings
This is minor, but an ideal study Bible would have chapter and verse indications but no editorialized headings for paragraphs and sections such as "The Lord's Prayer" and "The Great Commission." Such headings can be useful to locate material in the text, but they tend to bias the reader.

Cross-references
They can be helpful for comparing Scripture with Scripture.

Paper quality and binding
If you study Scripture the way I suggest in this book, you're going to give your Bible a real workout. You'll be flipping from passage to passage, writing in the margins, using the maps in the back, and moving back and forth between the Bible and secondary sources. So you

need an edition that will stand up to serious use. That means high-quality paper and a binding that won't let go of the cover. Ask someone at a bookstore who knows about book manufacturing to explain what sort of workmanship has gone into the Bible you are considering.

A concordance in the back

A concordance is a list of the words in the text, with references for where to find them. I'm going to talk more about concordances in chapters 34 and 35. A brief concordance in the back of your Bible can be quite handy.

Maps

For serious Bible study, you need an atlas, which I'll also describe later. But a few maps in the back of your study Bible can be helpful for quick reference. It's always crucial to consider the place where the events in Scripture take place.

Make sure you get a complete Bible, one with both Old and New Testaments. If you use just a New Testament, you won't be able to go back and look at the Old Testament passages that shed light on the New. You'll also be tempted to become a "one-testament" Christian. Remember, both testaments are the Word of God. Both are inspired. All sixty-six books are profitable (2 Timothy 3:16). In Hebrews 4:12, the writer calls Scripture a two-edged sword. But some people try to work with a little pocket testament, which sort of reduces the sword of the Spirit to a penknife.

Of course you probably will want to work from English translations, unless you happen to know Greek or Hebrew. There are dozens available. They all have strengths and weaknesses and serve different purposes. For a good portion of my life, I've used the *New American Standard Bible* (NASB). It is one of the most accurate, though a bit wooden at times. But it is very helpful.

Some other contemporary translations are the *New International Version* (NIV), the *New King James* (NKJV), and the *New Revised Standard Version* (NRSV). Those are actual translations, as opposed to paraphrases such as the Good News Bible or Phillips's *New Testament in Modern English*. Whatever translation you choose, make sure you get a good study Bible, as described above.

And finally, don't hesitate to write in it. People say to me, "I don't want to mess it up." Well, I say mess it up, if that's what you call it. Write all over the thing. You ought to be going through a Bible every two or three years, if you are diligent in your study. Then you can get another one. It's wonderful to be able to look back at old Bibles and see the progress you've made in your spiritual life.

4

AN OVERVIEW OF
THE PROCESS

J eanne and I were vacationing on the West Coast several years
ago with our son Bill. We had a friend there who owned a
plane, and one day he asked if we wanted to fly with him to
Santa Catalina Island. We accepted, and the next morning we
were zooming down a runway, heading up into the skies over Orange
County.

After we leveled off over the Pacific, our friend turned to Bill,
who was riding copilot, and shouted over the whine of the engine,
"How'd you like to try your hand at flying?"

Always one for adventure, he replied, "Sure." Bill had never flown
a plane in his life—but what difference did that make?

Our friend gave him some brief instruction in the art of flying—
sort of a "crash course," you might say. Then he handed over the
controls, and Bill was in command. Things went along uneventfully
as long as we flew straight ahead. But after a couple of minutes the
pilot shouted, "Why don't you try a turn."

Bill banked to the left, and suddenly I felt a bit dizzy. A moment
later our friend said, "OK, try the other way," and the plane banked
to the right. Now Jeanne and I both felt dizzy. We were quite
relieved to see the pilot eventually rest his hand on the controls and
level us off before taking over again.

"Not bad," he shouted to Bill, who was smiling like a Top Gun.
"We only dropped about a thousand feet."

Obviously learning to fly takes a lot more than just handing the controls to someone and shouting, "Have fun." It requires skills that take years to develop fully. Apart from gaining that experience, you're taking your life in your hands.

The study of God's Word is no different. Learning to do it properly is a process that can't happen overnight. Yet that's exactly what we do with new believers when we tell them to get into the Scriptures, hand them a Bible, and expect them to take it from there. No wonder so many believers give up in frustration.

In this chapter I want to give an overview of the Bible study process. First, I want to define what method in Bible study involves. Then I'm going to show the big picture of where the process leads and where you'll end up by following it.

THERE'S METHOD TO THE MADNESS

Let's begin with a definition. I define method in Bible study with three statements. First of all, *Method is "methodicalness."* That is, it involves taking certain steps in a certain order to guarantee a certain result. Not just any steps; not just any order; not just any result.

The result governs everything. What is the product of methodical Bible study? What are you after? All along I've been saying that personal Bible study has a very specific aim—namely, life-change.

So, then, how will you get there? What process will lead to that result? I propose a three-step approach that will guarantee life-change—three crucial steps carried out in a particular order.

1. Observation

In this step, you ask and answer the question, *What do I see?* The moment you come to the Scriptures you ask, What are the facts? You assume the role of a biblical detective, looking for clues. No detail is trivial. That leads to the second step.

2. Interpretation

Here you ask and answer the question, *What does it mean?* Your quest is for meaning. Unfortunately, too much Bible study begins with interpretation, and furthermore, it usually ends there. But I'm going to show you that it does not begin there. Before you understand, you have to learn to see. Nor does it end there, because the third step is…

3. Application

Here you ask and answer the question, *How does it work?* not, Does it work? People say they're going to make the Bible "relevant."

But if the Bible is not already relevant, nothing you or I do will help. The Bible is relevant because it is revealed. It's always a return to reality. And for those who read it and heed it, it changes their lives.

IT TAKES FIRSTHAND KNOWLEDGE

So method is methodicalness. But let me add a second statement to the definition: *Method is methodicalness, with a view to becoming receptive and reproductive.*

Do you want to make an impact on your society? First the Scripture has to make an impact on you. It's the analogy of the sperm and the egg. Neither the male sperm nor the female egg is capable of reproduction. Only when the sperm impacts and is embraced by the egg is there conception and reproduction.

So it is in the spiritual realm. When God's Word and a receptive, obedient individual get together, watch out. That's a combination that can transform society. And that's what personal Bible study is designed to do—to transform your life, and as a result, transform your world.

A third statement completes our definition: *Method is methodicalness, with a view to becoming receptive and reproductive, by means of firsthand acquaintance with the Word.*

Once again, there's nothing to beat prolonged personal exposure to the Bible. It's vital. Without it, you'll never be directly involved with what God has to say. You'll always have to depend on an intermediary. Imagine dealing with your spouse on that basis. How long do you think your marriage would last? The same is true with God. There is no substitute for firsthand exposure to His Word.

BEGIN WITH OBSERVATION

Now that you know where you are going, take a closer look at how you are going to get there, at the process itself. Recall that the first step is Observation. That's where you ask and answer the question, What do I see? You need to look for four things.

1. Terms

A term is more than just a word. It's a key word that is crucial to what an author has to say. For instance, in the gospel by John, the word *believe* appears no less than seventy-nine times, always as a verb

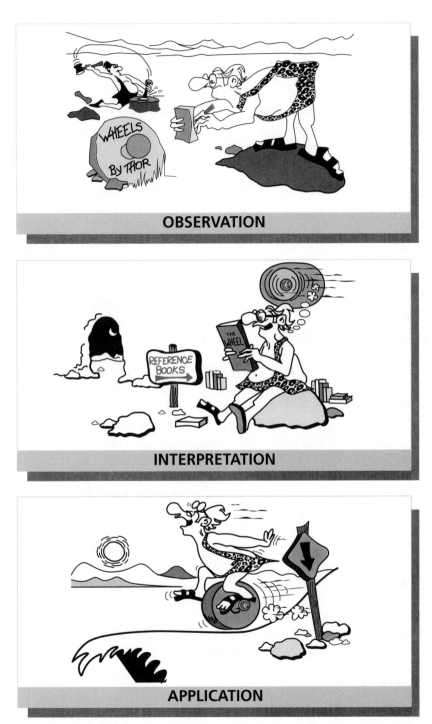

B.C. characters used by permission of Johnny Hart and Creators Syndicate Inc., with apologies to Johnny Hart.

and never as a noun. Do some investigation, and you'll discover that John uses *believe* very purposefully. It's a term that unlocks his meaning. In fact, the book would be altogether different without it.

The same principle applies to every book in the Bible. They are all filled with terms. You've got to learn to recognize them and pay close attention to them because they are the basic building blocks with which you construct meaning.

2. Structure

Contrary to popular opinion, the Bible is not a collection of random sayings and stories that somehow fell together, willy-nilly. Rather, it's a library of carefully constructed books that display—to those who look for it—two basic kinds of structure.

First, there is grammatical structure. I can almost hear the groans: "Do we have to get back into that? I gave that up in seventh grade." But if you want to learn how to study Scripture effectively, you must learn to read it with the grammar in mind. What is the subject of the sentence? What is the object? What is the main verb? The more you know about grammar, the more you can get out of a passage.

There is also literary structure. There are questions and answers. There is a climax and resolution. There is cause and effect. I'll show you a variety ways that the authors have structured their works.

3. Literary form

It's amazing to me how people ignore genre when they come to the books of the Bible. They treat them all the same.

Yet there's a vast difference between the Hebrew poetry of the Psalms and the tightly argued epistles of Paul; between the grand, sweeping narrative of Genesis and Exodus, and the simple, poignant stories of the parables. There is allegory and love poetry, satire and apocalyptic, comedy and tragedy, and much more. The Holy Spirit used each of these forms to communicate His message. So if you want to grasp that message, you must read each kind according to its proper "rules." I'll show you how to do that in later chapters.

4. Atmosphere

Reading for atmosphere involves picking up the setting and feelings from the biblical text. What was it like to be in the author's shoes?

For instance, Paul says, "Rejoice in the Lord always; again I will say, rejoice." (Philippians 4:4). Sounds good. But where was he? In the Ritz Carlton? Not exactly. He was in a foul-smelling Roman prison. And life looks very different from behind bars.

You want to transport your senses into the passage. If there's a sunset, see it. If there's an odor, smell it. If there's a cry of anguish, feel it. Are you studying the letter to the Ephesians? Then join the church at Ephesus, and listen to Paul as he goes down on his knees to pray (Ephesians 3:14-21). This is an exercise for the imagination, not just the intellect. So it doesn't take professional training to recapture the atmosphere of a passage of Scripture.

MOVE ON TO INTERPRETATION

Observation leads to the second step, Interpretation. Here you ask and answer the question, What does it mean? Remember, your central quest is for meaning. I want to suggest three things that will help you get the meaning of a passage of Scripture.

1. Questions

If you want to understand a biblical text, you've got to bombard it with questions. The Bible is never embarrassed to be asked questions. That doesn't mean it will answer all of them. But you still need to ask them to determine if they can be answered. I'm going to give you a series of questions to lob at the text that will help you search for meaning.

2. Answers

Obviously, if you're going to ask questions, you've also got to look for the answers. Where will you find them? In the text. Observation will give you the basic building blocks out of which you will construct the meaning of a passage. The answers to your questions will come directly from the observation process.

That is why I say, the more time you spend in Observation, the less time you will need to spend in Interpretation, and the more accurate will be your results. The less time you spend in Observation, the more time you will need to spend in Interpretation, and the less accurate will be your results.

Read, Record, Reflect

Would you like to start gaining more from your time in the Scriptures? Here are three habits to cultivate that will increase your productivity. Use them every time you open your Bible.

READ

This may seem obvious. Yet too many "readers" are nothing but browsers. They turn pages the way they flip through channels on a TV set, looking for something to catch their interest. The Word doesn't lend itself to that  sort of approach. It requires conscious, concentrated effort. So read portions of the Bible over and over. The more you read them, the more clear they will become. Be sure to see chapters 8-10, where I've listed ten strategies to first-rate reading.

RECORD

In other words, write some notes. Jot down what you see in the text. Keep a record of your insights and questions. I don't know how many times someone has said to me, "Prof, what I have to write down is not very good." Yet the fact is, you can't build on something you don't have. So start where you are, even with very elementary things. Everyone starts at that same place. But be sure to write it down. Use a legal pad or a notebook to record what you see. In your own words, summarize your observations and insights so that later they will come back to you. Doing so will help you remember what you've discovered and use it.

REFLECT

 That is, take some time to think about what you've seen. Ask yourself: What's going on in this passage? What is it telling me about God? About myself? What do I need to do on the basis of what I'm reading here? As we're going to see, reflection, or meditation, is vital to understanding and applying God's Word.

3. Integration

Not only must you ask the text questions and look for answers, but you must put the answers together into a meaningful whole. Otherwise you end up with nothing but baskets of fragments.

One time I was asked to speak at a church. "Preach on anything you want," they told me. "Except Ephesians."

That seemed an odd request, until they explained why: "Our preacher has spent three years in Ephesians, and we're just into the second chapter."

I went out to lunch with some of those people, and I asked them, "What's the theme of the book of Ephesians?"

They didn't have a clue. They had all kinds of little details. But their pastor had never put all the data together into a meaningful whole. Result: despite three years of teaching, his congregation had never discovered the meaning of Ephesians.

Integration is the stage where you reconstruct the meaning of a passage after you've taken it apart to inspect the details.

KEEP GOING INTO APPLICATION

Observation and Interpretation lead to the third step in the process, the crucial step of Application. In application you ask and answer the question, How does it work? Again, not does it work, but how does it work? There are two areas to consider.

1. How does it work for me?

That can be a very convicting question. As George, the adult Sunday school teacher, told us in chapter 1, it's easy to study the Bible and say, "Oh, wow! That's just what my class needs. Man, I can hardly wait to get there and tell it to them." But by taking that approach, it is possible to ignore the more personal question, What does this have to say to me? How would this work in my life? Because if it isn't working in my life, then what authority do I have to share it with someone else? I have a credibility gap.

2. How does it work for others?

Of course, the Bible does have implications for others. And it is legitimate to ask, How would this transform their life? Their marriage and family? Their business and occupation? Every area of life. I'll point out some ways to make application of the Scriptures to others in your sphere of influence.

ALWAYS KEEP THE BIG PICTURE

So that is an overview of where we are going and how we're going to get there. Every time you come to a portion of God's Word, approach it in terms of the big picture:

Observation: What do I see?
Interpretation: What does it mean?
Application: How does it work?

That's the destination. Let's get started on the exciting journey.

Finding Your Way Around the Bible

Have you ever felt lost when a preacher or Bible teacher told you to turn to a particular passage of Scripture? Maybe it was in one of those odd-sounding Old Testament books, such as Nahum, Zephaniah, or Haggai. You fumbled around for a while, trying to act like you knew where to go. Eventually you turned to the table of contents and looked it up. But by the time you got to the indicated passage, the speaker had moved on, and you were lost once again.

Not knowing how to find a passage of Scripture can be as frustrating as wandering down a country road with no map. But there are two ways to overcome this problem.

Memorize the books of the Bible

That's not as hard as you may think. Look at the sixty-six books listed by categories on page 29. It's easier to memorize them by groups, and you can do it in just a couple of weeks' time.

Learn how Scripture references work

A Scripture reference is like an address. It tells you where the verse "lives" in the Bible. It's better than a page number because different versions of the Bible place the text on different pages.

By way of illustration, consider the reference, John 8:32. It is read, "John eight thirty-two." "John" is the name of the book, the gospel by John in the New Testament. The "8" refers to the eighth chapter in the book. The verse number is "32." That's all there is to it.

Or consider 1 Corinthians 4:2. It is read "first Corinthians four two." (Some church traditions call it "one Corinthians four two.") The book is 1 Corinthians, "4" is the chapter, and "2" is the verse.

Occasionally you might come across a reference such as John viii.32 or St. John viii.32, using Roman numerals for the chapters, and a period rather than a colon to separate chapter and verse. That's an older form of referencing, found particularly among works published in Europe. But the system is the same.

For multiple verses, you will find a hyphen connecting the first and last verses in the reference. John 8:32-42 indicates the section of John 8 from verse 32 through verse 42. If there are only two verses involved, the writer will separate them with a comma, as in John 8:32, 42. He may also separate two consecutive verses with a comma rather than a hyphen, as in John 8:32, 33.

A reference may also indicate a section that spans two or more chapters. If you see John 8:32–9:12, it means the section beginning at verse 32 of John 8, and continuing through verse 12 of John 9. If the reference is to entire chapters and there is no need to indicate verse numbers, you might see something like John 8-9.

Suppose, however, that the reference is to a book with only one chapter, such as Obadiah, Philemon, or Jude. In that case, the reference mentions only the book name and verse number. For instance, Philemon 21 refers to the twenty-first verse of Philemon.

Sometimes a writer may want to indicate only part of a verse, rather than the whole. In that case he may use a lower-case a or b (or sometimes even a c if the verse is lengthy) to further specify the reference. Romans 12:1a, for instance, refers to the first half of Romans 12:1. Isaiah 40:8b refers to the second half of that verse.

What about multiple references, indicating more than one passage? Conventions vary, but a common one is to show a list of references in the order in which they appear in the Bible, separated by semi-colons, and to show book names only once. For example: Genesis 3:17-19; Psalm 8:3-8; Ecclesiastes 3:12-13; 5:18; Ephesians 4:28; 6:5-9; and Colossians 3:22-4:1.

One final note: When referring to a particular chapter in Psalms, use the singular, "psalm," as in Psalm 23—not Psalms 23. The book of Psalms is a collection of psalms (plural); each individual chapter is a psalm (singular).

STEP 1
Observation

What do I see?

5

THE VALUE OF OBSERVATION

The first step in Bible study is Observation, where we ask and answer the question, What do I see? When the psalmist prayed, "Open my eyes, that I may behold wonderful things from Thy law" (Psalm 119:18), he was praying for the powers of observation. He was asking the Spirit of God to tear the bandages from his eyes so that he might see with sight and insight into the truth that God had revealed.

What makes one person a better Bible student than another? He can see more, that's all. The same truth is available to both of them in the text. The only difference between them is what either one can see in a cubic foot of space.

Have you ever gone to a Bible study or heard a message preached in a local church on a passage that you have read and studied—maybe even taught—but afterward you wondered, "Are we studying the same passage?" You were forced to ask, "Why can that person see more than I do? Why has he gotten so much more out of the text?"

The difference between you is the difference that Sherlock Holmes was fond of pointing out: "You see, but you do not observe."

The ability to see is a developed process. Louis Agassiz, the renowned nineteenth-century naturalist of Harvard, was asked on one occasion, "What was your greatest contribution, scientifically?"

His answer: "I have taught men and women to observe."

And he used a fascinating process to do that. He would place a malodorous fish on a dissecting tray, stick it beneath the nose of a freshman, and command, "Observe this specimen, and write down everything you see."

The student would start out enthusiastically, writing down twenty or thirty things. Meanwhile, the professor would disappear until the next day, when upon returning he would ask, "How are you doing?"

"Oh, I saw thirty-seven things," the student would boast.

"Wonderful," the master teacher would cry. "Continue to observe."

And the student would think, *Man, I've seen everything there is to see on that fish!* But since the professor told him to keep at it, he'd go back and look some more.

This process would continue for two weeks. Nothing but looking at the fish. You see, the genius of the professor was his awareness that the basis of scientific inquiry is the process of seeing. And the same is true for good Bible study.

In the pages that follow, I'm going to give you a number of pointers on how you can boost your powers of observation when you read Scripture. I'm also going to give you plenty of opportunities to test your skills on various portions of the Word. But for now, here's a little exercise to make the point that seeing is not the same as observing. Answer the following questions from memory. Then go find out whether your perceptions are correct:

1. Think of a stairway or the steps to a building that you use regularly. How many steps are there?

2. How many stoplights do you pass on your way to work?

3. Which of the following inscriptions is not found on the back side of a dollar bill?
    (a) In God We Trust
    (b) *annuit coeptisnouus ordo secorum*
    (c) The Department of the Treasury, 1789
    (d) *e pluribus unum*

4. Think of someone you live with or work with closely. Describe in detail what that person was wearing the last time you saw him or her.

Without lifting your pen from the paper, draw four straight, connected lines that go through each dot only once. After you've tried two different ways, consider what restrictions you might be setting up for yourself in solving this problem.

How many squares do you see below?

5. How many pages are there in this book, within ten pages?

6. What was the exact title of your pastor's sermon last Sunday? What was the text, if he used one?

7. Was your mother right-handed or left-handed? How about your father?

8. If you are married: Which side of his face does your husband start shaving first? Or, which side of her face does your wife start putting makeup on first?

9. How many miles has it been since you changed the oil in your car, within 1,000 miles? How many miles since you got new tires? How many miles since you had the engine tuned?

10. Which phase was last night's moon closest to: new, first quarter, full, or last quarter?

How did you make out? Do you have an eagle eye for detail? Or are you blind as a bat? Of course, none of the items in these ten questions is a matter of life and death (except maybe the oil in your car).

Yet it's funny how the little things so often make the difference in a fictional mystery or a real-life police investigation. Everything turns on a "minor" detail—the color of a suspect's eyes, the time of day, a mispronounced word. The facts are there for anyone to see, yet only the master sleuth notices them. "You see, but you do not observe."

Let me give you a chance to start observing Scripture. In the next chapter we'll look at one verse and ask the simple question, What do I see? You may be surprised at the result.

You Try It

Observation is one of the most useful skills you can acquire. It can also be a lot of fun. Here's an exercise to try with young people. It will develop their powers of observation, and teach you a lot about the observational process.

Apart from the children's presence, arrange a group of objects on a table, such as:

    a rock
    a paperback
    a pen
    two or three seashells
    a toy car
    five crayons
    a Lego building block
    a leaf
    a magnet in the shape of a number or letter
    a multicolored scarf
    a necktie
    a toothbrush

It doesn't really matter what you select to put on the table. Just be sure they are things that the kids will recognize. And pick objects that have distinctive, interesting features, such as unique shapes or colors.

Once you've arranged the items on the table, cover them with a sheet or tablecloth. Then call the participants into the room and give each one a pencil and paper. Tell them to write down what they see on the table. Pull off the cover and reveal the objects for about sixty seconds. Then re-cover them.

Ask the children to tell you what they saw—or what they think they saw. Ask them to describe specifics, such as size, color, markings, and so forth. Make a list of their observations. Then pull the cover off the objects and show them to the group. Everyone will be amazed at what was and was not observed. They'll realize that there's a vast difference between merely seeing and carefully observing.

The Watch

"I have heard you say it is difficult for a man to have any object in daily use without leaving the impress of his individuality upon it in such a way that a trained observer might read it. Now, I have here a watch which has recently come into my possession. Would you have the kindness to let me have an opinion upon the character or habits of the late owner?"

I handed him over the watch with some slight feeling of amusement in my heart, for the test was, as I thought, an impossible one, and I intended it as a lesson against the somewhat dogmatic tone which he occasionally assumed. He balanced the watch in his hand, gazed hard at the dial, opened the back, and examined the works, first with his naked eyes and then with a powerful convex lens. I could hardly keep from smiling at his crestfallen face when he finally snapped the case to and handed it back.

"There are hardly any data," he remarked. "The watch has been recently cleaned, which robs me of my most suggestive facts."

"You are right," I answered. "It was cleaned before being sent to me."

In my heart I accused my companion of putting forward a most lame and impotent excuse to cover his failure. What data could he expect from an uncleaned watch?

"Though unsatisfactory, my research has not been entirely barren," he observed, staring up at the ceiling with dreamy, lack-lustre eyes. "Subject to your correction, I should judge that the watch belonged to your elder brother, who inherited it from your father."

"That you gather, no doubt, from the H.W. upon the back?"

"Quite so. The W. suggests your own name. The date of the watch is nearly fifty years back, and the initials are as old as the watch: so it was made for the last generation. Jewellery usually descends to the eldest son, and he is most likely to have the same name as the father. Your father has, if I remember right, been dead many years. It has, therefore, been in the hands of your eldest brother."

"Right, so far," said I. "Anything else?"

"He was a man of untidy habits—very untidy and careless. He was left with good prospects, but he threw away his chances, lived for some time in poverty with occasional short intervals of prosperity, and finally, taking to drink, he died. That is all I can gather."

I sprang from my chair and limped impatiently about the room with considerable bitterness in my heart.

"This is unworthy of you, Holmes," I said. "I could not have believed that you would have descended to this. You have made inquiries into the history of my unhappy brother, and now you pretend to deduce this knowledge in some fanciful way. You cannot expect me to believe that you have read all this from his old watch! It is unkind and, to speak plainly, has a touch of charlatanism in it."

"My dear doctor," said he kindly, "pray accept my apologies. Viewing the matter as an abstract problem, I had forgotten how personal and painful a thing it might be to you. I assure you, however, that I never even knew that you had a brother until you handed me the watch."

"Then how in the name of all that is wonderful did you get these facts? They are absolutely correct in every particular."

"Ah, that is good luck. I could only say what was the balance of probability. I did not at all expect to be so accurate."

"But it was not mere guesswork?"

"No, no; I never guess. It is a shocking habit—destructive to the logical faculty. What seems strange to you is only so because you do not follow my train of thought or observe the small facts upon which large inferences may depend. For example, I began by stating that your brother was careless. When you observe the lower part of that watch-case you notice that it is not only dinted in two places but it is cut and marked all over from the habit of keeping other hard objects, such as coins or keys, in the same pocket. Surely it is no great feat to assume that a man who treats a fifty-guinea watch so cavalierly must be a careless man. Neither is it a very far-fetched inference that a man who inherits one article of such value is pretty well provided for in other respects."

I nodded to show that I followed his reasoning.

"It is very customary for pawnbrokers in England, when they take a watch, to scratch the numbers of the ticket with a pint-point upon the inside of the case. It is more handy than a label as there is no risk of the number being lost or transposed. There are no less than four such numbers visible to my lens on the inside of this case. Inference—that your brother was often at low water. Secondary inference—that he had occasional bursts of prosperity, or he could not have redeemed the pledge. Finally, I ask you to look at the inner plate, which contains the keyhole. Look at the thousands of scratches all round the hole—marks where the key has slipped. What sober man's key could have scored those grooves? But you will never see a drunkard's watch without them. He winds it at night, and he leaves these traces of his unsteady hand. Where is the mystery in all this?"

SOURCE: From Sir Arthur Conan Doyle, *The Sign of the Four*.

6

LET'S START
WITH A VERSE

A re you ready to get into Scripture for yourself? I hope so. In
this chapter I want to start small by observing one verse, Acts
1:8. I'm going to demonstrate the observational process so
that you can see it in action. Follow along in your Bible as I ask
questions of the text (in boldface below), to see what I can discover.
Remember that my main concern in observation is, What do I see?

You'll notice on the following pages that I have rewritten the text
in a way that facilitates the process. It clarifies not only the grammar
but also the ideas that the writer wants to communicate to us.

START WITH TERMS

We said in chapter 4 that when we observe, we need to start by
looking for some terms. **What is the most important term in this
verse?** It's the first word I see, *But*. Mark that word in your Bible.

The word *but* indicates contrast. Later we'll see that contrasts are
always important in Scripture. They indicate a change of direction.
Here, **what does the word *but* force me to do?** To go back to the
preceding context, another crucial aspect of Bible study that we'll
come back to. I'm breaking into this chapter at verse 8. And we
never want to study something in isolation, but always in relation to
something else. Since we're so close to the beginning of the book of
Acts, let's go back and pick up the context from the start.

Verse 1 begins by mentioning "the first account," which upon investigation turns out to be the gospel by Luke. So right away I discover that Acts is by the same writer, Dr. Luke. (An important question that I'll ask but let you answer is, **Who was Luke?** Make a list of everything you can discover about him.) Luke-Acts forms a two-volume set. The gospel of Luke gets the story started; Acts is the sequel.

Furthermore, I find that Luke and Acts have the same subject: "all that Jesus began to do and teach." That's a clue that Acts is going to give me a continuation of Christ's ministry through His apostles.

Not only do Luke and Acts have the same subject, they are addressed to the same reader, a man named Theophilus. **Who was Theophilus?** If I go back to Luke 1:3, I discover that he is called "most excellent Theophilus," which may indicate that he had a title and position of great prominence in Roman society. But here he is called simply Theophilus. Perhaps in the interval between the writing of Luke and Acts, he had come to know Christ and lost his position. Or maybe Luke just uses the shorter form because of greater familiarity. At any rate, Luke had a particular individual in mind as he wrote.

The Acts account begins with a discussion. In verse 6, I find the Lord and His disciples talking about the kingdom of God. The text says, "And so when they had come together, they were asking Him." The first thing they do is raise a question: "Is this it?" Is what it? "Is this the time when you are going to restore the kingdom to Israel?"

Jesus answers their question. First, He answers negatively by saying, in effect, "That is not for you to know" (v. 7). Then positively (v. 8)—and here's where the word *but* figures so prominently— "But this is your responsibility." So verse 8 is part of a dialogue in which the disciples are asking questions and the Lord is answering them.

So that's the preceding context. Let's also look at what follows in verses 9-11, because they recount the ascension of our Lord. Remember that in addition to terms, you should look for atmosphere. These verses create tremendous atmosphere, because if this is the ascension, then Jesus' words in verse 8 are His last words to His disciples. In effect He's giving them their marching orders. "Now the job is yours," He is telling them. And then, while they are looking, He goes up into heaven. He's gone—and they're on.

Whenever you study any verse of Scripture, be sure to place it in its context. See it both in terms of what goes before and what follows.

CONTEXT

CONTRAST

DIALOGUE / QUESTION
ANSWER { NEGATIVELY
{ POSITIVELY

But you shall receive power

when the Holy Spirit has come upon you;

and you shall be My witnesses

both in Jerusalem,

and in all Judea

and Samaria,

and even to the remotest part of the earth.

WHO ARE THE PEOPLE INVOLVED?

Having done that, let's go back to verse 8. I noted the importance of *but* as a contrast. **There's a second key term to notice; what is it?** The word *you*. Observe that it is repeated: "You shall receive power...you shall be My witnesses."

That raises the question, **Who are these people?** The context tells me that they are the apostles (v. 2). From there I could make a list of general information that I already know about these individuals. For instance:

1. They have walked with Jesus for about three years during His ministry.
2. Jesus has chosen them.
3. They are anxious, which is probably why they ask the question about the kingdom.
4. They are all Jewish.
5. Many of them are, or have been, fishermen.

I could add more. The point is, when you come to something like this, re-create in your mind who the people are. In this case, they are people who have heard the teaching, seen the miracles, and spent a lot of time with the Lord. Now they have the opportunity to ask Him the most crucial question of their lives.

Another question to ask is, **What is the main verb in this verse?** Here, it is "shall receive." **What tense is it?** Future tense. That looks ahead to something that is going to happen later.

What are they going to receive? "Power." That word could be translated—and in some translations you will see it this way—"ability." Jesus is not talking about physical power; He's talking about the ability of the apostles to accomplish what He wants them to.

WATCH FOR CAUSE-EFFECT RELATIONSHIPS

A crucial phrase comes next: "When the Holy Spirit has come upon you." **What does that add to the verse?** First, it indicates a cause-effect relationship. The power won't come until the Holy Spirit comes. Second, it answers the question of time. It tells us that the receiving of power will happen when the Holy Spirit comes upon them.

Earlier I observed that the word *you* indicates the apostles. Here I run into another person, the Holy Spirit. **Who is He?** Again, I could generate a list of what I know about Him. For one thing, He's the third Person of the Trinity; He is supernatural. And He's the Person linked with the power. So we're talking about supernatural power.

Did the apostles need that? Definitely. The last thing they had done was to let down their Lord at the crucifixion, at the crucial time. So they needed the ability—the power—that only the Holy Spirit could give.

Notice that Jesus says that the Spirit is going to come "upon" them. The power does not exist within them but rather is going to come from outside. There will be an invasion of supernatural ability on otherwise ordinary human beings. That says a lot about the task to which Jesus is calling them.

A moment ago we saw a cause-effect relationship in terms of timing. Here I want you to see one in terms of two statements, "You shall receive power" and the next phrase, "And you shall be My witnesses." The apostles are going to receive power; that's the cause. The effect is that they are going to be something—"witnesses."

CONTEXT

CONTRAST   DIALOGUE / QUESTION
                              ANSWER   NEGATIVELY
                  WHO?   FUTURE   POSITIVELY
But you shall receive power | ABILITY

C/E   SUPERNATURAL   NOT w/IN – w/o
    TIME **when the Holy Spirit has come upon you;**

                              NB. ORDER!
and you shall be My witnesses

both in Jerusalem,

and in all Judea

and Samaria,

and even to the remotest part of the earth.

(9–11) ASCENSION
            ATMOSPHERE — LAST WORDS

I notice that that is also in the future. That becomes very significant, it turns out. It's not, "You are going to be witnesses and then receive power," but the other way around: "You are going to receive power, the result of which is, you are going to be witnesses."

That's an interesting point, because often we spend a lot of time trying to urge people to witness concerning the faith. Yet nothing inside of them would ever warrant their doing that. They have nothing to share with others, and if they tried, they would be doing nothing but putting on an act.

By contrast, suppose one of my female seminary students gets engaged over the summer. In the fall, she walks into my class, and the first thing you know she's waving her ring finger in front of my face. I never have to beg her to show me her ring. No, there's something inside that compels her to take the initiative. She's in love with a man, and she's got to share it. She can't keep it to herself.

That's the kind of dynamic Luke wants us to see in this passage. As a result of what the apostles receive, they are going to be witnesses. **But whose witnesses?** Christ's witnesses. His by personal identification. They are going to represent Him.

DEFINE THE TERMS

What is a "witness"? A simple definition would be someone who has seen and can tell others about an event, person, or circumstance. A witness is someone who has experienced something. That is exactly what these apostles are going to be. For three and a half years they have lived intimately with the Savior. Now, as a result of their contact with the Holy Spirit and the provision of His power, they are going to be totally different people.

Until now, they have lived pretty much in their own strength. In fact, their performance has not been too impressive, if you read the gospels. They fall flat on their faces over and over again, particularly at the critical moment. Yet now that the Spirit is going to give them power, they are going to be the Savior's witnesses.

What does the next phrase begin with? "Both in Jerusalem." If I tell you "both" of us are going downtown, you assume that there are two of us. But there are more than two things here. In fact, there are four different places mentioned. That's odd. It's one reason to look up this passage in a commentary by someone who knows the Greek and explains why Luke uses this phrase. I'll talk more about commentaries under Step Two: Interpretation.

I've looked it up and learned that the word translated "both" is an interesting term. It indicates the beginning of a series. There may be two in the series, there may be twenty-two. There are only four here. "Both" begins a series of four places where the apostles are going to be witnesses for Christ.

THE IMPORTANCE OF PLACE

The first is Jerusalem. What do I know about Jerusalem? Let's start a list:

1. It's a city.
2. The Temple is there.

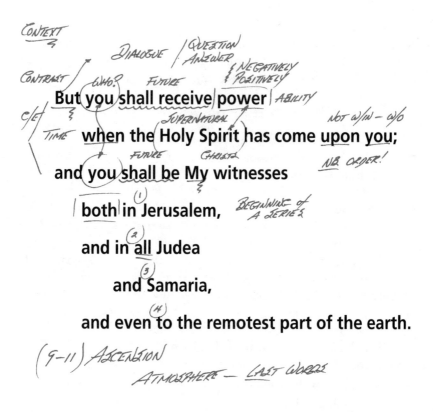

But you shall receive power

when the Holy Spirit has come upon you;

and you shall be My witnesses

both in Jerusalem,

and in all Judea

and Samaria,

and even to the remotest part of the earth.

3. It's where they are at this moment.
4. It also has become their home. They are to begin witnessing at home. An easy place to start, right? Hardly! Have you ever tried sharing your faith with the people in your own home? It's one thing to go down the street and tell some stranger that you don't even know about Jesus Christ. But try it with your kids, or your parents, or somebody else who knows you well. They are likely to react, "Don't put your religious trip on me." Nevertheless, Jesus tells the apostles they are going to start right there in Jerusalem, which is particularly interesting because of a fifth point:
5. It is where the crucifixion took place. They are known there. So a hostile environment is to be the starting point for evangelism.

After starting in Jerusalem, though, they are to go to Judea. **How can I relate Jerusalem and Judea?** A glance at a good atlas shows me that it's what a city is to a state, such as Dallas, Texas, or Chicago, Illinois. Jerusalem was the city within the larger province called Judea. So the Lord is moving from the city to the province.

Three provinces were central in the apostles' thinking: Judea in the south; Galilee in the north; and in between, Samaria. There was also a fourth one on the eastern side of the Jordan River called Peraea. Jesus tells them to begin in Jerusalem and go to Judea.

But notice the little connective, "and," which brings them to the third place—Samaria. They loved Samaria, right? No way.

Remember the woman at the well in John 4? The text says that Jesus *had* to pass through Samaria (v. 4). He was in the south; He wanted to go to Galilee in the north. The Jews would have said, "No, you must not go through Samaria." Instead, they would have routed Him east, across the Jordan River, up the east bank, and eventually back west into the Galilee. To return, He'd have to take the same steps in reverse. In other words, He was supposed to take the long way around. Under no circumstances was He ever to go through Samaria. Why? John 4:9 explains, "For Jews have no dealings with Samaritans."

But in Acts 1:8, Jesus says that the very area that the apostles would normally avoid, He wants them to invade. "Go to the place that is out-of-bounds for you, off-limits, the despised area."

The next phrase tells them where else they are to go: "even to the remotest part of the earth." Jesus uses a word for "earth" that means the inhabited earth. Consulting a Bible dictionary, I've found that several words for "earth" are used in the New Testament. Later I'll show you how to look up words and discover their significance and the differences between them. Here, Jesus is talking about the populated earth. He's not telling them to go everywhere in the world but everywhere there are people.

RELATE THE VERSE TO THE BOOK AS A WHOLE

Let's say this is the first time I've ever studied this verse. What have I discovered? Well, two things that are usually separated—Judea and Samaria—are actually linked together as one. I've also seen that the apostles are not to stop until they go to the very last part of the inhabited earth. And I've noted that these are the last words of the Lord.

So the question I ask is, **Is it possible that this verse is in any way an outline for the book? Do the apostles actually follow this pattern?** When I study the book as a whole, I discover that the answer to both questions is yes. Did they start out in Jerusalem? Acts 2 shows that they did. Then did they go to Judea? Exactly— but not by choice. Persecution got them started on their journey outward (8:1), until by the end of the book they are well on their way toward reaching the inhabited world of their day.

CONTEXT

CONTRAST *DIALOGUE / QUESTION ANSWER* *NEGATIVELY POSITIVELY*

C/E *WHO?* *FUTURE*

But you shall receive power *ABILITY*

SUPERNATURAL *NOT w/in – w/o*

TIME **when the Holy Spirit has come upon you;** *NB ORDER!*

FUTURE *CHRIST*

and you shall be My witnesses

both in Jerusalem, *BEGINNING of A SERIES*

OUTLINE **and in all Judea** *LINKED / USUALLY SEPARATED*

and Samaria, *cf JOHN 4:9*

INHABITED

and even to the remotest part of the earth.

(9–11) ASCENSION

ATMOSPHERE — LAST WORDS

THERE'S NO LIMIT TO OBSERVATION

Now look at all that we've observed in this exercise. Count them, and you'll find that I've come up with at least thirty observations from Acts 1:8. (And this is only one verse. I haven't studied a paragraph, or a chapter, or even the book of Acts—just one verse.) Yet each time I come back to it, I'll see more. In fact, an assignment I give my seminary students is to list as many observations as they can from this single verse. So far they've come up with more than six hundred different ones.

Imagine what fun you could have with six hundred observations on this passage. Would you like to see Scripture with eyes like that? I'd like to help you gain that skill. I assure you, it's the essential first step in Bible study method. Come with me into the next few chapters, and I'll show you some ways to increase your powers of observation.

You Try It

Now that you've seen me observe Acts 1:8, try the process yourself. Observe the following passage, Joshua 1:8:

This book of the Law shall not depart from your mouth,

> **but**
> **you shall meditate on it day and night,**

> **so that**
> **you may be careful to do**
> **according to all that is written in it;**

> **for**
> **then you will make your way prosperous,**
> **and**
> **then you will have success.**

Remember, in Observation your main concern is, What do I see? Pay special attention to terms and grammatical structure. Also look at the context. Use a pen or pencil to record your observations in and around the text. See what you can find in this fascinating passage.

7

YOU MUST LEARN
TO READ

Have you ever closed your Bible in frustration, wondering why you don't get more out of your study of Scripture? In chapter 1 Wendy told us that was her experience. Perhaps like her you've made an honest effort somewhere along the way to sit down and study God's Word. You heard others talk about mining the riches there, and you wanted to grab a few nuggets for yourself. But after pouring a lot of time and energy into the process, things just didn't pan out. The few specks of gold you did find weren't worth the trouble. So in the end, you walked away from Bible study. Maybe others were profiting by it, but not you.

May I suggest two reasons you failed to hit pay dirt: First, you didn't know how to read. Second, you didn't know what to look for.

Now I don't mean to insult you, but I do mean to instruct you. Our culture has made a radical shift in the last century from a word-based society of readers to an image-based society of viewers. The medium of our time is television, not books. As a result, unlike our forebears of a few generations ago, we don't know how to read. To a large extent, we've lost that art.

And yet the Bible is a book, which means it must be read to be understood and appreciated. We've got to recapture the skills of reading if we want to become effective Bible students. So in this and the next few chapters, I want to offer instruction on how to read. Then I'll talk about what you need to look for.

On eleven different occasions, Jesus said to the most well-read people of His time, "Have you never read?" Of course they had. They spent their lives reading. But they didn't understand what they read.

They were like a student I once came across in the library, dead asleep in front of a book. I thought I'd have some fun with him, so I stuck my head right down next to his ear and said, "Boo!" He just about went through the ceiling.

"What in the world are you reading?" I asked him after he had rallied. "If it's that exciting I want to be sure to assign it for one of my classes."

He laughed.

"Is it funny?" I asked him.

"It's tragic," he replied.

"What do you mean?"

"Well, I just realized I'm on page thirty-seven, and I don't have the foggiest idea of what I'm reading."

He's right. That is a tragedy. If you don't understand what you are reading, then you are not reading—you are wasting time. I'm afraid that many people come away from the Word having basically wasted their time, because if their life depended on it, they couldn't tell you what they read.

Is that the case for you? If so, let me give you three suggestions to help you to learn how to read.

LEARN TO READ BETTER AND FASTER

There is a direct correlation between your ability to observe Scripture and your ability to read. So anything you can do to improve your reading skills will be a quantum leap in the direction of improving your observation skills as a student of the Bible.

Yet I've discovered that an increasing number of graduates from our nation's high schools and colleges have a very hard time reading. In fact, I asked one of my seminary classes, "If you graduate from the university and you can't read, you can't write, and you can't think, what can you do?"

One wag hollered out, "Watch television!"

Sad, but true. One of my children was halfway through first grade before I realized they weren't teaching him how to read. So I went to complain to the teacher.

"You don't understand, Mr. Hendricks," she told me. "The important thing is not that your child know how to read but that he be happy."

Against my better judgment, I decided to let it go for a while. But at the end of the year I discovered that my child was disgustingly happy, yet couldn't read. In fact, I went back to the teacher and said, "Did it ever occur to you that children might be happier if they knew how to read?"

It cost me a month's salary to put my youngster in a remedial reading program. But it was one of the best investments I ever made. Today he reads better and faster than I can, which is very fast and reasonably well. That's why I believe that one of the most important things you can do for people is help them in the process of reading.

Suppose you want to study the book of Ephesians. You happen to be a slow reader, so it takes you one half hour to read the entire six chapters. But suppose you learned to read it in fifteen minutes and also to double your comprehension. Then for the same amount of time—one-half hour—you would increase your effectiveness fourfold. That's worth the investment.

I'd like to recommend a book that will help you get started in this process. It's a book that changed the whole course of my life, the classic by Mortimer J. Adler called *How to Read a Book*. Now available in paperback, it's a tool you can't afford to be without. It will revolutionize your life.

I graduated from high school with honors. I even received the English award. Then I went to college—one of those strange schools where they expected us to study. Unfortunately, I'd never studied in high school. I'd never even taken home a book. So after arriving on campus, I took an aptitude test, and they put me in the lowest English section in the school. This, despite my English award. Pretty humiliating. (It turned out to be the best thing that could have happened, because they gave us remedial students the best professor in the place.)

Well, all I did for the first six weeks was study. No dates. No athletics. Yet I still managed to flunk three courses. That has a way of getting your attention. I thought, *I'm never going to make it.*

So I went to see my professor. He was very straightforward with me: "Howie, your problem is you don't know how to read." And he introduced me to Mortimer Adler's book. I read it, and it transformed my study skills. In fact, it changed the course of my life. And that's what it can do for you in terms of Bible study.

Adler covers practical skills such as how to classify books, how to discover an author's intentions, how to outline a book, and how to find the key terms. He tells what the four questions are that every reader should ask, what the difference is between sentences and propositions, and what good books can do for you. He tells you how to read practical books, imaginative books, historical books, and more. He even includes a recommended reading list of the great books that are worth your while to read. In short, even though *How to Read a Book* is about books in general, it's an outstanding resource for Bible study because it teaches you how to read.

Another good tool is Norman Lewis's *How to Read Better and Faster*. It's really a workbook that promises to help you read 50 to 60 percent faster than you do now, and with better comprehension. Lewis has material on how to read for main ideas, how to think along with the author, and how to read with a questioning mind. He's included forty-two work sessions with dozens of exercises to get you involved in the process. I highly recommend his book.

LEARN TO READ AS FOR THE FIRST TIME

It is often said that familiarity breeds contempt. Well, something else it breeds is ignorance. The moment you come to a passage of Scripture and say, "Oh, I know this one already," you're in trouble. Instead you need to come to every text as if you'd never seen it before in your life. That's quite a discipline. It involves cultivating a mind-set, an attitude toward the Word.

It helps to read the Bible in different versions. If you've been reading the same translation for years, try something fresh and contemporary for a change, such as J. B. Phillips's *New Testament In Modern English*, or *The Living Bible*. If you really want to stretch yourself, check out the *Cotton Patch Version* of the gospels. On the other hand, if you are unfamiliar with the classic King James Version, you really owe it to yourself to read it. Reading an unfamiliar version jars your attention so that you see the Bible with a new set of eyes.

The point is, do whatever it takes to approach the Word with a fresh perspective. One of the great killers of Bible study is the statement, "I already know that."

Test Your Reading Skills

How sharp are your reading skills? Here's an exercise to test them. In ninety seconds or less, read the following material and circle T or F for each statement (without looking back at the article). Set a timer or have someone call time in exactly ninety seconds. Stop when time is over, finished or not.

DRY ICE

Can you imagine ice that does not melt and is not wet? Then you can imagine dry ice. Dry ice is made by freezing a gas called carbon dioxide. Dry ice is quite different from ordinary ice, which is simply frozen water.

Dry ice was first manufactured in 1925. It has since fulfilled the fondest hopes of its inventor. It can be used for making artificial fog in movies (when steam is passed over dry ice, a very dense vapor rises), and for destroying insects in grain supplies. It is more practical than ordinary ice because it takes up less space and is 142 degrees colder. Since it evaporates instead of melting, it is cleaner to use. For these reasons it is extremely popular, and many people prefer it to ordinary ice.

Dry ice is so cold that, if you touch it with your bare fingers, it will burn you!

Respond

1. Dry ice is made from water, but because
   it is specially treated it does not melt.   T   F
2. The first dry ice was manufactured in the
   1950s.   T   F
3. Dry ice has more uses than ordinary ice.   T   F
4. Dry ice is not as cold as ordinary ice.   T   F
5. Artificial fog can be made by passing
   steam over dry ice.   T   F

Did you make it in ninety seconds? Feel no anxiety if you did not—you are at the start of your practice in reading quickly and responding accurately. Your aim is to improve gradually and surely, not to become an expert at once.

[Correct answers to the five questions can be found on page 73.]
From Norman Lewis, *How to Read Better and Faster,* 4th ed. (New York: Harper & Row, 1978), pp. 14-15.

READ THE BIBLE AS A LOVE LETTER

Have you ever fallen in love? I hope so. I fell in love with the woman who became my wife, Jeanne, through a correspondence courtship. Five years I chased that women until she finally caught me.

So guess what I did when one of her letters would arrive? Did I mumble, "Oh, no, another letter from Jeanne (sigh). I guess I better read it"? Did I sit down, read the first paragraph, and then say, "Well, that's enough for today. I can check that item off my list"?

No way! I used to read every single letter four or five times. I'd stand in line, waiting to get into the dining room at college, reading her letters there. At night I'd read them before I went to bed. I'd tuck them under the pillow so that if I woke up in the middle of the night, I could pull them out and read them all over again. Why? Because I was in love with the person who wrote them.

That's the way to come to the Word of God. Read it as though it were His love letter to you.

When Mortimer Adler's book first came out, it was advertised in *The New York Times* under the slogan "How to Read a Love Letter." A picture showed a puzzled adolescent perusing a letter, with the following copy underneath:

This young man has just received his first love letter. He may have read it three or four times, but he is just beginning. To read it as accurately as he would like, would require several dictionaries and a good deal of close work with a few experts of etymology and philology.

However, he will do all right without them.

He will ponder over the exact shade of meaning of every word, every comma. She has headed the letter, "Dear John." What, he asks himself, is the exact significance of those words? Did she refrain from saying "Dearest" because she was bashful? Would "My Dear" have sounded too formal?

Jeepers, maybe she would have said "Dear So-and-So" to anybody!

A worried frown will now appear on his face. But it disappears as soon as he really gets to thinking about the first sentence. She certainly wouldn't have written *that* to anybody!

And so he works his way through the letter, one moment perched blissfully on a cloud, the next moment huddled miserably behind an eight-ball. It has started a hundred questions in his mind. He could quote it by heart. In fact, he will—to himself—for weeks to come.

Then the advertisement concluded,

If people read books with anything like the same concentration, we'd be a race of mental giants.[1]

Likewise, if people read Scripture with anything like the same concentration, we would be a race of spiritual giants.

If you want to understand the Bible, you've got to learn to read— better and faster, as for the first time, and as if you were reading a love letter. Just think of it: God wanted to communicate with you in the twentieth century—and He wrote His message in a Book.

1. From Robert A. Traina, *Methodical Bible Study: A New Approach to Hermeneutics* (Wilmore, Ky.: Robert A. Traina, 1952) pp. 97-98.

Four Versions of 1 Corinthians 13

KING JAMES

Though I speak with the tongues of men and of angels, and have not charity, I am become as sounding brass, or a tinkling cymbal.

And though I have *the gift of* prophecy, and understand all mysteries, and all knowledge; and though I have all faith, so that I could remove mountains, and have not charity, I am nothing.

And though I bestow all my goods to feed *the poo*r, and though I give my body to be burned, and have not charity, it profiteth me nothing.

Charity suffereth long, *and* is kind; charity envieth not; charity vaunteth not itself, is not puffed up,

Doth not behave itself unseemly, seeketh not her own, is not easily provoked, thinketh no evil;

Rejoiceth not in iniquity, but rejoiceth in the truth;

Beareth all things, believeth all things, hopeth all things, endureth all things.

Charity never faileth: but whether *there be* prophecies, they shall fail; whether *there be* tongues, they shall cease; whether *there be* knowledge, it shall vanish away.

For we know in part, and we prophesy in part.

But when that which is perfect is come, then that which is in part shall be done away.

When I was a child, I spake as a child, I understood as a child, I thought as a child, but when I became a man, I put away childish things.

For now we see through a glass, darkly; but then face to face: now I know in part; but then shall I know even as also I am known.

And now abideth faith, hope, charity, these three; but the greatest of these *is* charity.

THE NEW KING JAMES

Though I speak with the tongues of men and of angels, but have not love, I have become as sounding brass or a clanging cymbal. And though I have *the gift of* prophecy, and understand all mysteries and all knowledge, and though I have all faith, so that I could remove mountains, but have not love, I am nothing. And though I bestow all my goods to feed *the poor*, and though I give my body to be burned, but have not love, it profits me nothing.

Love suffers long *and* is kind; love does not envy; love does not parade itself, is not puffed up; does not behave rudely, does not seek its own, is not provoked, thinks no evil; does not rejoice in iniquity, but rejoices in the truth; bears all things, believes all things, hopes all things, endures all things.

Love never fails. But whether *there are* prophecies, they will fail; whether *there are* tongues, they will cease; whether *there is* knowledge, it will vanish away. For we know in part and we prophesy in part. But when that which is perfect has come, then that which is in part will be done away.

When I was a child, I spoke as a child, I understood as a child, I thought as a child; but when I became a man, I put away childish things. For now we see in a mirror, dimly, but then face to face. Now I know in part, but then I shall know just as I also am known.

And now abide faith, hope, love, these three; but the greatest of these *is* love.

Holy Bible, *New King James Version* (Nashville, Tenn.: Thomas Nelson, 1982), pp. 1107-8.

PHILLIPS' NEW TESTAMENT IN MODERN ENGLISH

If I speak with the eloquence of men and of angels, but have no love, I become no more than blaring brass or crashing cymbal. If I have the gift of foretelling the future and hold in my mind not only all human knowledge but the very secrets of God, and if I also have that absolute faith which can move mountains, but have no love, I amount to nothing at all. If I dispose of all that I possess, yes, even if I give my own body to be burned, but have no love, I achieve precisely nothing.

This love of which I speak is slow to lose patience—it looks for a way of being constructive. It is not possessive: it is neither anxious to impress nor does it cherish inflated ideas of its own importance.

Love has good manners and does not pursue selfish advantage. It is not touchy. It does not keep account of evil or gloat over the wickedness of other people. On the contrary, it shares the joy of those who live by the truth.

Love knows no limit to its endurance, no end to its trust, no fading of its hope; it can outlast anything. Love never fails.

For if there are prophecies they will be fulfilled and done with, if there are "tongues" the need for them will disappear, if there is knowledge it will be swallowed up in truth. For our knowledge is always incomplete and our prophecy is always incomplete, and when the complete comes, that is the end of the incomplete.

When I was a little child I talked and felt and thought like a little child. Now that I am a man I have finished with childish things.

At present we are men looking at puzzling reflections in a mirror. The time will come when we shall see reality whole and face to face! At present all I know is a little fraction of the truth, but the time will come when I shall know it as fully as God has known me!

In this life we have three lasting qualities—faith, hope and love. But the greatest of them is love.

J. B. Phillips, *The New Testament in Modern English*, rev. (New York: Macmillan, 1955), pp. 361-62.

COTTON PATCH VERSION

1 Atlanta 13

Though I speak with the tongues of men and of angels, but have no love, I am a hollow-sounding horn or a nerve-wracking rattle. And though I have the ability to preach, and know all the secrets and all the slogans, and though I have sufficient faith to move a mountain, but have no love, I am nothing. Even though I renounce all my possessions, and give my body as a flaming sacrifice, but have no love, I accomplish exactly nothing. Love is long-suffering and kind. Love is not envious, nor does it strut and brag. It does not act up, nor try to get things for itself. It pitches no tantrums, keeps no books on insults or injuries, sees no fun in wickedness, but rejoices when truth prevails. Love is all-embracing, all-trusting, all-hoping, all-enduring. Lover never quits. As for sermons, they shall be silenced; as for oratory, it shall cease; as for knowledge, it will vanish. For our knowledge is immature, and our preaching is immature; but when that which is immature arrives, it supersedes the immature. For example, when I was a child, I was talking like a child, thinking like a child, acting like a child, but when I became an adult, I outgrew my childish ways. So, on the childish level [i.e., *without love*] we look at one another in a trick mirror, but on the adult level [i.e., *with love*] we see face to face; as a child [i.e., *without love*] I understand immaturely, but as an adult [i.e., *with love*] I'll understand just as I'll be understood. Now these three things endure: faith, hope and love; but the greatest of all is love. Seek diligently for love.

Clarence Jordan, *The Cotton Patch Version of Paul's Epistles* (New York: Association Press, 1968), pp. 66-67.

Answers to reading test questions, page 68: 1. F; 2. F; 3. T; 4. F; 5. T. What percentage did you answer correctly?

TEN STRATEGIES TO FIRST-RATE READING

Read Thoughtfully
Read Repeatedly
Read Patiently
Read Selectively
Read Prayerfully
Read Imaginatively
Read Meditatively
Read Purposefully
Read Acquisitively
Read Telescopically

8

READ THOUGHTFULLY

T he step of observation requires you to assume the role of a biblical detective, searching for clues as to the meaning of the text. But as any detective will tell you, there is more than one way to crack a case.

Sherlock Holmes, the master sleuth, can sometimes be found on his hands and knees, inspecting the floor for cigar ashes or footprints. Other times he broods for hours, rolling things over and over in his mind, straining for answers. He assumes disguises, feigns sickness, conducts experiments—whatever it takes to solve the mystery.

In the same way, finding clues in the biblical text demands more than one approach. The Bible must be read to be understood. But there is more than one way to read it. In fact, I'm going to give you ten strategies that can turn you into a first-rate reader. Each one yields different clues about what the text means. The first one is:

READ THE BIBLE THOUGHTFULLY

Thoughtful reading involves study. Not boredom. Far from it. When you come to the Bible, put your thinking cap on. Don't throw your mind into neutral. Apply the same mental discipline that you would to any subject in which you take a vital interest. Are you a stockbroker? Then use the same mental intensity to study Scripture that you would *The Wall Street Journal*. Are you a pilot? Then pay as much attention to the Word as you would to a flight plan or a weather advisory. Are you a nurse? Then look for the "vital signs" in the biblical text just as you would with any patient on your floor. The Bible does not yield its fruit to the lazy.

Proverbs 2:4 gives an interesting insight concerning the richness of God's Word. It likens biblical wisdom to precious ore, found not lying around on the surface but at a deeper level. A good analogy for our own day would be the many oil deposits under the parched deserts of the Middle East. For millennia, people wandered across those trackless wastes, unaware that only a few thousand feet away lay resources of unimaginable value.

So it is with Scripture. The very truth of God is there, able to transform your life. But you must probe for it. You've got to penetrate the surface with more than just a cursory glance. In other words, you've got to think.

To change the metaphor, your objective needs to be to develop a spiritual "cud" so that you've got something to think about, something to chew on. In effect, you need to program your mind with God's truth.

THE BOOK THAT REFUSED TO BE WRITTEN

One of the best examples I know of thoughtful Bible reading is the story of Frank Morison. An English journalist at the turn of the century, Morison set out to disprove the resurrection of Jesus Christ:

> When, as a very young man, I first began seriously to study the life of Christ, I did so with a very definite feeling that, if I may so put it, His history rested upon very insecure foundations.[1]

Morison had been heavily influenced by certain scholars of his day who were out to debunk the biblical narrative and destroy the credibility of Scripture. Moreover, science seemed to undermine Scripture at many points.

> It was about this time—more for the sake of my own peace of mind than for publication—that I conceived the idea of writing a short monograph on what seemed to me to be the supremely important and critical phase in the life of Christ— the last seven days....

1. Frank Morison, *Who Moved the Stone?* (London: Faber and Faber, 1930), p. 9.

It seemed to me [...] f I could come at the truth why this man died a cruel de[ath at] the hands of the Roman Power, how He Himself regard[ed th]e matter, and especially how He behaved under the [...] should be very near to the true solution of the proble[m].

The "problem" that M[orison] was out to solve was the problem many modern people have [...] can anyone believe in supernatural miracles when the world i[s obvio]usly governed by natural laws and forces? The supreme miracle [of Scr]ipture is the resurrection of Christ. If one can explain that away, t[he othe]rs will surely fade away with it.

Morison's quest to dispro[ve the] resurrection took him directly to the four gospels. He studied t[he life] of Christ in extraordinary detail, paying particular attention [to the] final seven days before His crucifixion. He analyzed the tr[ial of] Jesus before the Jewish leaders and before the Roman governo[r Pilat]e. He evaluated the timing of events and the physical space in [which] they occurred. He considered the psychological factors behind [the be]havior of Pilate and his wife, Claudia. He compared the beha[vior of] those who deserted Christ with those who remained by His s[ide].

Morison also asked a preemin[ent qu]estion: What was it that caused the entirety of Jesus' follow[ers to] quickly and unanimously claim that He had risen from the [dead?] He looked at two of the disciples in detail: Peter the fisherm[an an]d James, the brother of Jesus. He also examined the conver[sion an]d conviction of Saul of Tarsus.

In short,

the opportunity came to *study* the li[fe of C]hrist as I had long wanted to *study* it, to *investigate* the o[rigins] of its literature, to *sift* some of the evidence at first han[d, and] to form my own *judgment* on the problem which it prese[nts. I w]ill only say that it effected *a revolution in my thought*. Thi[s em]erged from that old-world story which previously I [...] have thought impossible. Slowly but very definitely th[e convi]ction grew that the drama of those unforgettable weeks o[f huma]n history was stranger and deeper than it seemed. It wa[s the s]trangeness of many notable things in the story which fi[rst arres]ted and held

2. Morison, p. 11.

my *interest*. It was only later that *the irresistible logic of their meaning* came into view.[3]

Can you see how involved Morison's mind was in this Bible study process? Here was a man reading thoughtfully. He was applying the same mental process to his study of the New Testament as he did to his journalism.

Result: The book that he started out to write turned out to be "the book that refused to be written." Instead, integrity demanded that he write *Who Moved the Stone?* Published in 1930, it is still one of the best defenses of the resurrection of Christ ever produced. It's really the story of Morison's conversion to Christianity. And it's a quintessential illustration of the first strategy of Bible reading: Read thoughtfully.

3. Morison, pp. 11-12, italics added.

You Try It

Here is a project that will help you cultivate the skill of reading Scripture thoughtfully. It involves the little book of Philemon in the New Testament. Only twenty-five verses long, Philemon records Paul's advice to an old friend whose slave, Onesimus, had run away. Onesimus encountered Paul in Rome, became a believer, and now Paul sends him back to his master with the letter in hand.

Read Philemon according to the principles of thoughtful reading. Barrage the text with questions. What can you find out about the relationships between Paul, Philemon, and Onesimus? Reconstruct the situation. What feelings might be involved? What practical considerations? What questions remain unanswered as you read this letter? What problems does it create? What issues does it speak to? Why do you think it is significant enough to be included in the Bible? What issues do we face today that this book might speak to? How would you communicate this book and the insights you gain from it to someone else?

9

READ REPEATEDLY

Years ago I read a book in which the author wrote, "When I read this passage for the one hundredth time, the following idea came to me...."

I thought, *You've got to be kidding!* In those days, if I read a portion of Scripture twice, it would be incredible. If I read it three or four times, it would be miraculous. But here was this great, seasoned Bible student telling me that I needed to read it over and over again—not once or twice but a hundred times, if necessary, to gain insight.

Today I realize that he was wisely practicing the second strategy to first-rate Bible reading:

READ THE BIBLE REPEATEDLY

The genius of the Word of God is that it has staying power; it can stand up to repeated exposure. In fact, that's why it is unlike any other book. You may be an expert in a given field. If you read a book in that field two or three times, you've got it. You can put it on the shelf and move on to something else. But that's never true of the Bible. Read it over and over again, and you'll still see things that you've never seen before.

Let me suggest several ideas to help you in this process.

Read entire books at one sitting

I know what you're thinking. You're thinking about books such as Isaiah and Jeremiah, and you're saying "Man, I'd die before I got through them." But may I remind you that the bulk of the books in Scripture are no longer than two or three ordinary columns in a newspaper. And even the longer books are shorter than most novels. So go ahead and read books of the Bible at one sitting.

The value here is that you'll be able to appreciate the unity of each book. That's what most people miss when they skip from passage to passage. They never get a sense of the whole. Consequently, their perception is fragmented. It's like switching from channel to channel on a TV set, catching a few scenes or snatches of dialogue but never watching an entire program.

I remember one time when I was studying the book of Matthew. I had studied it before and even taught it. But frankly, I had never quite grasped where the writer was going. So I carved out a slice of time one Saturday morning and read the entire twenty-eight chapters. For the first time in my life, I finally began to understand what Matthew was trying to communicate in his book.

The same is true for the rest of the books. Each one was written as a unit that only hangs together when read in its entirety. Reading it at one sitting will help you grasp that big picture.

Start at the beginning of the book

Often readers dive into the middle of a book in the Bible, and then they can't figure out why the text makes no sense. They wouldn't think of starting a novel in the fifth or sixth chapter, and then condemning it as dull and uninteresting. But that's exactly what they do to the Scriptures. They take a passage, rip it out of its context until it virtually screams, and then wonder why they can't understand it.

Remember our study of Acts 1:8? Fortunately the first word, "but," warned us to go back and check out the context. And since we were only eight verses into the book, it was no problem to pick up the narrative from the beginning. Doing so helped us discover some fascinating things about the purpose of the book, the writer, the man to whom it was written, and the setting in which verse 8 takes place.

But suppose we had chosen to study Acts 2:8, or 8:8, or 28:8. Standing by themselves, these verses make little sense. It is not until we link them with their surrounding paragraphs, and those paragraphs with their surrounding sections, and those sections with the entire book of Acts, that they take on significance.

So we're back to the same issue: the books of the Bible were written as units. If you cut them anywhere, they bleed. So if chapter 7 has the measles, you can be sure that chapters 6 and 8 have got the same disease.

Read the Bible in different translations

The danger in reading repeatedly is familiarity with the text. After a while you can put yourself to sleep. One way to avoid that is to use a variety of translations so that once you're on intimate terms with one, you can try another. It keeps the experience alive, and you're bound to notice new things.

Listen to tapes of Scripture

One of the most exciting developments of the last few years is the proliferation of audiocassettes of the Bible. You can get almost any translation you want. I like to listen to them in the car, but there's nothing to prevent you from listening to them while you're working in the yard, painting the garage, tanning at the beach, or jogging down the street.

The values of this habit are many. First, you change the sensory experience from the visual to the audible. For many portions of Scripture, this is closer to the way the material was originally presented than it is in its current, written form. For instance, all of the teaching of Jesus, including the parables and the Sermon on the Mount, was presented verbally. The book of Job was probably recited long before it was written down. And the psalms were mostly sung, not read. Hearing the words is a far more involving experience than reading them.

The voice of the reader helps, too. No two people read Scripture exactly the same way. So hearing the tapes is like encountering a new translation. The words may be the same, but the emphases are different. Furthermore, if the reader knows what he's doing, he can bring the text alive in an engaging way.

A final benefit of audiotaped Scripture is that you can play the tapes over and over to gain the value of repetition. I mentioned the man who had read a particular passage at least a hundred times. Imagine hearing a passage one hundred times. You think you might remember something of the truth in that passage?

Read the Bible out loud

This follows from everything I have said. There's nothing like the sound of your own voice to get you involved in Scripture. Reading out loud forces you to pay attention to every word.

Furthermore, there's actually a biblical precedent for doing so. Deuteronomy 6:7 instructs parents, especially fathers, to "teach [the words of Scripture] diligently to your sons and...talk of them when you sit in your house and when you walk by the way and when you lie down and when you rise up." In other words, God's Word should be part and parcel of your conversation at home. In light of this principle, I ask, when was the last time your kids heard you read the Bible to them?

Actually, I encourage you to let your whole family get in on the act. Have your kids read to you, then you read to them. Work your way through the gospels, or the Old Testament histories, or perhaps one of the epistles. Use a translation that is easy to read. I guarantee you'll drive biblical truth where it belongs—into your memory.

Set up a schedule for Bible reading

This idea has been around for years, and with good reason. Many of us feel exhausted just looking at the Bible. We figure we'll be in our rocking chairs by the time we read the entire thing. But the truth is that it's possible to read through the whole Book in a year's time if we read a few chapters a day. Many Bibles even have a schedule for that in the back.

Imagine sticking to a program like that year after year. It wouldn't take long to read every verse ten, twenty, or even thirty times.

Of course, you don't have to take a through-the-Bible-in-a-year approach. You could try reading a psalm in the morning and a psalm at night. That would take you through the entire book of Psalms almost five times in a year. Or read a chapter of Proverbs every day— the entire book every month. Or concentrate on one book for one month: a chapter of Ephesians or Galatians every day on Monday through Saturday, four times; or a chapter of 1 John every day for thirty days.

You can create your own schedule for completing these books. Or come up with a plan of your own. The point is, devise a way to help you mark your progress. If you're a person who needs structure or who likes to achieve goals, this is a great way to read Scripture repeatedly.

Here's a year-long plan,
beginning in the fall,
that will take you through
eleven different
kinds of books.

You Try It

Are you convinced of the value of repeated Bible reading? Here's an exercise to dispel any lingering doubts: Read through the entire Old Testament book of Esther once a day for seven days in a row. It should take about half an hour or so each day. Use some of the suggestions in this chapter, such as reading it in different versions, reading it out loud, or perhaps even listening to it on audiocassette. Of course, you should also use the other skills of Observation I mentioned earlier. See how many new things you can see on each successive day. Make a list of your observations, or record them in your Bible. At the end of the week, see if you can reconstruct the story clearly and accurately by telling it to someone else. Also, what insights have you gained from the story?

10

READ PATIENTLY

There's an old saying that nothing good happens fast. I don't know if that's altogether true, but it does pertain to Bible study. Unless you have highly developed habits of reading, it's unlikely that you can just dip into the Word for five minutes and come away with much of significance. In fact, highly skilled readers devote a lot more than five minutes to the task. They've learned to approach Scripture using the third strategy of first-rate reading:

READ THE BIBLE PATIENTLY

That's a hard assignment for most of us. We live in an instant society. The things we used to want tomorrow, we now want right now. And the things we used to need right away, we now need yesterday. So it's no surprise that if we do decide to open our Bibles, we expect results instantly and effortlessly. If we don't hit the jackpot in short order, we're liable to get very frustrated, very quickly.

But the fruit of the Word takes time to ripen. So if you are the least bit impatient, you're liable to bail out early and miss a rich harvest. Many people do that. They get disillusioned with the process. Perhaps they are looking for entertainment rather than enlightenment. People tell me, "Look, I tried to read the Bible, but it's like plowing through concrete."

Others give up on the biblical text and turn instead to secondary sources. The moment they think they are in over their heads, they make a mad dash for a commentary to find out what some other significant saint has to say about the passage. In the process, they ruin the experience because they quit too soon. They are usually right on the verge of paydirt when they go to secondary sources. There's nothing wrong with using secondary sources—after you have drenched your mind with what the biblical text says.

IN IT FOR THE LONG HAUL

When I was in college I ran track. I ran low hurdles, which makes sense since I'm built so close to the ground. In those days a man named Gil Dodds was the world's indoor mile champion.

I'll never forget the first time I met him. We were standing on the track when he tapped me and said, "C'mon, Howie. Let's go around." So I took off. I found myself several paces in front of him, which puzzled me. I thought, *If you're supposed to be the world's indoor mile champion, why don't you run a little faster?*

What I didn't realize was that he was planning to go around again. I was running as fast as I could. But when I finally got around the track he tapped me again and yelled, "C'mon, Howie. Only three more to go."

I thought, *Good night, I'm going to die right here!*

You see, there's a vast difference between running sprints and running cross-country. To do the latter you need to develop the kicker, the second wind. You've got to prepare for the long haul. So it is with patient Bible reading. You have to develop some stamina, some staying power to hang on with a text until you start to make some progress. Let me suggest a few things to help.

Work with one book for one month

I find that there's a rhythm to life, and for many of us the cycle takes about a month to six weeks. We can stick with something for about that long, but then we need a change of pace.

In Bible study, five weeks with a book is usually enough time to make some significant headway. In five weeks you can read the book through several times. You can also observe its structure, identify the key terms, investigate the central characters, do some background work with secondary sources, and decide on some practical ways to apply the truths of the book to your life. I'll discuss all of these tasks in later chapters.

The point is that in a month's time, you can begin to take ownership of a book of the Bible. One book may not seem like much, but it may be one more than you currently understand. In a year's time, you can have twelve books under your belt; in five-and-a-half years, sixty-six. Can you believe that you could be less than six years away from having a firsthand grasp of the entire Bible?

Any book will fit into a five- or six-week study plan, but a few suggestions to get you started are Nehemiah, Jonah, the gospel by Mark, 1 Corinthians, Philippians, James, or 1 Peter. Nehemiah, Jonah, and Mark are "user-friendly" narratives, with plot and characterization. The four other books mentioned are letters to Christians that are short and practical. You won't have much trouble figuring out what the writers are trying to say.

Zoom in and zoom out

A month may seem like a long time to spend with a single book, but it's really not that much time. And since there is so much to see in any passage (remember, we identified no less than thirty observations in Acts 1:8 alone), you have to settle for limited objectives.

One strategy is to use a zoom lens for your approach. Start with a wide angle. Back off and get the big picture by reading the book in its entirety. See if you can detect a flow in the material, a progression of events or ideas. Then zoom in on something that seems prominent. If you use the month-long approach, spend a week or so on that one event or idea.

For instance, in Genesis, the first eleven chapters sweep through the creation of the universe, the Flood, and the confusion of tongues at Babel. Then the next thirty-nine chapters cover just four generations, led by four men—Abraham, Isaac, Jacob, and Joseph. That's the big picture of Genesis. But some events worth zooming in on are the creation narrative (chapters 1-2), the Flood (chapters 6-10), the sacrifice of Isaac (chapter 22), and Jacob's prophecy concerning his sons (chapter 49).

Once you spend some time on one of these smaller events, you can zoom in even more and study one particular feature in detail. For example, in the creation account, God establishes marriage (2:18-25). This is a passage worth intensive study because the principles established here carry throughout the Scriptures. Jesus refers to this passage (Matthew 19:4-6), as does Paul (Ephesians 5:31). Its presence here also forces you to ask, What place does marriage have in Genesis?

After you've zoomed in to study a particular event or concept or word, make sure you zoom back out to recall the big picture. Remember, you don't want to end up with a lot of disconnected fragments but rather with a unified whole in which all the details fit in with the overall message of the book.

Alter your approach

As we're seeing, there is more than one way to study Scripture. The more strategies you use, the more insight you will gain. And the way to hang in there for the long haul of Bible study is to vary your approach, just as runners vary their pace. In subsequent chapters we'll talk about some different techniques you can use with different kinds of material.

TWO PRINCIPLES OF PATIENCE

The keys to reading the Bible patiently are: Be patient with the text, and be patient with yourself. I've suggested some ways to be patient with the text to give it a chance to reveal its message.

Perhaps a more difficult principle, especially for the inexperienced Bible student, is to be patient with yourself. Often a person will attend a church service or a Bible conference where he hears a speaker deliver an incredible exposition of the Word. In response, he becomes a real eager beaver who can't wait to get into the text. He's so motivated to discover truths for himself that he can't see straight. And that's wonderful.

But what he forgets is that the speaker has been studying the Scriptures diligently for years. There's no way that a novice can start out at that level. Remember my "race" with Gil Dodds? I started out like a flash of lightning. But the champion knew what it took to go the distance. I didn't.

So as you dive into the Word for yourself, relax and enjoy the experience. God's truth is there, and you'll find it if you just give yourself time to read patiently.

11

READ SELECTIVELY

M y sons will tell you that I'm not much of a fisherman. I love to fish, but I don't catch very much. Our family used to take vacations in Colorado, and we'd go to a little pond where there were trout about half the size of a canoe! But do you think I could hook one of those babies? No way!

I tried every gimmick the tackle shops had to sell. No luck. Those fish would come right up to the shore, and I dangled the hook right in front of their noses. But all in all, I caught very little.

The frustrating thing was, just down the shoreline were always a couple of old duffers with two or three rigs, and they couldn't reel the fish in fast enough. We'd be talking to them while they were pulling one in, and meanwhile one of their other lines would be dancing with a strike.

What was their secret? Not only did they know the pond and not only did they know trout, they knew what bait to use.

They illustrated the fourth strategy of first-rate Bible reading:

READ THE BIBLE SELECTIVELY

Selective Bible reading involves using the right bait when you troll the Scriptures. Here are six "lures" that you can use with any text, six questions to ask any passage of Scripture.

Who?

Who are the people in the text? That's a pretty simple question to answer. Just read the text. But once you've identified who is in the passage, I suggest you look for two things.

First, what is said about the person or people? For example, Joshua 2:1 introduces Rahab, but it identifies her as "a harlot whose name was Rahab." And from then on she is known as "Rahab the harlot." How would you like that hung around your neck? She never shows up again in the account without that full title.

Or how about Andrew, Simon Peter's brother. Do you know anyone with a famous brother or sister, or a famous parent? Every time he's introduced, it's, "This is Andrew. You know, Peter's brother." It's as if he has no identity of his own. That was Andrew's predicament. The point is, whenever anything is said about a person, make a note of it.

And be sure to consult other passages to learn everything you can about the person. For example, the preface to Psalm 88 tells us that the psalm is a "Maskil of Heman the Ezrahite." (By the way, those prefatory notes are considered part of the biblical text.) Who in the world was Heman the Ezrahite? The psalm doesn't tell you. You have to go back to the historical books to find out. When you do, you can begin to piece together a fascinating portrait that explains why Psalm 88 is so dark and disturbing.

Or take Hebrews 11. It lists more than a dozen figures from the Old Testament. But unless you go back and study what was said about them there, you'll never appreciate what Hebrews contributes.

A second thing to look for is, what does the person say? Take Peter on the Mount of Transfiguration (Matthew 17:1-8). There he is, enjoying one of the most incredible experiences ever committed to a human being. What does he say? "Lord, it is good for us to be here." (That must be the understatement of the first century.) "Let's build three tabernacles—three lean-tos—and stay up here and perpetuate the conference." You see, Peter was the kind of guy whose motto was: Don't just stand there—say something.

You may wonder, why does God clutter the biblical text with this sort of stuff? Why so many inane, off-the-wall comments and details? The reason is because He wants you to see the process people went through in order to come to the conclusions they came to.

What?

A second question to ask is, what is happening in this text? What are the events? In what order? What happens to the characters? Or, if it's a passage that argues a point: What is the argument? What is the point? What is the writer trying to communicate?

Another What? question is, what's wrong with this picture? There are a number of these in the Old Testament. For example, King Saul makes war against the Amalekites in 1 Samuel 15. He wipes them out, captures their king, plunders their spoils, and prepares to praise God with sacrifices. But what's wrong with this picture? Samuel puts his finger on the problem (15:19): "Why did you not obey the Lord?" Saul had obeyed, but not completely. And in God's economy, partial obedience is disobedience.

Where?

This gives you the location. Where is the narrative taking place? Where are the people in the story? Where are they coming from? Where are they going? Where is the writer? Where were the original readers of this text?

The question Where? is one reason to have a set of maps or an atlas whenever you study the Bible. That's why at the end of many Bibles you'll find several maps. It isn't because the publishers couldn't find their way. It's to show you where the biblical events took place.

Are you are studying a journey? Then trace it on a map. Are you studying 1 Corinthians? Find Corinth on a map. Are you in Acts 8 with Philip and the Ethiopian eunuch? Find out about the road south from Jerusalem to Gaza and what sort of country the official was traveling through.

I taught a class once in which there was a woman who had several advanced degrees. Right in the middle of one of the sessions she put up her hand and asked, "Dr. Hendricks, what part of South America is this taking place in?" We were studying the gospel by Mark.

Here was an obviously intelligent, informed individual. But I had overlooked the fact that she had no idea of New Testament geography. She's not alone. This has become a blind spot in our culture. When you read about places in the Bible, don't assume anything; you'll seldom be disappointed. Most people don't have a clue as to where biblical events took place.

When?

This is the question of time. When did the events in the text take place? When did they occur in relation to other events in Scripture? When was the writer writing?

In short, always determine what time it is. For example, in Mark 1:35, we read, "And in the early morning, while it was still dark, [Jesus] arose and went out and departed to a lonely place, and was praying there." It's easy enough to tell when this happened: "in the early morning." But which morning? It was the morning after the busiest day recorded in the life of our Lord. There are only fifty-two of them in the gospels. That particular day was jam-packed with miracles, teaching, and healing.

May I say it reverently? Jesus had every reason to sleep in that morning. He even could have used the excuse, "I was about your business, Father." But so high on His priority list was intercourse with the infinite God, that He got up a great while before daylight and went to a solitary place and prayed. Now if Jesus Christ, who had unbroken fellowship and communion with the Father, needed to pray, what must my need be? What must your need be?

We learn this sort of thing by asking a simple question: When did this take place?

Why?

There is an infinity of Why? questions to ask the biblical text. Why is this included? Why is it placed here? Why does it follow that? Why does it precede that? Why does this person say that? Why does someone say nothing? Why? is a question that digs for meaning.

For example, the parable of the prodigal son is found only in the gospel by Luke—not in Matthew, Mark, or John. Why? Why does Luke alone record this powerful parable?

Or, we come to the book of Acts, and frankly, there's no ending. Paul is in Rome, teaching and preaching. But we never find out what happens to him, or to the early church, or to the rest of the apostles. Why? Why did Luke not continue the narrative? Why did no one else pick up where he left off?

The question Why? probes the text more than any other. Asking it will inevitably lead to new insights.

Wherefore?

I like to paraphrase this question, So what? What difference would it make if I were to apply this truth?

Wherefore? is the question that gets us started doing something about what we've read. Remember, the Word of God was not written to satisfy our curiosity; it was written to change our lives. So with any passage of Scripture, we need to ask, So what? When we get to the step of Application, I'm going to show you a number of ways to answer that question.

SELECTIVE READING AT THIRTY THOUSAND FEET

Can those six questions really unlock the Bible for you? After all, they are really very simple. Reporters have been using them for years to get the facts for their stories. So how powerful can they be?

One time I was flying from Dallas to San Francisco on a 747. There were eight passengers and fifteen flight attendants. After we got up in the air, I was reading my New Testament when one of the flight attendants came down the aisle. When she saw me with my Bible open, she stopped and asked, "Oh, are you a believer?"

"I certainly am," I said. "How about you?"

"Yes, I am, too," she replied with a smile.

We got into a conversation about spiritual things. Finally I said, "Would you mind if I asked a question?"

"Of course not."

"Do you have a regular Bible study program?"

"No, sir, I'm afraid I don't."

"Why not?"

She said, "I don't know how. I don't know where to begin."

So I asked, "Would you like to learn?"

"I'd love to."

"Have you got some time?"

She had time to burn on that flight. So I took out one of those sickness bags (they make wonderful notepads) and wrote the six questions mentioned above: Who? What? Where? When? Why? Wherefore?

Then we went through Mark 4:35-41, the stilling of the storm. I asked her to read the passage, and then we went through the questions: Who are the people involved? What is happening in this paragraph? Where is it taking place? When is it taking place? Why do you think God put it in the narrative? And what difference would this make in your life?

I've rarely seen someone so excited. When we finished she asked me, "How is it that I've been a Christian now for seven years, and nobody ever taught me how to study the Bible?"

That's a good question. But it's really a tragedy. The church today is leading people to Christ, but sometimes they are in the faith for ten, fifteen, or even twenty years without learning how to study the Bible. The reason? They don't know where to begin. They don't know how to go about it.

They are a lot like I was at that pond in Colorado—looking at the fish, but unable to land any of them for myself. That's no big deal when you're just on vacation. But when you are starving spiritually—and most people are—you need to learn how to fish.

I suggest you try the six lures of selective Bible reading that I've mentioned. They'll help anyone catch a few big ones.

You Try It

The six questions of selective Bible reading are especially fun when you study the stories of Scripture. Luke 24:13-35 records one of the most fascinating—the account of Jesus meeting two of His disciples on the road to Emmaus following His resurrection. Read that passage two or three times, and then probe it with the six questions presented in this chapter. Don't forget to write down your observations.

12

R EAD PRAYERFULLY

A fifth strategy to use in unlocking Scripture is:

READ THE BIBLE PRAYERFULLY

We tend to think of Bible study and prayer as separate disciplines, but the fact is, they are integrally related. Prayer is really a key to effective Bible study. Learn to pray before, during, and after your reading of the Scriptures.

Prayer is especially crucial when you come to a place in your study where you are hung up and confused. That's a good time to stop and carry on a conversation with God. "Lord, I can't make any sense out of this passage. I don't understand it. Give me insight. Help me to discover Your truth."

However, most of us struggle when it comes to prayer. Do you? Do you want to learn how to pray? Here are a couple of suggestions — something to avoid and something to do:

Don't try to imitate other Christians

If you listen too much to the prayers of other believers, you will only pick up all of the clichés, all of the lingo, all of the shibboleths to get you over Jordan. Without question, Christians should pray corporately. But that doesn't mean they should pray identically.

I've discovered there are two groups of people who can teach you the most about praying. Number one, children. They are refreshing and realistic. How many churches do you suppose recite the Lord's Prayer week after week? And week after week it's the same old thing—the same words, the same rhythm, the same corporate mumble. But what a difference when a four year old launches into a simple, eloquent rendition before dinner or bedtime.

The other group to listen to is new converts. They haven't learned all of the jargon. A man in our church came to Christ and decided to show up for a prayer meeting and Bible study on Wednesday night. We had the study, and then we broke into groups for prayer.

"Hey, Howie. Where are we going?" he asked me as we headed down the hall.

"We're going down here to pray," I said.

"Good night, I've got a problem," he exclaimed.

"What's your problem?"

"I can't pray. I mean, I can't say it the way you guys say it."

I said, "Friend, that's no problem. Thank God for that."

So we began praying. I knew he wanted to participate, but he was a little hesitant. Finally, I reached over and prompted him to go ahead. I'd give anything to have a recording of what happened next.

He said, "Lord, this is Jim. I'm the one that met You last Thursday, remember?" (I thought he was going to give God his zip code.) "I'm sorry I can't say it the way the rest of these guys say it, but I really love You. Honestly, I do. And hopefully, after I know You a while, I'll be able to say it a lot better. Thanks a lot. I'll see you later."

You know what that man did? He turned on a prayer meeting. You see, the rest of us were saying prayers. As usual, we were reviewing our theology, taking our tour of the mission field, scraping the Milky Way. This guy was praying. Just talking to God. Without realizing it, he was way ahead of the rest of us because he was honest before his heavenly Father. The only thing that ever moves Him is our heart.

Do turn Scripture into prayer

God loves to be reminded of what He has promised. So tell Him. Remind Him. Claim His promises.

Let me give you a beautiful illustration of this from Nehemiah. We're going to come back to this man in chapter 18, when we look at how to study a paragraph. But for now, I want you to see how Nehemiah turns God's Word into prayer. If you want to learn to pray, study his prayer. It's a classic. (You can find it printed on pages 131-32, or turn to Nehemiah 1:4-11.)

To set the context, Nehemiah is a highly placed Jewish official in the Babylonian court. Messengers arrive to tell him that his hometown, Jerusalem, is in dire straits. Its walls are broken down, and the people are in distress.

So Nehemiah goes to his knees. His instinctive response is to pray. There's a lesson right there. As he prays, the first thing he does is to adore God:

> And I said, "I beseech Thee, O Lord God of heaven, the great and awesome God, who preserves the covenant and lovingkindness for those who love Him and keep His commandments." (1:5)

We can put the label "adoration" next to that verse. Before he gets to anything else, Nehemiah occupies himself with who God is.

Is that the way we pray? No, we're more likely to say, "Oh, Lord, am I ever in a jam. Please bail me out." We focus on ourselves.

But the prayers of the Bible have one characteristic in common: they always focus on the Person to whom the prayer is addressed. Whenever we write out a check, we first need to ask how much we have in the bank. That's also what we need to do in terms of prayer. Looking at what we need, we should ask, Who are we talking to? What kind of a Person is this? Nehemiah fills his mind with who that Person is.

Then he changes his prayer. Having occupied himself with God, his next step is to confess his sin as well as his people's sin:

> I and my father's house have sinned. We have acted very corruptly against Thee and have not kept the commandments, nor the statutes, nor the ordinances which Thou didst command Thy servant Moses. (1:6-7)

We can put a second label next to these verses, "confession." The prayer is now focused on sin — not only the people's sin, but Nehemiah's sin, too. If you have children, you probably know they are prone to confess the sins of their brothers and sisters. But Nehemiah sets a different pattern. He says, in effect, "The first thing I want the Lord to know is that we have sinned." It's not those sinners out there, but it's us in here.

Do you notice any connection between Nehemiah's focus on sin following his focus on God? It's pretty clear, isn't it? A recognition of our sinfulness always follows a perception of God's holiness. You see, the reason we think we're such capable individuals is that we really don't know what kind of God we're related to. But when we fill our minds up with who God is, then our true condition comes to light.

Pay close attention to the next verses because they pinpoint the whole prayer. Nehemiah started with adoration, focusing on who God is. Then he moved to confession. Now he concludes by claiming God's promises:

> O Lord, I beseech Thee, may Thine ear be attentive to the prayer of Thy servant and the prayer of Thy servants who delight to revere Thy name, and make Thy servant successful today, and grant him compassion before this man. (1:11)

Nehemiah moves to what we call "petition." His focus is on the needs of his people. And in making his request, he leans on the promises of God. It's obvious that he was a good Bible student, because in verses 8-9 he recalls several passages from the first five books of the Bible where God had set forth conditions for blessing or punishment, based on the faithfulness or unfaithfulness of His people. Nehemiah reminds Him of that: "OK, Lord. Remember what You promised? Well, I'm asking You to perform it."

There's a great lesson in that. Always pray on the basis of the promises of God. After all, the question with any promise is, who made it? I can say to you, "Bill, I'm going to give you a million dollars for your cause." Great promise. But who made it? A guy who probably has about ten bucks right now. When a person makes a promise, always ask, who is making this promise?

Do you want to know how to pray? Nehemiah shows you: Begin with adoration. Occupy yourself with who God is. That will lead you to confession because you'll see yourself in proper perspective. Then you are ready to petition God with your need.

By the way, try a comparison study of passages such as Exodus 3 and Isaiah 6. You'll find this pattern for prayer from Genesis to Revelation.

A PSALM OF PRAYERFUL BIBLE STUDY

There's a powerful precedent for prayerful Bible study in Psalm 119. Significantly, it's the longest psalm in the Bible. In fact, it has more verses (176) than any other chapter in the canon. And every one of them has something to say about the Word of God—its purpose, its benefits, its value. I heartily recommend that you study it in detail.

A number of verses relate specifically to reading Scripture prayerfully. For instance, the psalmist uses the Word in praising God (v. 12). He asks God to help him become an observant reader (v. 18). He prays for understanding of God's truth (vv. 27, 34). He asks for help in applying that truth to his life (vv. 33, 35-36, 133). He points out that God's law is being broken; therefore, it is time for God to act (v. 126). He prays for mercy on the basis of God's character (v. 132). He bases his petitions on God's promises (vv. 169-170). He prays for forgiveness after reflecting on God's commands (v. 176).

What a brilliant example of prayerful Bible study. Imagine what might happen if Christians today approached the Word in this manner.

You Try It!

Of all the strategies to first-rate Bible reading, prayerful reading probably requires the most cultivation. Here are three projects to help you get started:

Psalm 23

Psalm 23 may be the most famous passage in Scripture, and for good reason: It paints a beautiful picture of the tender relationship between God and one of His children. You can turn this psalm into a personal prayer by inserting your name wherever you see the first-person pronouns, "my," "me," or "I."

Isaiah 40:28-31

Here's another passage that you can make your own through prayer. Look at the tremendous promises of God in this text! Do you need Him to deliver in your experience what He offers here? Turn this passage into your own prayer, asking God to do that.

Philippians 4:8-9

Here is another set of promises—and conditions—that you can read and study prayerfully. Review Paul's list of qualities, and ask yourself: What are some illustrations of these in my life? Then, on the basis of verse 8: What do I need to start practicing in order to know God's peace? Talk to God about the things mentioned in these verses and your response to them. Where does He need to change you? What attitudes and thoughts do you need His help to cultivate?

13

READ IMAGINATIVELY

I t is sad but true that the average person thinks that reading the Bible is dreadfully boring. In fact, the only thing more boring would be listening to someone teach from the Bible. Yet I'm convinced that the reason Scripture seems dull to so many people is that we come to it dully. How different things would be if we employed the sixth strategy for first-rate Bible reading:

READ THE BIBLE IMAGINATIVELY

"Why don't you read the Bible?" I've asked people.

"The Bible?" they reply incredulously. "C'mon, I've got better things to do with my time." You get the feeling that if you handed them a Bible, they'd stop to blow the dust off before they opened it.

And no wonder. Often when we come to the Scriptures, we use the least imaginative, most overworked approaches possible. For instance, how many times have you been in a group where the leader says, "Let's all turn to such-and-such a passage." You wait while everyone finds the place. That takes a while.

Then the leader goes on: "OK, we're going to read this passage together. Jim, why don't you start with verse 1. Then, Suzy, you take verse 2, and we'll work our way around."

So Jim starts in. Unfortunately, he's not such a good reader, and he's brought a King James Version with the old thees and thous. He stumbles all over the text trying to make sense of the king's English. By the time he's done, everybody else is nearly out cold.

Then Suzy takes her turn with an exotic modern translation, and no one else can follow along. Catastrophe strikes when the next person reads verse 3—but it's verse 3 in a different chapter. And so it goes. In the end, nobody has the foggiest idea what the passage really says. But it doesn't matter—most have already checked out mentally.

By contrast, our church used to have a pastor who was a master at dramatic presentations of Scripture. He had a background in theater, and he used it to advantage. Frequently he assumed the role of a biblical character in front of the congregation. He put on makeup and a costume. He did all kinds of background studies to give us a feel for the cultural setting. And then he told the character's story in the first person, using simple, everyday language.

As a result, by the time he finished, we were not simply entertained, we were instructed. Our imaginations kicked into gear, and we entered into the text. We understood how biblical truth and human experience could mingle.

One of the things I'd love to see more people do when they study the Bible is to pray this simple prayer: "Lord, clothe the facts with fascination. Help me crawl into the skin of these people—to see through their eyes, to feel with their fingers, to understand with their hearts, and to know with their minds." Then the Word of God would come alive.

Here are a number of suggestions for how to read imaginatively.

Use different translations and paraphrases
I'll mention this again and again. Reading different versions of the Bible is an excellent way to stimulate your imagination.

We are incredibly blessed to have such a variety of translations today. Until recently, Christians basically had one English version to read. In fact, prior to John Wycliffe's translation in 1382, there were none. But thanks to major developments in our understanding of ancient Hebrew and Greek, we now have some extraordinarily accurate translations, as well as some very readable ones.

One of my favorites is J. B. Phillips's *New Testament in Modern English* (revised edition). Phillips has a flowing style that does an excellent job of catching the atmosphere of the text. For example, let's compare how Paul's encounter in Acts 17:16-21 with the philosophers of Athens reads in Phillips as opposed to the *New American Standard Bible*, a very accurate translation. Here's the NASB:

Now while Paul was waiting for them at Athens, his spirit was being provoked within him as he was beholding the city full of idols. So he was reasoning in the synagogue with the Jews and the God-fearing Gentiles, and in the market place every day with those who happened to be present. And also some of the Epicurean and Stoic philosophers were conversing with him. And some were saying, "What would this idle babbler wish to say?" Others, "He seems to be a proclaimer of strange deities,"— because he was preaching Jesus and the resurrection. And they took him and brought him to the Areopagus, saying, "May we know what this new teaching is which you are proclaiming? For you are bringing some strange things to our ears; we want to know therefore what these things mean." (Now all the Athenians and the strangers visiting there used to spend their time in nothing other than telling or hearing something new.)

Compare that with Phillips's rendering:

Paul had some days to wait at Athens for Silas and Timothy to arrive, and while he was there his soul was exasperated at the sight of a city so completely idolatrous. He felt compelled to discuss the matter with the Jews in the synagogue as well as with the God-fearing gentiles, and he even argued daily in the open market-place with the passers-by. While he was speaking there some Epicurean and Stoic philosophers came across him, and some of them remarked,

"What is this cock-sparrow trying to say?"

Others said,

"He seems to be trying to proclaim some more gods to us, and foreign ones at that!"

For Paul was actually proclaiming "Jesus" and "the resurrection." So they got hold of him and conducted him to their council, the Areopagus. There they asked him,

"May we know what this new teaching of yours really is? You talk of matters which sound strange to our ears, and we should like to know what they mean." (For all the Athenians, and even foreign visitors to Athens, had an obsession for any novelty and would spend their whole time talking about or listening to anything new.)

See how imaginative Phillips' version is? If you've grown bored by overexposure to a particular translation of the Bible, I encourage you to pick up something fresh to stimulate your mind.

Rewrite the text in your own paraphrase

This is an extension of what we've just looked at. Translators have to use a lot of imagination to render the original text of Scripture into English. In the same way, it will challenge your imagination to rewrite the English text into words that make sense to you.

For instance, in the New American Standard version of Acts 17:16 above, the translators describe Paul's feelings about the idols with the words, "his spirit was being provoked within him." Phillips offers, "his soul was exasperated." How would you say it? That "he was really upset"? "He was ticked off"? "He was churned up"? "He felt sick to his stomach"? "He was tearing his hair out"?

Try rewriting Acts 17:16-21 in your own words. See if it doesn't spark your creativity and your interest in the text.

Read Scripture in a different language

If you know a language other than English, read a translation of the Bible in that language. You'll make all kinds of discoveries in the text. This approach has the same advantages as using varying translations and paraphrases.

Have someone read the text out loud

I mentioned in an earlier chapter that the human voice has a way of bringing life to words on the page. Be sure to let your children read the stories of Scripture out loud. And if you know a foreign exchange student or someone else who grew up in a culture different from your own, invite that person over and ask him or her to read the text for you. The accent will dress the passage in altogether different clothing, to great advantage.

Vary your setting

I'm a firm believer in the value of having a set time and place to study the Scriptures. But if you want to stir up the embers of your imagination, explore different environments in which to read the Word.

For example, many of Jesus' parables were given by the Sea of Galilee. So if you live near a lake or the seashore, consider taking your Bible there to read and reflect on the Lord's teaching. Likewise, many of the psalms were composed by David when he was a shepherd, out in the fields. You might drive out to the country to spend some time studying those passages.

The idea here is to do whatever it takes to see the Word from a different perspective. If we always read Scripture in the same way and in the same place time after time, we run the risk of making it into a routine exercise with little interest or excitement. What a tragedy, especially when we consider that history's greatest works of art and music have been created by people who learned to read the Bible imaginatively.

You Try It

Here's a chance to stretch your creativity. See what you can do with these projects in imaginative Bible reading.

Acts 16:16-40
This is the lively account of Paul and Silas in Philippi. Carefully read and observe the events that happen in this section, and then act them out in dramatic form with your family or friends.

Psalm 19
This psalm praises the works of God and the Word of God. Observe it carefully, and then try rewriting it for a university physics or philosophy class.

1 Samuel 17
This is the epic account of David and Goliath. However, though most people know of the story, they know little of what actually happens in it. Read the chapter carefully, then rewrite it in a way that would relate to a gang of inner city youths.

Acts 15:22-29
Luke reprints a letter that the church council at Jerusalem sent to new believers in Phoenicia and Samaria. Study the context carefully, then rewrite this passage as a fax to a new group of believers meeting downtown in your city.

A Cotton Patch Christmas

Here's a fascinating illustration of reading the Bible imaginatively. It's the Christmas story (Luke 2:1-20) from Clarence Jordan's irreverent paraphrase, *The Cotton Patch Version of Luke*. Writing from Americus, Georgia, Jordan gives a "Southern twang" to the familiar account. See if he doesn't achieve his purpose of rendering the Scriptures in a way that "help[s] the modern reader have the same sense of participation in them which the early Christians must have had."

It happened in those days that a proclamation went out from President Augustus that every citizen must register. This was the first registration while Quirinius was Secretary of War. So everybody went to register, each going to his own home town. Joseph too went up from south Georgia from the city of Valdosta, to his home in north Georgia, a place named Gainesville, to register with his bride Mary, who by now was heavily pregnant.

While they were there, her time came, and she gave birth to her first boy. She wrapped him in a blanket and laid him in an apple box. (There was no room for them at the hospital.)

Now there were some farmers in that section who were up late at night tending their baby chicks. And a messenger from the Lord appeared to them, and evidence of the Lord was shining all about them. It nearly scared the life out of them. And the messenger said to them, "Don't be afraid; for listen, I'm bringing you good news of a great joy in which *all* people will share. Today *your deliverer* was born in the city of David's family. He is the Leader. He is the Lord. And

here's a clue for you: you will find the baby wrapped in a blanket and lying in an apple box."

And all of a sudden there was with the messenger a crowd of angels singing God's praises and saying,

"Glory in the highest to God,
And on earth, *peace* to mankind,
The object of his favor."

When the messengers went away from them into the sky, the farmers said to one another, "Let's go to Gainesville and see how all this the Lord has showed us has turned out."

So they went just as fast as they could, and found Mary and Joseph, and *the baby lying in an apple box*. Seeing this, they related the story of what had been told them about this little fellow. The people were simply amazed as they listened to what the farmers told them. And Mary clung to all these words, turning them over and over in her memories. The farmers went back home, giving God the credit and singing his praises for all they had seen and heard, exactly as it had been described to them.

SOURCE: Clarence Jordan, *The Cotton Patch Version of Luke and Acts: Jesus' Doings and Happenings* (New York: Association Press, 1969), pp. 18-19.

14

Read Meditatively

The seventh strategy to becoming a first-rate reader of the
Bible is a hard one for most of us:

READ THE BIBLE MEDITATIVELY

In other words, learn to reflect on it. That's hard, because more and
more of us are living in the "laser lane." In the old days, if people
missed the stage coach they'd say, "That's OK. We'll get it next
month." Today, if a guy misses a section of a revolving door it throws
him into a tizzy.

As a result, meditative Bible reading has fallen out of favor. I can
remember a hymn we used to sing, "Take Time to Be Holy." But I
don't hear it much anymore, and I can understand why. Time is
exactly what it takes to become holy. We can't be holy in a hurry.
And yet, we live in an instant society. You want television? Just press
a button, and you've got instant color and sound. You want coffee?
Just dissolve some crystals in boiling water, and you've got instant.
But there's no such thing as instant spirituality.

That's why Scripture speaks so frequently about meditation. I
want to give you five passages to whet your appetite in this regard.

Joshua 1:8

This book of the Law shall not depart from your mouth, but
you shall *meditate* on it [When?] day and night, [please note] so

that you may be careful to do [not to know; to do] according to all that is written in it; for then you will make your way prosperous, and then you will have success. (italics added)

That verse shows that there is a close connection between meditating on God's Word and acting on it. That's going to be key when we get to Step Three, Application. Here I want to point out the frequency with which biblical truth should percolate through your mind: "day and night." That leads me to ask, What portion of Scripture was I thinking about this morning as I started my day? While I was at work? On my way home? For that matter, when was the last time I consciously reflected on biblical truths and principles?

Proverbs 23:7

One day I was reading through Proverbs when a phrase leaped off the page at me: "For as [a person] thinks within himself, so is he." That really grabbed me, perhaps because I had just seen a sign in someone's office that read, "You are not what you think you are. What you think, you are." Scripture teaches the basic principle that you become what you think. So be careful what you think.

Psalm 1:1-2

The first psalm has a similar message:

How blessed is the man who does not walk in the counsel of
the wicked,
Nor stand in the path of sinners,
Nor sit in the seat of scoffers!
But his delight is in the law of the Lord,
And in His law he *meditates* day and night. (italics added)

There's that day-and-night pattern again. That's typical of meditation. It's not an exercise that you carry out for a few minutes and then check off your list. It's a mental discipline that you carry throughout your day. It's a mind-set and a lifestyle in which the Word courses through your mind.

That's what makes biblical meditation altogether different from meditation as we know it in our society. Meditation as popularly taught by the Eastern philosophies tells you to empty your mind—the exact opposite of what the Scriptures say. Biblical meditation means filling your mind with the truth that God has revealed.

Psalm 119:97

Psalm 119 reinforces that idea, as the psalmist cries,

> O how I love Thy law!
> It is my *meditation* all the day. (italics added)

Have you ever observed that most of us waste an awful lot of time? Time doing routine things: waiting on the phone, standing in line, driving to work. I asked a friend in Los Angeles how much time he spent commuting. "One and a half hours going to work, one and a half hours coming from work," he told me. That's three hours every day, five and sometimes six days a week—a massive amount of time. Millions of commuters spend that much or even more time getting to work and back.

The question is, what are they doing with their minds during that time? I suspect that most of them drive along with their minds in neutral, listening to the radio and getting steamed at all the other drivers around them. But what a great time to put one's mind into gear.

That's why I've started using tapes of Scripture when I'm on the road, as I indicated in chapter 9. It's unbelievable what listening to God's Word does for me, especially to prepare me for the day's activities. It allows the truth to wrap itself around my heart.

Psalm 19

Psalm 19 offers some profound insight into Scripture. You must study that passage. It focuses on the Word of God, telling you what its characteristics are: "The law of the Lord is perfect.... The statutes of the Lord are trustworthy.... The precepts of the Lord are right," and so on (vv. 7-8, NIV).

It also tells you what the effects of the Word are. For example, it "revives the soul." Ever feel like you're out of gas? The Word of God can get you going again. It also "makes wise the simple." It doesn't matter whether you've been to college or what your IQ is. What matters is how teachable you are, how willing you are to program your mind with the wisdom that Scripture provides.

The climax to the psalm is the prayer,

May the words of my mouth and the *meditation* of my heart
    be pleasing in your sight,
    O Lord, my Rock and my Redeemer. (v. 14, NIV, italics
added)

That's a revealing prayer. It shows that the psalmist viewed meditation as an absolute necessity to his spiritual life. But if that was the case for him in his day, how much more essential must it be for those of us living in this generation, facing the pressures of our society. We need to bathe our minds in the waters of the Word so that our words and our thoughts become pleasing in God's sight.

Use your time—at the beginning of the day, at coffee break, during your lunch hour, riding home from work, before you go to sleep at night—to reflect upon the truth that you study.

To be honest, the greatest changes that God has brought about in my life have come through the process of meditation—just allowing the Word of God to filter and percolate through my mind and into my life. I've learned that first-rate Bible reading calls not for snapshots but for timed exposures.

You Try It

If you are not in the habit of reading the Bible meditatively, here's a suggestion to get started: Set aside a day when you can get away from your routine—no work, no interruptions, no commitments. Perhaps you have a favorite spot in the country or by the seashore, or access to a lake house. Wherever it is, find a place where you can spend several hours alone.

Devote your time to meditating on John 4:1-42, the account of Jesus visiting Samaria. Begin by asking God to help you gain insight into His Word and show you how to apply it. Then read the passage several times. Use the suggestions for repeated Bible reading in chapter 9.

Examine the sections before and after John 4 to place it in context. Then look carefully at the passage to answer such questions as: Who are the people in this story? Who were the Samaritans? Why was it unusual for Jesus to talk to this woman? What was the reaction of her neighbors? Of the disciples? What does Jesus tell them when they return? What lessons does this passage teach about telling the gospel story to others?

After you've got a grasp of the story, think about what implications it might have for you. For instance, what kinds of people do you normally stay away from? Why? How would those people respond to the gospel? Is there anything you could do or say that would help them come closer to Christ and ultimately to trust in Him? When it comes to evangelism, are you a sower or a reaper vv. 36-38? Or neither? With which of the characters in the story do you most identify? Why?

How did you come to faith in Christ? Who told you about Jesus? What was your response? Whom have you told about Jesus? What did you say? What was the response? Are there principles in this story that you could use the next time you tell people about Christ?

You can come up with additional questions. The goal is to chew on the Word, looking for insights, and to examine yourself, looking for ways to apply Scripture. Be sure to write down everything you observe in the passage, as well as your conclusions. And spend time in prayer. On the basis of what you've studied and meditated on, what is God telling you? What do you need to tell Him? Where do you need His resources and help? What opportunities for evangelism would you like Him to open for you?

15

READ PURPOSEFULLY

Remember 2 Timothy 3:16-17, a passage we looked at in chapter 2? It says that all Scripture is given by divine inspiration and is "profitable." In other words, it serves a purpose—four purposes, as a matter of fact: teaching, reproof, correction, and instruction in righteous living. This suggests an eighth strategy for first-rate reading of Scripture:

READ THE BIBLE PURPOSEFULLY

Purposeful reading looks for the aim of the author. There isn't a verse of Scripture that was thrown in by accident. Every word contributes to meaning. Your challenge as a reader is to discern that meaning.

How can you do that? One of the keys is to look for structure. Every book of the Bible has both grammatical and literary structure. Let's see these in action and consider how they contribute to meaning.

PURPOSE THROUGH GRAMMATICAL STRUCTURE

Many biblical authors communicate their mind through carefully selected grammar. I know that there's a growing trend today to dismiss grammar as the bugaboo of officious schoolmarms of whatever gender or occupation. But the Bible is not so cavalier in its choice of words and their order. In fact, grammar is determinative for doctrine. So we need to pay careful attention to the following grammatical features of the text.

Verbs

Verbs are critical. They're the action words that tell us who is doing what. For instance, in Ephesians 5:18 Paul writes, "Be filled with the Spirit." The verb "be filled" is passive. He doesn't say, "Fill yourself with the Spirit." He challenges us to open ourselves up to the Spirit's control, to yield to His will. That's an important observation because Ephesians tells us what life in the Spirit looks like in the church.

Another interesting use of a verb is found in Genesis 22:10, where Abraham takes his son, Isaac, up Mount Moriah to offer him as a sacrifice: "And Abraham stretched out his hand, and took the knife to slay his son."

You can't detect it in the English translation, but a commentary will tell you that the verbs here indicate a completed act, as if Abraham actually slays his son. In his mind, the deed is done; he has obeyed God to the uttermost. That's crucial to understanding the writer's purpose. He's showing us Abraham's faith—faith illustrated by total obedience. As Paul says later in Romans, Abraham's trust in God was such that even if he sacrificed his son, God could raise him from the dead in order to preserve an heir (4:16-21).

Subject and Object

The subject of a sentence does the acting, and the object is acted upon. It's important not to confuse them. Philippians 2:3 exhorts us, "Let each of you regard one another as more important than himself." The order is crucial. "Regard" is the verb; "each of you" is the subject; "one another" is the object. Paul is writing some challenging words about the humility of Christ that ought to mark the relationships of believers.

A related verse is Galatians 6:4: "But let each one examine his own work, and then he will have reason for boasting in regard to himself alone, and not in regard to another." This is the "fruit inspector's verse," because many of us have a tendency to inspect other people's spiritual fruit, when we need to pay more attention to our own.

Again, the verb is "examine"; the subject is "each one," and by inference, "each one of you believers"; the object is "his own work." So Paul is arguing for some self-reflection, which has an important bearing on this portion of Galatians. He is talking about believers intervening with other believers when they have sinned.

Modifiers

Modifiers are descriptive words such as adjectives and adverbs. They enlarge the meaning of the words they modify, and quite often they make all the difference. For instance, in Philippians 4 Paul thanks the Philippians for a gift they had sent him. We don't know exactly what the gift was, but Paul encourages those who sent it with the oft-repeated promise: "My God shall supply all your needs according to His riches in glory in Christ Jesus" (v. 19).

This verse is routinely ripped out of its context and made to appear as if God promises to supply all of our wants rather than all of our needs. But it was never intended to stimulate materialism. Instead, it is Paul's statement of confidence in God's provision. How confident was he? The modifier "all" is definitive: "my God shall supply all your needs," literally, "every need of yours." He doesn't shortchange us. He not only supplies what we need, He supplies *all* that we need.

Prepositional phrases

Prepositions are the little words that tell you where the action is taking place: *in, on, upon, through, to,* and so on. Consider a few of the many prepositional phrases that appear in Scripture, and you'll see how important it is to mark them when you see them: "in Christ," "in the beginning," "by the Spirit," "according to the Spirit, "in the flesh," "under the law," "by faith," "according to the Word of the Lord."

Connectives

Two of the most powerful words in the Bible are *and* and *but*. We saw how crucial *but* was in Acts 1:8. Look up Numbers 13:31, 2 Samuel 11:1, Luke 22:26, John 8:1, and 1 John 3:17, and you'll see some more illustrations of its potency.

And is just as crucial: "Delight yourself in the Lord; and He will give you the desires of your heart" (Psalm 37:4); "Abide in Me, and I in you (John 15:4); Paul and Barnabas (Acts 13:42-43); "Draw near to God and He will draw near to you (James 4:8).

Another important connective is *therefore*. Whenever you see a *therefore*, go back and see what it's there for. Romans is full of *therefores*, as Paul works his way through a tightly structured argument. The Old Testament prophets use *therefore* extensively. Over and over they state their case against the people, and then cry, "Therefore, thus says the Lord."

PURPOSE THROUGH LITERARY STRUCTURE

In addition to grammatical devices, the biblical writers communicate their purposes through literary structure. Even if you are inexperienced as a reader, you are probably familiar with literary structure. Television screenplays use the same ones over and over.

For instance, think how many mystery shows and action thrillers use this structure: (1) introduction of the characters and the setting; (2) commitment of the crime, usually murder or robbery; (3) investigation by the protagonist; (4) evasion by the criminal(s); (5) crisis, such as a car chase or shoot-out; and (6) resolution, as when the perpetrators are led away in handcuffs and the protagonist gets the girl. That's a common structure for screenplays.

The Bible has literary structure, too, though it's usually more sophisticated. When we get to Step Two: Interpretation, we'll see how different kinds of literature use different kinds of literary structure. But for now, here are five kinds to look for.

Biographical structure

Commonly found in the narrative books, biographical structure builds on the key persons in the story. As I've pointed out, Genesis 12-50 focuses on the experiences of the four patriarchs, Abraham, Isaac, Jacob, and Joseph. Judges structures itself around the leaders of Israel in the period between Joshua and the nation's first king, Saul. In 1 and 2 Samuel, the narrative moves from Samuel to Saul to David. In Acts, the apostle Paul commands the action in the later portions of the book.

Geographical structure

Here the key is place. The structure of Exodus depends heavily on the places that Israel visits on its way from Egypt to the Promised Land.

Historical structure

Key events are the basis of historical structure. The book of Joshua is a good example. The book opens with Joshua receiving his charge from the Lord. Then the people cross the Jordan. Then they take Jericho. Then they face defeat at Ai. And so it goes throughout the book, as the people go in and possess the land.

The book of John also uses historical structure to make its point. The gospel presents seven key miracles that promote one central purpose:

Jesus did many other miraculous signs in the presence of his disciples, which are not recorded in this book. But these are written *that you may believe* that Jesus is the Christ, the Son of God, and that by believing you may have life in his name. (20:30-31, NIV, italics added)

One of the most interesting uses of historical structure occurs in the Revelation. John tells us at the outset that the book records a vision that God gave to him after he had been banished to the island of Patmos. In the vision, startling events of global proportion take place, and the narrative progresses from incident to incident until it reaches a climax at chapter 21, with the presentation of a new heaven and new earth.

Chronological structure
Closely related to historical structure is chronological structure, where an author organizes material around key times. There is temporal progression; the events of the story happen sequentially. 1 and 2 Samuel use biographical structure, as I pointed out, but they also employ chronological structure. The narrative moves like a diary through the early days of Israel's kingdom. Incident after incident begins with the word, "Then...," "Then...," "Then...."

Ideological structure
Most of Paul's letters to churches are structured around ideas and concepts. Romans is a classic in this regard. It argues forcefully and comprehensively for one main idea, as summarized in 1:16: the gospel is the power of God for salvation. In presenting his case, Paul touches on concepts such as sin, the law, faith, grace, and life in the Spirit.

Ideological structure makes it easy to outline a book. Once you understand the central theme and purpose, you can determine what each part contributes to the understanding of that theme and purpose.

THE QUEST FOR MEANING
Detecting structure is a critical step in the Bible study process. When we get to Interpretation, we're going to ask, What does this text mean? But we'll never be able to answer that question accurately until we've answered the observational question, What do I see? Structure is the doorway to understanding an author's purpose.

You Try It

The books of the Bible are filled with statements that express the purpose of the writers. John 20:30-31 is one of the most straightforward. Others are less obvious. But an observant reader can usually find them. Here are a number of purpose statements. Read each one carefully, then skim the rest of the book in which it is found. See how the writer accomplishes his purpose in the way he presents his material.

- Deuteronomy 1:1; 4:1; 32:44-47
- Proverbs 1:1-6
- Ecclesiastes 1:1-2; 12:13-14
- Isaiah 6:9-13
- Malachi 4:4-6
- Luke 1:1-4
- 2 Corinthians 1:8; 13:1-10
- Titus 1:5; 2:15
- 2 Peter 3:1-2
- 1 John 5:13

The Laws of Structure

LAW	DESCRIPTION	EXAMPLES
Cause & effect	One event, concept, or action that causes another (key terms: *therefore, so, then, as a result*)	Mark 11:27–12:44 Rom. 1:24-32; 8:18-30
Climax	A progression of events or ideas that climb to a certain high point before descending	Ex. 40:34-35 2 Sam. 11 Mark 4:35–5:43
Comparison	Two or more elements that are alike or similar (key terms: *like, as, too, also*)	Ps. 1:3-4 John 3:8, 12, 14 Heb. 5:1-10
Contrast	Two or more elements that are unlike or dissimilar (key terms: *but, yet*)	Ps. 73 Acts 4:32–5:11 Gal. 5:19-23
Explanation or reason	The presentation of an idea or event followed by its interpretation	Dan. 2, 4, 5, 7-9 Mark 4:13-20 Acts 11:1-18
Interchange	When the action, conversation, or concept moves to another, then back again	Gen. 37-39 1 Sam. 1-3 Luke 1-2
Introduction & summary	Opening or concluding remarks on a subject or situation	Gen. 2:4-25; 3 Josh. 12 Matt. 6:1
Pivot or hinge	A sudden change in the direction or flow of the context; a minor climax	2 Sam. 11-12 Matt. 12 Acts 2
Proportion	Emphasis indicated by the amount of space the writer devotes to a subject	Gen. 1-11; 12-50 Luke 9:51–19:27 Eph. 5:21–6:4
Purpose	A declaration of the author's intentions	Jn. 20:30-31 Acts 1:8 Tit. 1:1
Question & answer	The use of questions or questions and answers	Malachi Mark 11:27–12:44 Luke 11:1-13

LAW	DESCRIPTION	EXAMPLES
Repetition	Terms or phrases used two or more times	Ps. 136 Matt. 5:21-48 Heb. 11
Specific to general, general to specific	Progression of thought from a single example to a general principle, or vice versa	Matt. 6:1-18 Acts 1:8 James 2

Adapted from an unpublished chart by John Hansel. Used by permission.

16

READ ACQUISITIVELY

O ne morning years ago I got up, went into the bathroom, filled the basin with water, and proceeded to shave. But when I went to put my razor into the water, I discovered there was no water there. I thought, *Well, it is a little early.* So I filled up the sink again and continued shaving. But once more the water drained out. So I decided to do a little observing. Examining the stopper, I discovered that one of my creative children had taken an ice pick and punched five of the nicest holes you have ever seen—in the form of a star.

That's a good illustration of what has happened to many of us in getting an education. We've got holes in our minds, and as a result they've become like sieves. They don't retain much—at least little of value. We read a book and a week later can't recall what it was about. We attend a class and afterward haven't the foggiest idea what the teacher presented. We hear a sermon on Sunday morning, and by Sunday night we don't even remember what passage it was from. It's as if we have Teflon-coated brains: nothing sticks.

But we've got to learn a different approach if we want to take possession of biblical truth. We need to read with the ninth strategy of first-rate Bible reading:

READ THE BIBLE ACQUISITIVELY

That is, read not only to receive it but to retain it; not merely to perceive it but to possess it. Stake a claim on the text. Make it your own property.

How can that happen? The key is personal, active involvement in the process. There's an old proverb to that effect: "I hear, and I forget. I see, and I remember. I do, and I understand."

Modern psychological studies back that up with scientific data: We remember at most only 10 percent of what we hear; 50 percent of what we see and hear; but 90 percent of what we do, see, and hear.

That is why I have never given an exam in any of my Bible study methods courses during more than forty years of teaching them. Students can't believe it. (Neither can some of the other professors.) But you see, I'd much rather get students involved in the process— the process of studying Scripture, not studying for an exam. What do I care if a kid can ace a test? The real question is, can he or she work with the text of the Word in order to understand it, possess it, and apply it?

Instead of a final exam, I ask my students to devise a creative way to study and present a passage. They can work separately or in teams. On the last day of class, they present their projects to the entire group. I have yet to be disappointed.

For instance, one group of six guys worked out a skit based on Acts 1:8, in which they played the part of three pairs of feet taking the gospel to the ends of the earth. They used their creative writing skills to inject humor, drama, and insight into their presentation.

Another team developed an entire puppet show to demonstrate biblical principles. I've seen audiovisual presentations, magic shows, paintings, even creative dance. I've heard poems, songs, dramatic readings, short stories. All based on Scripture. All accurate to the text.

Now please note: these are not games or gimmicks. Sure, one could use them that way. But for the students involved, they were exercises in acquisitive Bible study. I guarantee that if you polled them today, the ones who made a real effort in the assignment could still tell you not only what they did but what they learned by doing it. (How many assignments can you remember from high school, college, or graduate school?)

GET INVOLVED IN THE PROCESS

In the same way, this book will have value to the extent that it gets you involved in the process. What difference does it make whether you've read every page, and maybe even underlined parts of the text, if in the end you leave your Bible on the shelf and never get into it for yourself? My goal—and I hope yours as well—is to see life-change as a result of your personal interaction with God's Word.

What ideas can you come up with to make permanent your work with the biblical text? Are you studying Elijah on Carmel? How about acting out the story with your family or some friends? A group of camp counselors did that for their campers—complete with fire from heaven. Those kids have never forgotten it.

Or try rewriting texts such as Ecclesiastes 3:1-8 ("To everything there is a season"), Luke 19:1-10 (Zaccheus), or 1 Corinthians 13 (the love chapter) in your own paraphrase.

Or try a concentrated, month long biographical study of a particular character in Scripture. Look up every reference to that person in the text. Get a Bible dictionary, and read about the cultural and historical background in which he or she lived (see chapter 34 for more on Bible dictionaries). Locate the places in an atlas where the person lived and traveled.

Also develop a psychological profile: What sort of person was he? What attitudes and feelings did he have? What biases? What ambitions? What was his family background? What motivated him? Become a specialist in the life of that individual so that if you met him on the street you'd know him at a glance.

In short, do whatever it takes to become an acquisitive Bible reader. Marry the truth of the Word with your own interests and experience—through personal engagement in the process—so that you do more than remember Scripture—you make it your own.

You Try It

Here's an idea for making a passage of Scripture your own. Turn to Numbers 13, the story of the spies sent by Moses into the Promised Land. Read the account carefully, using all of the principles we've covered so far. Then write your own paraphrase of the story. Here are a few suggestions:

1. Decide what the main point of the story is. What happens? Why is this incident significant?

2. Think about any parallels to what happens here in the history of your own family, church, or nation, or in your own life.
3. Decide on the "angle" you want to use. For instance: the report of a task force for Israel, Inc. (a business angle); a tribal council (a Native American angle); a political contest between two factions (a political or governmental angle). The point is, choose something that fits the situation and will make this incident memorable for you.
4. Rewrite the story according to the angle you have chosen. Use language that fits that motif. Make the characters sound real-to-life. Change names and places to fit the style. (See Clarence Jordan's *Cotton Patch Version of Luke* on pages 108-9.)
5. When you're finished, read your paraphrase to a friend or someone in your family.

17

READ TELESCOPICALLY

The tenth and final strategy for developing first-rate skill as a student of Scripture is:

READ THE BIBLE TELESCOPICALLY

Telescopic reading means viewing the parts in light of the whole.

Sony president Akio Morita came to Texas recently to answer the question, Why are the Japanese reluctant to build consumer products in the United States? His answer: They can't find American parts that meet their quality control standards.

Take the Sony camcorder, he explained. Sony has a production standard that tolerates only one out of a hundred of them to fail. That seems easy to meet—until you realize that the device is made up of two thousand component parts. With that many parts, each one must work flawlessly—one failure in a hundred thousand, or even a million—in order for the whole unit to meet the standard. The whole is far greater than the sum of the parts.

So it is with the Bible. It is not simply a collection of parts. It is an integrated message in which the whole is greater than the sum of its parts. That's bad math, but it's good method. Yet what happens in a lot of Bible study and Bible teaching is that we keep breaking it down and breaking it down, until we have nothing but baskets of fragments. What we need today are people who can put the parts back together again into a meaningful and powerful whole.

So every time you read and analyze Scripture, every time you take it apart, realize that you've only done half the job. Your next task is to put it back together again.

How can you do that?

Look for the connectives

In chapter 15 we looked at the power in the little words *but, and,* and *therefore.* These and other words are "connectives" in that they link the text together. They are the coupling pins in a train of associated words that work together to communicate meaning. Telescopic reading demands that you pay attention to these links, so that you tie the author's message together in your mind.

Pay attention to context

We saw how important context can be when we studied Acts 1:8. We'll come back to it in detail when we get to Step Two, Interpretation. But the principle to remember is that whenever you study a verse or a paragraph, always consult the neighbors of that verse or paragraph to find out what the broader context is. Telescopic reading is based on this principle. It never settles for close-ups alone; it always demands the wide-angle lens of perspective. It always asks, What is the big picture?

Evaluate the passage in light of the book as a whole

This is the ultimate extension of checking the context. It's like flying a plane over some land in order to evaluate distances and relationships.

For instance, if you were to slug your way through Mark verse by verse, you'd probably enjoy the narrative, but you'd miss the author's message. Obviously the story is about Jesus. But so are three other books in the New Testament. What makes this one distinctive?

It's not until you back off and evaluate the book as a whole that you discover that Mark breaks his account into two major sections. From 1:1 through 8:26, you have the Person of Christ; from 8:31 through 16:20 you have the purpose of Christ. The hinge of the book is 8:27-30, where He asks the crucial question, "Who do people say that I am?" All kinds of insights flow out of this structure. But it is something you can detect only by examining a satellite photograph of the book.

Look at the historical context of the book

I happen to think that history is one of the most fascinating subjects there is. History lends relevance to otherwise insignificant details. For instance, we're all familiar with the Christmas story, which begins: "And it came to pass, in those days, that there went out a decree from Caesar Augustus, that all the world should be taxed" (Luke 2:1, KJV).

But how many of us appreciate the fact that Caesar Augustus was the first emperor of Rome? How did that come about? Perhaps you've seen or read Shakespeare's tragedy *Julius Caesar* and know that Caesar was murdered in 44 B.C. He had become a dictator. But previously Rome had been a republic, much like our own United States. A power struggle ensued in the aftermath of Caesar's death, and a man named Octavius emerged as the victor. A mere thirty years before Christ, Octavius was named emperor and assumed the title Caesar Augustus.

Another interesting fact is that Rome annexed Judea—the birthplace of Christ—in 6 B.C.

So when Luke opens chapter 2 with reference to Caesar Augustus, he's reminding the reader of the extraordinary political changes underway at that time. Does that have any bearing on his account? Does it give us any insight into the circumstances surrounding Jesus' life and death? Does it shed light on the Acts narrative, which continues the story? Does it give us any clues as to who Luke was writing for, and what might have mattered to the fellow he calls Theophilus in Luke 1:3 and Acts 1:1?

Whenever you come to a book of the Bible ask, Where does this book fit historically? When was it written? When did the events take place? What was happening elsewhere in the world at that time?

Also ask, Where does this book fit in the flow of the Bible? Does it come before, during, or after Christ? How much of the Bible was complete when this material was written? In other words, how much did the writer and the people in the book know about God?

You'll probably have to use secondary sources to discover the historical context of the biblical books. I'll talk about some of those in chapter 34. For now, keep in mind that God is the God of history. He works in and through real people in the real world to accomplish His purposes. You can discover a lot about those purposes if you read His Word telescopically.

You Try It

To read a book of the Bible telescopically, you have to get the big picture. You have to start by reading synthetically, not analytically. That is, survey the terrain before you dig any holes. Get an overview of what the writer covers and especially how much space he devotes to each subject.

A good book to study in this manner is Judges. It covers the period just after Joshua's death, before Israel had a king. God raised up individual leaders, called judges, to lead the people as they settled in the Promised Land.

To gain the broad perspective, read the entire book at one sitting and make a list of who the major characters are—the judges—and where they start appearing in the text. (A key phrase is "Then the sons of Israel did evil in the sight of the Lord.")

Next, create a chart that shows where each one appears in the book and how much space is given to him or her. (See chapter 25 for examples of different kinds of charts. I recommend that you develop something like the chart of Luke on page 185.)

When you complete this exercise, you'll have an excellent start on reading the book of Judges telescopically. You'll have the big picture so that when you read the stories of the individual judges you'll have a context in which to place them.

Some other Old Testament books to read in this way are 1 and 2 Samuel, 1 and 2 Kings, and 1 and 2 Chronicles.

18

WORK WITH A
PARAGRAPH

I began our discussion of Observation by focusing on one verse, Acts 1:8. Now I want to step up to a paragraph. The paragraph is the basic unit of study—not the verse, not the chapter. Certainly a paragraph may be as short as one verse or comprise an entire chapter. In any case, the paragraph represents a complete thought. It is a group of related sentences and statements that deal with one main topic or idea. That makes it ideal for observational study.

By the way, originally the Scriptures were not divided into chapters, paragraphs, and verses. They were just long, unbroken passages (see page 140). Twelve hundred years after Christ, scholars began carving them up into the divisions we have today. They did so to enhance Bible study, but their efforts were by no means inspired by the Holy Spirit. In fact, many of the breaks are artificially imposed on the text. So sometimes we have to ignore them in order to read the books properly.

THE PRAYER OF NEHEMIAH

The paragraph we're going to study is Nehemiah 1:4-11. I suggest you turn to it in your own Bible, but here's the paragraph:

> 4Now it came about when I heard these words, I sat down and wept and mourned for days; and I was fasting and praying before the God of heaven.

[5]And I said, "I beseech Thee, O Lord God of heaven, the great and awesome God, who preserves the covenant and lovingkindness for those who love Him and keep His commandments,

[6]"let Thine ear now be attentive and Thine eyes open to hear the prayer of Thy servant which I am praying before Thee now, day and night, on behalf of the sons of Israel Thy servants, confessing the sins of the sons of Israel which we have sinned against Thee; I and my father's house have sinned.

[7]"We have acted very corruptly against Thee and have not kept the commandments, nor the statutes, nor the ordinances which Thou didst command Thy servant Moses.

[8]"Remember the word which Thou didst command Thy servant Moses, saying, 'If you are unfaithful I will scatter you among the peoples;

[9]"'but if you return to Me and keep My commandments and do them, though those of you who have been scattered were in the most remote part of the heavens, I will gather them from there and will bring them to the place where I have chosen to cause My name to dwell.'

[10]"And they are Thy servants and Thy people whom Thou didst redeem by Thy great power and by Thy strong hand.

[11]"O Lord, I beseech Thee, may Thine ear be attentive to the prayer of Thy servant and the prayer of Thy servants who delight to revere Thy name, and make Thy servant successful today, and grant him compassion before this man."

Now I was the cupbearer to the king.

As I discuss this paragraph, I'll highlight the questions that I ask the text in boldface, as I did in chapter 6.

CHECK THE CONTEXT

Verse 4 begins, "Now it came about when I heard these words." **What is the significance of the word *Now*?** It's a connective. It links this paragraph with something else. Furthermore, the phrase *these words* compels me to ask, **what words?** So both of these questions force me to go back to the beginning of the book to check out the context.

The beginning of verse 1 gives me an introduction to the book. **What do I find there?** Three very important clues—clues that most people ignore. First of all I discover something about the nature or contents of the book—these are the words of a particular man. Second, I find out who that man is—Nehemiah. Third, I learn about the family from which Nehemiah came, which is especially helpful because the name *Nehemiah* appears elsewhere; but it is a different Nehemiah.

In the last part of verse 1 I read, "Now it happened," and **then what do I notice?** Three prepositional phrases: "in the month Chislev, in the twentieth year, while I was in Susa the capitol." So I ask, **what does this refer to? What word could I put beside the first two statements?** *Time*, because they tell me the month and the year.

A Bible dictionary can help me find out what month Chislev is. I discover that the ancient Hebrews had a calendar altogether different from ours. They didn't go by January, February, March, and so on. Chislev was their ninth month, beginning in November and extending into December. So assuming that the events in this narrative are taking place in the northern hemisphere, the time is early winter.

I also discover that the Hebrews' calendar differed from that of the Persians, which becomes significant when I learn that Nehemiah was an exile in Persia. In fact, he had a very high position in the government. But he was marking time by the Jewish calendar.

Next he points out that this is taking place "in the twentieth year." That forces me to ask, **the twentieth year of what?** I can't answer that here. It is not given to me until I get to the beginning of chapter 2.

Finally, **what does "Susa the capitol" tell me?** That answers the question, Where? but I still have to wonder, What is Susa the capitol? When I look it up in a Bible dictionary, I discover that there were two palaces in this kingdom. Susa was the winter palace. (Remember, this is taking place in November/December.) There was a summer palace, too, in Ek-batana. But Nehemiah was at the one in Susa—and it was no shack! In fact, it covered five thousand acres, and it was extremely plush.

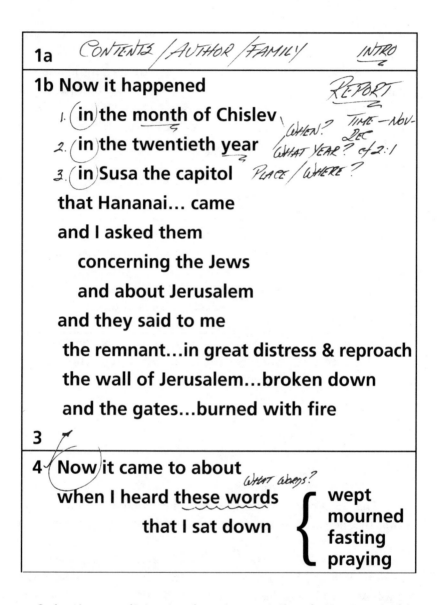

1a CONTENTS / AUTHOR / FAMILY   INTRO

1b Now it happened   REPORT

   1. (in) the month of Chislev   WHEN? TIME —Nov-DEC

   2. (in) the twentieth year   WHAT YEAR? cf 2:1

   3. (in) Susa the capitol   PLACE / WHERE?

   that Hananai... came

   and I asked them

     concerning the Jews

     and about Jerusalem

   and they said to me

     the remnant...in great distress & reproach

     the wall of Jerusalem...broken down

     and the gates...burned with fire

3

4 (Now) it came to about   WHAT about?

   when I heard these words   { wept

     that I sat down   mourned

          fasting

          praying

So here's a man living in a luxurious, privileged situation. And he gets a report (v. 2): Hanani comes to him. What does Nehemiah do? He asks something. What two things does he ask? First of all, "concerning the Jews." That has to do with his people. And then he asks "about Jerusalem." That has to do with the place, his home.

Verse 3 gives Hanani's response. So I notice a dialogue here, a question-and-answer session. **What relationship does the answer have to the question?** Nehemiah asks about the people and the place. The brothers give him a three-part answer: (1) "The remnant...are in great distress and reproach" (that has to do with the people); (2) "the wall of Jerusalem is broken down" (that's the place); and (3) "its gates are burned with fire" (also having to do with place).

So the order of the answer is exactly the same as the order of the question: the people first, then the place. I think that says something about Nehemiah. His first concern was for people, not places. Later I discover how much that figures into what happens in the book.

LABEL YOUR OBSERVATIONS

OK, I've plugged into the context. Now I come to my paragraph at verse 4. Once he hears about the people and the place, what does Nehemiah do? Four things: he weeps, mourns, fasts, and prays.

Can I find a way to gather these together? Well, weeping and mourning have to do with emotions. What about fasting and praying? They indicate a spiritual response.

One of the things you need to do in your Bible study is to hang some labels on your observations. They will help you get a handle on the material. For instance, beside verse 1*b* I can put *report*. If you prefer a different word, use it; but choose something that summarizes the contents for you.

If verse 1*b* is the report, verse 4 is the "response." Nehemiah has a total response, emotionally and spiritually, to the report.

Moving along to verse 5, I find a prayer. Or, to keep the pattern, I could label it the request that Nehemiah made. We've already looked at this prayer in chapter 12. Remember the pattern? Nehemiah starts with adoration (v. 5). He praises God for His steadfast love. Then he moves to confession (vv. 6-7). Seeing God as He really is always helps us to see ourselves as we really are—sinners in need of His mercy. Then, after confessing his sin and the sin of his people, Nehemiah begins to petition God on the basis of His promises.

Nehemiah's prayer is a model for how we can approach God. But looking at it in context, I notice how it ties directly to the report of Hanani and the brothers. They come and say, "The people are in great distress, and the walls are in ruins." And Nehemiah's

---

1a CONTENTS / AUTHOR / FAMILY   INTRO

1b Now it happened   REPORT

   1. (in) the month of Chislev \ WHEN? TIME — Nov-

   2. (in) the twentieth year / WHAT YEAR? cf 2:1

   3. (in) Susa the capitol PLACE / WHERE?

   that Hananai... came

Q **and I asked them**

    { *1.* **concerning the Jews** PEOPLE

    { *2.* **and about Jerusalem** PLACE

A **and they said to me**

PEOPLE **the remnant...in great distress & reproach**

PLACE **the wall of Jerusalem...broken down**

   and the gates...burned with fire

3

4 **(Now) it came to about** WHAT about?   RESPONSE

  when I heard these words   { ¹**wept** \ EMOT-

      that I sat down   { ²**mourned**
                    { ³**fasting** \ SPP
                    { ⁴**praying**

---

immediate response is prayer, but it is prayer based on the Word of God. God had promised that if Israel disobeyed Him, He would scatter them; if they returned to Him, He would restore their land (vv. 8-9). Nehemiah hears the report, he reviews God's Word, and then he falls to his knees in prayer.

NO DETAIL IS TRIVIAL

Is that the end of the paragraph? No. **What should I notice in the last part of verse 11?** Nehemiah adds an interesting detail: "I was the cupbearer to the king." That's terribly important. Yet most people pass right over that crucial statement. But in the step of observation, I'm asking, What do I see? I assume the role of a biblical detective—and no detail is unimportant.

What was a cupbearer? I've found that most people figure he was a guy walking around carrying a cup, as if he had nothing better to do. But here again is where a good Bible dictionary will help. Looking up "cupbearer," I find that his title derives from the fact that he was responsible for tasting the king's wines. As you might imagine, this was an era of intrigue and constant attempts to eliminate people. So rulers trusted no one—except the cupbearer.

The cupbearer was virtually the prime minister, the second-in-command. He had a personal expense account and direct access to the king.

So the Holy Spirit includes this detail about Nehemiah to show me how God accomplished His purpose. Later in the book I discover that it was because Nehemiah was the cupbearer that the king gave him permission to go back to the land and rebuild the walls and the city. God had His man in a strategic position. Nehemiah was able to leverage that position to accomplish God's purposes.

Have you ever asked yourself where God has placed you? Maybe you're a school teacher, a nurse, a computer expert, a carpenter, or a doctor. Whatever your situation, what opportunity has God given you to accomplish His purposes? I guarantee that He places every one of His children in a strategic position. He wants to use you for His honor and glory.

"I DON'T KNOW WHERE TO BEGIN"

There are many more observations to be made about this paragraph. In fact, this book is one of the most fascinating I've ever studied in the Word of God. But I didn't start out seeing things in the text the way I do now. Far from it.

Not long after I became a Christian, someone encouraged me, "Now that you've come to faith, you need to get into the Word."

"Wonderful," I said. "Where do I start?"

1a CONTENTS / AUTHOR / FAMILY   INTRO

1b Now it happened   REPORT

1. (in) the month of Chislev   WHEN? TIME — Nov-Dec

2. (in) the twentieth year   WHAT YEAR? cf 2:1

3. (in) Susa the capitol   PLACE / WHERE?

that Hananai... came

Q and I asked them

1. concerning the Jews   PEOPLE

2. and about Jerusalem   PLACE

A and they said to me

PEOPLE the remnant...in great distress & reproach

PLACE the wall of Jerusalem...broken down

and the gates...burned with fire

3

4 Now it came to about   WHAT WORDS?   RESPONSE

when I heard these words

that I sat down

{ 1 wept   EMOT
2 mourned
3 fasting   SPIR
4 praying }

5 And I said   REQUEST

I beseech thee

ADORATION (5)
CONFESSION (6-7)
PETITION (8-11)

11a CUPBEARER

"Start anywhere, brother. It's all profitable."

So I went home and opened my Bible—and landed in Ezekiel. Right in the middle of the wheels. I struggled with that passage for a while, until I thought, *This has to be an exception.* So I tried the other end of the Bible—Revelation. Bowls and vials and wrath completely confused me. So, I'm ashamed to say, I closed the Book for one solid year. I was convinced that what the priests had taught me was true—you needed a professional milkman to dispense the Word.

By God's grace someone came along and asked, "Hey, Hendricks, are you in the Scriptures?"

"No, as a matter of fact I'm not," I told him.

"How come?"

My answer was straightforward: "I don't know how to go about it. I don't know where to begin."

By now, you know infinitely more than I did when I began studying God's Word for myself. You've seen how to observe a verse, and now a paragraph. You've also discovered that you've got to learn to read better and faster, as for the first time, and just as you would a love letter. And you've been exposed to ten strategies that are guaranteed to turn you into a first-rate Bible reader.

But not only must you learn to read, you must learn what to look for. In the next few chapters, I'll give you six clues that will help you further unlock the biblical text.

You Try It

In this chapter I've worked with a paragraph, observing how Nehemiah responded to the report of Hanani and the brothers. Now it's your turn. Below is a paragraph from Paul's letter to Titus, who was a first-century pastor on the Mediterranean island of Crete.

Read the paragraph carefully, using the ten strategies to first-rate reading and paying attention to terms and grammatical structure. See what you can discover here about the lifestyle that should characterize all believers, and especially leaders.

The reason I left you in Crete was that you might straighten out what was left unfinished and appoint elders in every town, as I directed you. An elder must be blameless, the husband of but one wife, a man whose children believe and are not open to the charge of being wild and disobedient. Since an overseer is entrusted with God's work, he must be blameless—not overbearing, not quick-tempered, not given to drunkenness, not violent, not pursuing dishonest gain. Rather he must be hospitable, one who loves what is good, who is self-controlled, upright, holy and disciplined. He must hold firmly to the trustworthy message as it has been taught, so that he can encourage others by sound doctrine and refute those who oppose it. (Titus 1:5-9, NIV)

Courtesy of Dr. John Hellstern, Aledo, Texas.

This manuscript Bible is believed to have been produced by hand on vellum at Cambridge, England in about 1180. Like all Bibles of its day, it originally had no chapter breaks or verse numbers. Chapter numbers (in color) were added later. It would take a scribe about two years to produce a Bible like this one.

SIX THINGS TO LOOK FOR

Things that are emphasized
Things that are repeated
Things that are related
Things that are alike
Things that are unlike
Things that are true to life

19

THINGS THAT ARE EMPHASIZED

Have you ever gone to a doctor with a sore throat? The first thing he asks you to do is to stick out your tongue. He takes a glance down your throat and says, "Aha." Right away he knows what's wrong. I could look in your mouth from now to eternity, but it would do no good because I don't know what I'm looking for.

The same principle applies to Bible study. You could spend hours paging through the Word, but it will be a complete waste of time if you don't know what you're looking for. That's why, in Observation, you ask and answer the question, What do I see? You assume the role of a biblical detective, searching for clues, and no detail is trivial.

There are six clues to watch for in Scripture. You'll hit pay dirt every time if you notice them. And God has provided an excellent tool to help you remember them—your hand. There's a clue for each of the fingers, and one for the palm of your hand. In this and the next four chapters, I'll show you how to spot these six important clues.

Start with your thumb. The first clue to look for is:

THINGS THAT ARE EMPHASIZED

The Bible uses several ways to emphasize material. Let me mention four.

Amount of space

A book can emphasize something by devoting a large portion of space to it. We've seen that in Genesis. It has fifty chapters. The first eleven cover the creation, the Fall, the Flood, the tower of Babel, and other details. All of those major events are compressed into just eleven chapters. By contrast, the writer devotes chapters 12-50 to the lives of four individuals: Abraham, Isaac, Jacob, and Joseph. Through this emphasis, the Spirit of God is teaching us that the most important thing in the book is the family that God chose to be His people.

We see the same thing when we come to the gospels. For example, of Matthew's 1,062 verses, at least 342 of them—one-third of the book—give us discourses of the Savior. That has a major bearing on the purpose of the book. Likewise, some gospels take much more space to cover the crucifixion than they do other events in the life of Christ.

In the epistles of Paul, we frequently find a section of doctrine followed by a section of practical applications based on that doctrine. For instance, Ephesians 1-3 tells us what God has done for us. Ephesians 4-6 tell us what we need to do as a result. That's an intriguing balance between theology and practice. The same pattern is found in Colossians. However, in Romans the ratio is eleven chapters of doctrine to five of applications, which gives us some idea of the emphasis Paul wants to make there.

So whenever you observe a portion of Scripture ask, How much space is given to this subject? What is the writer emphasizing?

Stated purpose

Another way the biblical writers may emphasize their points is by telling us straight out what they are up to. Remember, we saw a prime example in John 20:30:

> Jesus did many other miraculous signs in the presence of his disciples, which are not recorded in this book. But these are written that you may believe that Jesus is the Christ, the Son of God, and that by believing you may have life in his name. (NIV)

As I pointed out in chapter 15, John presents seven carefully selected signs in the narrative to accomplish this purpose—to show that Jesus is the Christ, the Son of God, and that He is therefore worthy of a person's trust.

Or take Proverbs. Solomon launches that fascinating collection of wisdom sayings by telling the reader why he ought to read the book:

> To know wisdom and instruction,
> To discern the sayings of understanding,
> To receive instruction in wise behavior,
> Righteousness, justice and equity;
> To give prudence to the naive,
> To the youth knowledge and discretion,
> A wise man will hear and increase in learning,

And a man of understanding will acquire wise counsel,
To understand a proverb and a figure,
The words of the wise and their riddles.

(Proverbs 1:2-6)

Those are impressive benefits. And the rest of Proverbs follows
through on those promises. By stating his purpose at the beginning,
the writer frames the reader's thinking as he or she approaches the
material. Whatever else you expect from Proverbs, you know that it
is going to emphasize wisdom.

Order

A third way to emphasize something is to give it a strategic
placement in the material. This comes before that; or this follows
that.

For instance, in Genesis 2, God places Adam and Eve in a garden
"to cultivate it and keep it," the text says (2:15). Then in chapter 3
the couple sin, and God drives them out of the Garden and curses the
earth (3:17-24). That order becomes important when we talk about
work, because some people believe that work is a part of the curse.
But the order of events in Genesis disallows that interpretation.

Another illustration comes from the life of Christ. In Luke 3 you
have the baptism of the Savior. In Luke 4 you have the temptation.
Notice the order: in the baptism He is approved by God; in the
temptation He is tested by Satan. The order is significant.

Or take a third illustration, also from Luke. Chapter 6 verses 14-
16 recount the choosing of the twelve. Look carefully at the order:
Simon Peter and Andrew; James and John; Philip and Bartholomew;
Matthew and Thomas; James the son of Alphaeus and Simon the
Zealot; Judas the son of James; and Judas Iscariot. Who is
mentioned first? Who is paired with whom? Who is last?

By choosing where to locate people, events, ideas, and so on, a
writer can call attention to something. So look for the order given. It
can yield major insights into the text.

Movement from the lesser to the greater, and vice versa

These are really special cases of what we've just looked at in terms of
order. Often a writer will build up to a climax, where he presents
some key information. In the life of David, 2 Samuel 11-12 records

what are probably the most crucial events of David's life—the murder of Uriah and his sin with Bathsheba. Those chapters form a sort of pivot to the book. Everything before leads up to them, everything after goes down from them.

Or take Acts 2. When you study the book of the Acts, you discover that chapter 2 is the pivot. It's the one chapter without which you couldn't have the book. Everything grows out of what happens there. It is Luke's way of emphasizing that material.

So the first clue to look for when you come to the Scriptures is that which is emphasized. The writers have gone to great trouble to hang out a sign that says, "Hey, this is important. Pay attention." Look for the four kinds of emphasis I've mentioned, and you'll quickly catch on to what matters in the text.

You Try It

Here are two sections of Scripture that you can observe for things emphasized.

1 and 2 Samuel
Develop an overview chart of these two books showing the relative space devoted to the principle characters, Samuel, Saul, and David. (You should have developed a similar chart at the end of chapter 17, page 130. There's a good example of the kind of chart I'm talking about at the bottom of page 185.) Which character was most important to the writer? What does that tell you about the purpose of 1 and 2 Samuel?

Acts 1:8
What is the order of the places mentioned? What relationship do these places have to each other? (We looked at this in chapter 6.) How does the order of these places in Acts 1:8 compare with the expansion of the gospel in the rest of Acts? See if you can determine the relative amount of space Dr. Luke devotes to each of these places, and the amount of time the apostles give to each one. What significance might this have for the purpose of Acts?

20

THINGS THAT ARE
REPEATED

There's probably no tool of teaching more powerful than repetition. If I want to make sure that you catch on to what I have to say, I'll repeat it over and over, again and again, time after time. Repetition reinforces. That's why the second clue to look for in the biblical text is:

THINGS THAT ARE REPEATED

Have you ever noticed how often Jesus repeats things to His disciples? The gospels record at least nine times that He said, "He that hath ears to hear, let him hear." And when John was recording the Revelation, what do you suppose the Lord told him to write to the seven churches? That's right: "He that hath ears to hear, let him hear."

That's a lot of emphasis. You get the impression that Jesus wanted His disciples (and us) to pay attention to what He had to say. By constantly using that formula to flag His words, He gave His listeners clues about the significance of His teaching.

Let me mention a few categories of repetition to look for.

Terms, phrases, and clauses
Scripture constantly repeats terms, phrases, and clauses to emphasize their importance. For example, in Psalm 136 we read,

> Give thanks to the Lord, for He is good.
> *His love endures forever.*

Give thanks to the God of gods.
His love endures forever. (vv. 1-2, NIV)

The psalmist repeats "His love endures forever" no less than twenty-six times in this psalm. Why? Did he have nothing else to say? No, he was emphasizing the fact that God's love endures forever. By the time you get through the psalm, you know the bottom line: "His love endures forever." In effect, the psalmist is saying, "What else do you need to know?"

Or take Hebrews 11, God's Hall of Fame—or Hall of Faith. The phrase "by faith...," "by faith...," "by faith..." appears eighteen times. The writer is talking about different people living in different times under different circumstances. But all of them have lived the same "by faith" lifestyle.

Again, look how important the little word *if* is to 1 Corinthians 15. Paul uses it seven times in verses 12-28, where he is talking about the critical importance of Christ's resurrection to our faith. "If" emphasizes the fact that everything we believe is conditioned on the resurrection. If that goes, everything goes.

Characters

Phrases and terms are not the only things that a writer repeats to make a point. Sometimes a character reappears.

Barnabas is a good example. We really don't know too much about the man. His given name was Joseph, but the apostles called him Barnabas, meaning Son of Encouragement (Acts 4:36). And that's really the most important thing about him: he was an encourager. Whenever somebody in the early church needed a hand, up would pop Barnabas to help him out: Saul (Acts 9:27); the believing Gentiles at Antioch (Acts 11:22); and John Mark (Acts 15:36-39). Luke brings Barnabas into the story at strategic points as a model of spiritual mentoring.

Incidents and circumstances

Sometimes a writer makes his point by repeating a particular incident or set of circumstances.

In the book of Judges, for instance, the writer begins each section with the words "Then the sons of Israel did what was evil in the sight of the Lord." That refrain sets up the situation in which God raises up judges who usually lead the people back to God—but never permanently. Sooner or later they fall away, and the cycle is repeated until the end of the book, where it gets to the heart of the

problem: "In those days there was no king in Israel; everyone did what was right in his own eyes" (21:25).

Another example of repeated circumstances occurs in Matthew. Throughout his gospel, the author builds a tension between Jesus and the Pharisees. Over and over the Lord does or says something that offends these leaders. Matthew uses these incidents to call attention to the power struggle going on between the old system of self-righteous legalism and the new way of salvation in Christ.

Patterns

A related situation is the creation of a repeating pattern. Bible students have long recognized the parallels between the life of Joseph and the life of our Lord. Likewise, there are parallels between the experience of Israel and that of Jesus.

Or take Saul and David in 1 and 2 Samuel: whatever Saul does wrong, David does right. The writer uses juxtapositions to show that Saul was the people's choice for king, whereas David was God's choice.

New Testament use of Old Testament passages

A final and obvious case of repetition is the citation of Old Testament Scripture by the New. That's a fascinating study in itself. Obviously, if the Spirit of God compels a New Testament writer to recall a passage from the Old Testament, it's likely because He wants to emphasize that portion of God's Word.

Take the story of Jonah. In the early days of the faith, some people didn't want it included in the canon of Scripture. But Jesus referred to it in a way that makes it indispensable to the divine revelation (Matthew 12:39-41).

Or look at Hebrews. It would be hard to imagine what that book would have to say were it not for its heavy reliance on Old Testament Scripture.

In short, whenever you study the Bible and notice that something is repeated—said more than once—mark it down. It's not because the writers couldn't think of anything else to say. It's their way of pointing out matters of crucial importance.

You Try It

Repetition is one of the most frequently used means of emphasis in the Bible. Let me suggest several projects that will help you unlock portions of the Word by looking for things repeated.

Psalm 119

In this psalm, David refers to the Word of God in every verse. Observe the psalm carefully, and catalogue all of the things that David says about Scripture.

Matthew 5:17-48

Observe how Jesus uses the formula "You have heard...but I say..." in this portion of the Sermon on the Mount. What structure does this phrase give to the passage? Why is it significant for Jesus to say this?

Arithmetic In Acts

Use a concordance to look up all of the "arithmetic" phrases in the book of Acts—numbers of people being "added" to the church, the believers "multiplying" themselves. There are even a few "divisions" and "subtractions." Can you find them? How does Luke use these terms to describe the growth of the early church?

1 Corinthians 15:12-19

Investigate the importance of the little word *if* to Paul's argument.

21

THINGS THAT ARE
RELATED

So far we've labeled the thumb with things that are emphasized and the index finger with things that are repeated. Now the third clue you need to look for—and this goes on your middle finger—is:

THINGS THAT ARE RELATED

By "related" I mean things that have some connection, some interaction with each other. You see, just because two things are next to each other does not make them related. They've got to work off of each other in some way. There must be a tie that somehow binds them together.

Look for three kinds of relationships in your study of Scripture.

Movement from the general to the specific

This is the relationship between the whole and its parts, between a category and its individual members, between the big picture and the details. We've seen this relationship a number of times before.

Let me give you an illustration out of Matthew 6, a part of the Sermon on the Mount. The chapter begins,

> Be careful not to do your "acts of righteousness" before men, to be seen by them. If you do, you will have no reward from your Father in heaven. (v. 1, NIV)

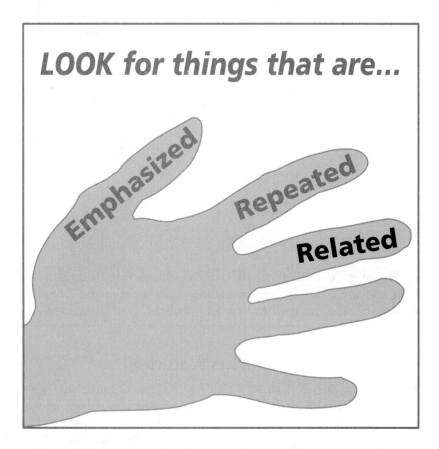

LOOK for things that are...

Emphasized

Repeated

Related

You will have a reward: when you do your righteous act to be seen by men, that will be your reward. But it will not be observed by the Father, Jesus says.

Then He moves from that general principle to three specific illustrations. First in the area of giving (vv. 2-4), then in the area of praying (vv. 5-15), and then in the area of fasting (vv. 16-18).

Another example can be found in Genesis 1. Verse 1 gives an overview: "In the beginning God created the heavens and the earth."

If the account ended there, you wouldn't have any of the details of how He created the heavens and the earth. You would just know that He did. But the rest of the chapter fills in the specifics: on day one He created light (vv. 3-5); on day two He separated the water from the skies (vv. 6-8); on day three He formed the dry land and caused vegetation to start growing (vv. 9-13); and so on.

Whenever you come across a broad, general statement in Scripture, look to see whether the writer follows with specific details that flesh it out in some way.

Questions and Answers

The question is one of the most powerful tools of communication. If I ask you a question, doesn't it more or less force you to think? Sure it does. Of course, if someone only asks questions and never provides answers, that can be very frustrating. You begin to wonder whether he knows what he's talking about. But we're going to discover that the biblical writers employ both—strategic questions and helpful answers.

The book of Romans is a classic example. It is written like a legal treatise, as if Paul were a lawyer. He's constantly raising questions and then answering them. For example, look at Romans 6:1: "What shall we say, then? Shall we go on sinning so that grace may increase?" (NIV). Then he answers that question: "By no means!"

At verse 15 he again uses a rhetorical question: "What then? Shall we sin because we are not under law but under grace?" (NIV). That's the question. Again the answer is, "By no means," and he goes on to spell it out in detail.

Sometimes a question itself carries so much weight that it needs no answer. Have you ever looked over the barrage of questions that God fires at Job? "Now gird up your loins like a man, and I will ask you, and you instruct Me!" (Job 38:3).

"I will ask you." That's sarcasm. God launches into a cascade of questions that continues for two chapters, until Job briefly interrupts (40:3-5). Then the torrent starts again. They are questions that carry their own answers.

How about the pointed questions that our Lord throws at the disciples: "Who of you by worrying can add a single hour to his life?" (Matthew 6:27, NIV). Or, "Why are you so timid? How is it that you have no faith?" (Mark 4:40). Or how about, "So, you men could not keep watch with Me for one hour?" (Matthew 26:40).

Questions and answers demand your attention. They are important keys to help you unlock a text.

Cause and Effect

This is the principle of the billiard balls. You strike the cue ball with your cue (that's the cause) in order to knock the colored balls into the pockets (that's the effect). In Scripture we find all kinds of cause-effect relationships ricocheting around the text.

I want to point out a dynamic illustration of this in Acts 8:1: "On that day a great persecution arose against the church in Jerusalem." You are led to ask, what day? Checking the context, you find that it was the day Stephen was martyred. That intensified the persecution, and all the believers except the apostles were scattered throughout Judea and Samaria. But verse 4 says, "Those who had been scattered went about preaching the word."

In other words, the persecution was the cause, and the preaching was the effect. The believers didn't stand around, crying, "What in the world is God doing to us now? Here we prayed that He would use us, and now all we've got is persecution." No, they used the pressure as leverage to get the gospel out to the ends of the earth.

In chapter 18 we studied a paragraph from Nehemiah 1. Remember Nehemiah's prayer? He reminded God of some promises that He had made back in the books that Moses had written. God had said that if the people disobeyed Him, He would eventually send them into exile. Sure enough, the people disobeyed (that was the cause), and God had kept His promise by allowing the Babylonians to carry them away (that was the effect).

As a matter of fact, Nehemiah was banking on that cause-effect relationship, because God had also promised that if the people repented (cause), He would return them to the land (effect). That's why Nehemiah was so interested in confessing sin. Did God respond? Yes, and He used Nehemiah to fulfill His promise.

What promises of God are you banking on? For instance, Psalm 1 says that the person who plants himself in the counsel of God's Word will flourish like a well-watered tree. Notice, that's a direct cause-effect link between Scripture and God's blessing. Are you experiencing that effect? The real question is, are you activating the cause by delighting and meditating, as it says, in what God has said?

As you do, look for things that are emphasized, things that are repeated, and as we've seen in this chapter, things that are related.

You Try It

One of the primary goals of observation is to see relationships in the biblical text. Test your observational skills on these three passages.

Matthew 1:1-18

Most people just skip over the genealogies. They are bored by the monotonous repetition of "So-and-so begat So-and-so." But genealogies are actually important ways that the biblical writers communicate their meaning.

Read through the list of names mentioned in Matthew 1. What relationship do these people have to Jesus? To each other? What four individuals stand out conspicuously? Why? What can you find out about the people mentioned here? Compare this list with the genealogy that Luke records (Luke 3:23-38). What is different? What is the same? What do you think Matthew's list has to do with the purpose of his book?

Amos

You'll need an atlas to discover the significance of the relationships in the Old Testament book of Amos. Find all of the places mentioned in chapters 1-4. Where does the prophet finally land in chapter 5? What's the relationship? What is Amos doing by mentioning these places in this manner?

22

THINGS THAT ARE ALIKE, AND UNLIKE

I have two granddaughters who are identical twins. In fact, they look so much alike that I absolutely cannot tell them apart. Neither can their father half the time. Only their mother seems to be able to distinguish between them. I've been with them in public and watched strangers react to them as if seeing double. They point and remark, "Look! Look! Twins." Why is that? Because the moment we see two of anything alike—especially when we least expect it—the similarity immediately draws our attention.

The same phenomenon is true in Bible study. Similarities stick out. And so do contrasts. That's why the fourth and fifth clues to look for whenever you observe Scripture are:

THINGS THAT ARE ALIKE AND THINGS THAT ARE UNLIKE

We've assigned things that are emphasized to the thumb, things repeated to the index finger, and things related to the middle finger. So things alike can go with the ring finger, and things unlike with the little finger.

Similes

The biblical writers give you a number of terms that flag similarities. The two most common words to look for are *as* and *like*. They indicate a figure of speech called a "simile," which is a word picture that draws a comparison between two things.

For instance, Psalm 42 begins, "*As* the deer pants for the water brooks, so my soul pants for Thee, O God" (v. 1, italics added). That's a grabbing image, isn't it? It creates atmosphere. The psalmist compares his longing for God to a hot, thirsty deer.

Think back to 1 Peter 2:2, a verse that we saw when we asked the question, Why study the Bible for ourselves? Peter uses a simile: "*As* newborn babes, long for the pure milk of the word, that by it you may grow in respect to salvation" (italics added). He draws a poignant comparison between the appetite of a baby for its mother's milk and the appetite of the believer for the nourishment of God's Word.

Consider one more comparison—actually, a comparison that cannot be made. In Isaiah 44:6-7, the Lord asks a pointed question:

This is what the Lord says—
Israel's King and Redeemer, the Lord Almighty:
I am the first and I am the last;
    apart from me there is no God.
Who then is *like* me?
(NIV, italics added)

Answer: nobody. God alone is God, uniquely supreme and sovereign. But the word *like*, which ordinarily signals similarity, in this case heightens the contrast.

Metaphors

A device related to the simile is the metaphor, where comparison is made without using *as* or *like*. Jesus says, "I am the vine, and My father is the vinedresser" (John 15:1). He's obviously talking figuratively, not literally. He's painting a picture that illustrates His relationship to the Father and to believers as well.

Jesus uses an extended metaphor in John 3 when He talks with Nicodemus. "You must be born again," He tells him (vv. 3, 5, 7). Jesus is making a comparison. "Just as you were born physically, Nicodemus, and received the equipment for this life, so you need to be born again spiritually to receive the equipment for eternal life."

That stumped Nicodemus. He was far from dull, but he was thinking only on the human level. So he asked, "How can I go through the birth process again?" (v. 4). You see, he hadn't caught on to Jesus' use of the metaphor. That's why the Lord responded, "You've got to be *born from above*, Nicodemus, or you'll never make it into the kingdom" (vv. 5-6).

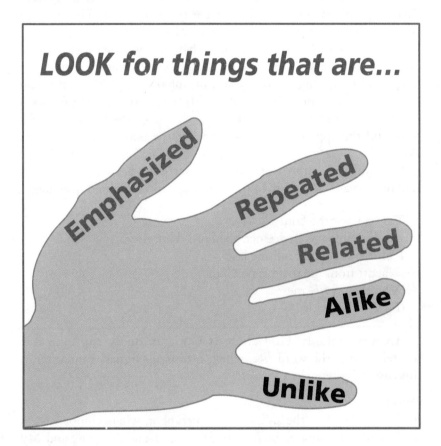

Then Jesus employed a simile: "And *as* Moses lifted up the serpent in the wilderness, even so must the Son of Man be lifted up" (v. 14, italics added). Now He was stepping onto Nicodemus' turf. Nicodemus was a Pharisee, so he knew better than anyone the significance of the bronze serpent in the wilderness (Numbers 21:4-9). Jesus was drawing a comparison between that incident and His own crucifixion to come.

Was Jesus' use of comparison effective? Apparently; later in the book, Nicodemus helps to place His body in the tomb (John 19:39)—a dangerous course of action, under the circumstances, and one that demonstrated his belief in the Savior.

We'll look at metaphors again later. For now, keep in mind that similarities have a way of drawing attention to themselves.

Nevertheless, get into the habit of looking for them. You'll find them especially in the wisdom literature, particularly in the psalms. Whenever you find one, mark it. The writer is trying to communicate with you through the effective tool of comparison.

THINGS THAT ARE UNLIKE

The flip side of comparison is contrast—things that are unlike. We could say that in Bible study, as in love, opposites attract. At least, they attract the eye of the observant reader. There are several ways the biblical writers signify contrast.

Use of *but*

The word *but* is a clue that a change of direction is coming. We've seen how crucial a term this is in several passages already. In the Sermon on the Mount, Jesus repeatedly says, "You have heard that it was said…but I say to you" (Matthew 5, italics added).

In Galatians 5, Paul writes, "Now the deeds of the flesh are evident" (v. 19), and he gives a list. Then in verse 22 he turns around and says, "*But* the fruit of the Spirit is…" and he lists those. So he sets up a contrast between what the flesh produces and what the Spirit produces.

Acts 1:8, a verse we looked at in detail, begins with "But." Remember how that led us to go back and look at the context, where we discovered the Lord in a discussion with the apostles? They wanted to know if He was about to establish the kingdom. He replied that it was not for them to know the time for that. *But*…and then comes all that we saw in verse 8.

Later in Acts, Philip begins a citywide evangelistic crusade in Samaria, with great success (8:5-8). In fact, the response is so overwhelming that the apostles in Jerusalem send Peter and John on a fact-finding mission to check it out. After they finish and are headed back home, verse 26 says, "*But* an angel of the Lord spoke to Philip saying, 'Arise and go south to the road that descends from Jerusalem to Gaza.' (This is a desert road.)" (italics added).

Again, the little word *but* signals a change of direction. It draws a contrast between Peter and John, headed from one city to another, and Philip, who suddenly finds himself commissioned to a wilderness ministry.

It would be as if I were preaching in Houston with the Billy Graham team, and folks are coming to Christ and the Spirit is at work and we're turning the city upside down with the gospel. Then one evening, the Lord says to me, "Hendricks, get on a bus, and head to West Texas. I'll tell you when to get off." You know, I'd sort of feel demoted. Here's all this exciting stuff going on in the big city, and I get sent to the minors.

But not Philip. He obeyed, and the Spirit brought him to an official from Ethiopia. He led the man to Christ, and the gospel spread to Africa. The word *but* in verse 26 sets all of this up by painting a contrast.

But is one of the most important words you'll ever come across in your study of Scripture. Whenever you see it, always stop and ask, what is the contrast being made?

Metaphors

Just as things that are alike can be shown through metaphors, so can things that are unlike.

Remember the parable of the unrighteous judge in Luke 18? A poor widow cries out day after day to a judge of little integrity, asking him to give her justice. But he turns a deaf ear. Finally, though, the woman's persistence drives him to rule in her favor.

What are we to make of this story? After all, the unrighteous judge is in the position that God is in. Does that make sense? Well, the key is to notice that Jesus is setting up an effective contrast. He is saying, in effect, "If a corrupt and indifferent human judge finally gives in to the persistent pleas of a widow, *how much more* will the heavenly Father respond to the petitions of His children?" The whole parable turns on the skillful use of contrast. (I'll talk about parables when we deal with figurative language in chapter 36.)

Irony

Let me show you one more outstanding case of contrast. This is also found in Luke's gospel. In chapter 8, Jesus is traveling around the Galilee region, teaching and healing. Great crowds are following Him. In fact, Luke makes a point of showing how many people are around Him: the twelve are there (v. 1); a group of women are supporting Him financially (vv. 2-3); and a "great multitude" follows after Him (v. 4).

Jesus leaves this mob for a while to go to the country of the Gerasenes, where He casts out the legion of demons (vv. 26-39). But as soon as He comes back, everyone is there waiting for Him (v. 40).

The pace picks up at this point as an official named Jairus comes up and places a "911" call to Jesus: "Lord, come quick! It's my daughter. She's really sick. In fact, she's not going to make it unless you get there fast."

That throws the crowd into a frenzy. It's a life-and-death situation involving a little girl. Will Jesus get there in time? Everybody wants to find out, and Luke is careful to tell us in verse 42 that "as He went, the multitudes were pressing against Him." Talk about ambulance chasers!

At this point an ironic contrast occurs. A woman with a chronic problem of bleeding—perhaps a gynecological malady, perhaps something else; the text doesn't tell us—somehow fights her way through the crowd and comes up behind Him. Upon touching Him, she's healed. And suddenly Jesus stops, and the surge of the crowd stops. He asks, "Who is the one who touched Me?" (v. 45).

The question is almost comical. In fact, it's fun to see the disciples' reaction: "Who touched you? Lord, people have been touching you since we got off the boat."

But Jesus has felt the touch of faith. And this is the contrast that Luke wants us to see: In the midst of a crisis, in the middle of a mob, an unknown woman privately and quietly approaches the Savior in faith—and He recognizes it. She stands out from the crowd because of her faith. Luke sets it up so that we notice her and benefit by her example.

Things that are alike and unlike make use of the strong human tendency to compare and contrast. As you study the Scriptures, listen to that voice inside your head saying, "Hey, this is like that passage I looked at yesterday," or, "This section is different from anything else in this book." Those are clear signals that the author is using things alike and unlike to communicate his message.

You Try It

John 11:1-46 makes an outstanding study in comparison and contrast. It's the story of the raising of Lazarus, but he's really just a background figure. John focuses his lens on Lazarus's two sisters, Martha and Mary.

Read the account carefully, then consider questions such as: What was the relationship between Jesus and these two women? Are there any other texts that shed light on this question? How do the two sisters approach Jesus? How does He respond to them? What does He say? Compare and contrast the faith of these two women. How do they compare to the disciples and to the people who observed this incident?

23

THINGS THAT ARE TRUE TO LIFE

There are two essential components to quality observation. First, you have to learn how to read. Second, you have to learn what to look for. We've seen five clues to look for when you open the Word of God. The sixth, and final, clue goes on the palm of your hand:

THINGS THAT ARE TRUE TO LIFE

The issue here is authenticity: What does this passage tell you about reality? What aspects of the text resonate with your experience?

This is where you need to use your sanctified imagination. You need to look for principles (more on that in chapter 43). We obviously live in a culture that is dramatically different from the cultures of the biblical era. Yet the same things that the biblical characters experienced, we experience. We feel the same emotions they felt. We have the same questions they had. They were real, live people who faced the same struggles, the same problems, and the same temptations that you and I face.

So as I read about them in Scripture, I need to ask: What were this person's ambitions? What were his goals? What problems was he facing? How did he feel? What was his response? What would be my response?

Often we study or teach Scripture as if it were some academic lesson, rather than real life. No wonder so many of us are bored with

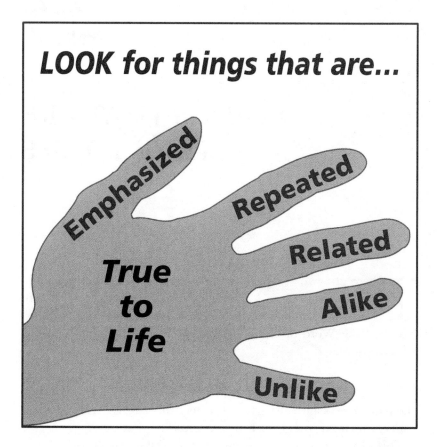

our Bibles. We're missing out on the best lessons of God's Word by failing to pick up on the experience of the people in it.

Let me mention a few individuals that I think help us see truth in realistic terms. What I love about the Bible is that it always returns me to reality. It never paints its characters with whitewash. If necessary, it hangs the dirty laundry right out the front window to tell me what really happened.

Abraham

In Genesis 22:2, God says to Abraham, "Take your son, I mean your only son, I mean the one whom you love, the seed—and offer him up as a sacrifice." So Abraham starts walking up Mount Moriah with his son, Isaac, who is about twenty-two years old. Isaac says to him, "Hey, Dad, we've got the wood. We've got the fire. But where's the sacrifice?" Abraham knows that his son is to be the sacrifice. How do you suppose he felt? How would you feel?

Moses

Moses was an incredible leader, probably the quintessential leader of all time. But he never gets into the Promised Land. Why? Because he struck a rock twice (Numbers 20:1-13). One act of bad temper, and he's eliminated from going in. How did that punishment affect him? How might it have made him feel toward God? Toward life? (See Psalm 90.) How do I respond to the consequences of my own sin?

Noah

Noah was a man of great righteousness. In a generation shot through with wickedness, he obeyed God and thereby saved his family from the Flood. And yet the account tells me that he also got dead drunk (Genesis 9:20-21). I think, *How was this possible?* Well, the Scriptures paint him not as a perfect individual but as a real, live person. Righteous? Honored by God? Absolutely. But also failing, weak, and sinful. What implications does that hold for me?

David

Of all the biblical characters, King David is probably my favorite to study. He is brilliant and gifted in many fields. He's an ultra-competent individual. I don't know about you, but whenever I study a person such as him, I almost feel inferior. Not only is he a great warrior, not only is he a great athlete, not only is he a great poet and musician, he's also a great leader. He seems to have it all. He's the one person in Scripture that God describes as "a man after [My] own heart" (1 Samuel 13:14).

Yet this choice man of God is shot down in flames one day, when he's home instead of out on the battlefield with his troops. It only takes one woman to wipe him out. What is the Spirit of God saying to us by including this tragedy in the narrative? What warning does it give us? What flags does it wave about our humanity?

Peter

The reason most of us like Peter is that he reminds us so much of ourselves. Every time we want to write him off we realize, "Good night, he's saying or doing exactly what I would have said or done." For instance, he's willing to take on a hundred men single-handedly to rescue the Lord (John 18:10). Yet one little gal comes up and says, "Hey, weren't you one of His disciples?"

He keeps repeating, "Who, me?"

"I know you were one of them," she insists.

"Drop dead, woman," he tells her. "I don't know what in the world you're talking about."

So finally she says, "I recognize the accent. You've got a Galilean accent. You were one of the disciples, weren't you?"

And Peter starts swearing and cursing at this young woman.

When we back up and look at that incident, we wonder, Who is saying that? Why, the man who told Jesus, "You can count on me." But at the moment of crisis he failed—just as you or I might have. Peter was human.

John Mark

John Mark is one of those characters that you are liable to miss because so little is said about him. He starts out with Paul and Barnabas on the first missionary journey. They sail from the coast of Palestine over to Cyprus and then eventually to Asia Minor. And as soon as they hit the mainland, John Mark takes off for home (Acts 13:13).

Later Paul and Barnabas decide to take another journey, and Barnabas suggests they take John Mark. But Paul says, "No way. We're not taking him. He flushed out the last time, and I don't want to run that chance again." The text says that they had such a strong disagreement (Don't water it down!) that they parted company (Acts 15:36-39).

It's not until the end of Paul's life that he writes, "Pick up Mark and bring him with you, for he is useful to me for service" (2 Timothy 4:11). How in the world did John Mark become useful? It certainly wasn't through Paul. No, it was Barnabas who took him and developed him and made him into a person that God could use.

There's a ring of authenticity to the accounts of all of these people. But it's easy to miss if your eyes are not looking for things that are true to life. When you study the Word of God, make sure you plug it into real life. Then you will discover that the people in the biblical narrative are just like you and me. They are cut out of the same bolt of human cloth.

Things to Look For

Speaking of things that are true to life, see how many things you can find hidden in this picture. (Answers on page 180.)

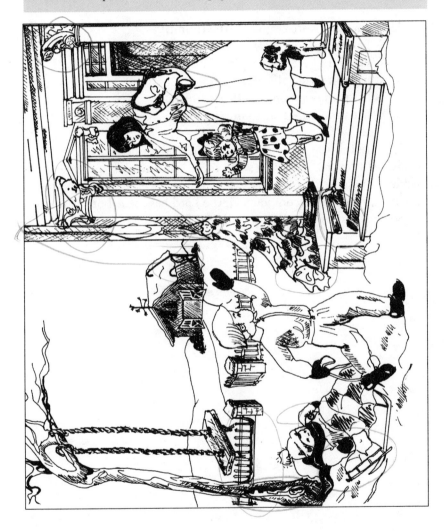

Well, there you have them: six clues to look for every time you open your Bible.

1. What things are emphasized? (thumb)
2. What things are repeated? (index finger)
3. What things are related? (middle finger)
4. What things are alike? (ring finger)
5. What things are unlike? (little finger)
6. What things are true to life (palm)?

Is there biblical precedent for asking those questions? I think so. Consider Proverbs 20:12. It's the most "audiovisual" passage in the Bible: "The hearing ear [that's the audio component] and the seeing eye [that's the visual component], the Lord has made both of them."

So your task is clear: Learn to listen. Learn to look.

24

GET THE BIG PICTURE

In this chapter we come to the college department in the school of Observation. Remember that we started out with a verse, Acts 1:8. That was a piece of cake. Then we moved up to a paragraph, Nehemiah 1:4-11, where we observed a collection of verses revolving around a common theme, Nehemiah's prayer.

Now we're going to look at what is called a segment, a collection of paragraphs united by a common theme. First I'm going to go through a section to show you what observation looks like on that scale. Then I'll list some specific suggestions to help you observe biblical sections on your own.

START WITH AN OVERVIEW

The section we're going to look at is Mark 4-5. I encourage you to open your Bible there, as the passage is too lengthy to reprint here. Take a few minutes now to read those two chapters before proceeding.

Two segments
Actually we have two segments in this portion. Mark 4:1-34 contains what I call the parable segment. Notice that chapter 4 begins with Jesus teaching by the Sea of Galilee. Verse 2 tells us, "He was teaching them many things in parables." So this is a teaching situation, and parables are the main medium of communication. In fact, in verses 33-34 we read,

And with many such parables He was speaking the word to
them as they were able to hear it; and He was not speaking to
them without parables; but He was explaining everything
privately to His own disciples.

Then, beginning at 4:35 and continuing through 5:43, we have
the miracle segment. This involves a series of four miracles: the
miracle of the storm (4:35-41); the miracle of the demoniac (5:1-20);
the miracle of the hemorrhaging woman (5:25-34) and the miracle
of Jairus's daughter (5:21-24, 35-43). What can we observe about
the order in which Mark has related these? Notice that they are
arranged climactically.

Now looking over the parables, what key expression is repeated?
"He who has ears to hear, let him hear" (4:9, 23). I still remember
the first time I came across that. I thought, *What in the world does
that mean?* After all, what else would you do with ears? Since then
I've discovered that people do all kinds of things with their ears—
put earrings on them, collect wax, everything but hear.

I'll let you examine this first segment in detail on your own.

CREATE A CHART

After Jesus finishes the teaching, He moves into the testing. You see,
He was a great teacher: He gave tests. But not the kind we give in
schools today, to see how much a student can cram into his bean and
then spill out on an exam. When Jesus gave tests He tested at the
reality level, at the level of life-experience. So we can say that the
first thirty-four verses of chapter 4 represent the lecture; then things
move into the laboratory. Jesus knew that you learn faith, not in a
lecture but in the laboratory of life.

I want to focus on the four miracles, and I want to do it in a
rather unique fashion. You are going to make a lot of discoveries in
the Observation phase of your Bible study. But that poses a problem:
how can you organize the material in order to make efficient use of
it? Let me suggest one strategy called a *grid chart*, shown on the next
page. When we have a lot of paragraphs and a lot of material, as we
do here, a grid chart can help us summarize it in a manageable way.

I've listed the four miracles down the left-hand column. Let's
compare them in five areas, as listed across the top: What was the

Mark 4:35–5:42

Miracle	Realm	People	Means	Results	Faith
Stilling of the Storm					
Demoniac					
Woman with the Hemorrhage					
Jairus' Daughter					

realm in which the miracle took place? Who were the people involved? What means did Christ use to effect the miracle? What was the result? And finally—and most important in light of the parables section—what was the component of faith?

The Realm

Let's begin with the stilling of the storm (4:35-41). Clearly that takes place in the physical realm. So we can write that on the chart. They are out on the lake when a tremendous storm comes up, and Jesus calms the storm.

What about the demoniac? That's a bit more difficult to say. Without question he was demon possessed, which is largely a spiritual problem. But I think most people would say that as a result he was mentally deranged and had a psychological problem.

What about the woman with the hemorrhage? She had an obvious physical affliction. But after trying for twelve years to find someone to help her, there was probably an emotional need as well.

What about the raising of Jairus' daughter? It really involves all three—physical, emotional, and spiritual. That's important to observe. It's why this miracle climaxes the section.

You see, someone could say about the stilling of the storm, "Well, that was just a fascinating coincidence." Someone else could say of the demoniac, "He lived before the days of psychiatric help. We could solve his problem if he were living today." Likewise, someone could say of the woman, "All she needed was a good gynecologist." But what can you say about the raising of Jairus's daughter? Who's solving that problem today? I don't find many people out at the local cemetery bringing them back.

So the miracles are arranged climactically: Jesus not only has power over the mental, psychological, and physical, He also has power over death.

The People

Let's move on to the people involved. Notice who experienced the stilling of the storm—the disciples. A number of them had been fishermen. It's very important to notice the connection between the realm of the miracle and the people involved in it. This was not a group of seminary professors scared spitless that the boat was going down. It was a group of professional fishermen. They had lived on this lake and seen storms before.

You see, in the Galilee region, prevailing winds come from the west, down valleys that act as funnels. The lake is 690 feet below sea level, so there are tremendous downdrafts. The phenomenon exists to this day. In fact, the last time I was visiting the Sea of Galilee, I watched a violent storm come up in less than ten minutes.

So these men had experienced storms all of their lives but never anything like this.

Notice who else was there: Jesus, fast asleep.

Let's look at the demoniac. Certainly Jesus is involved. But the obvious one is the man himself. His is an interesting story. Other people constantly tried to solve his problem but with no success.

There's another group—the townspeople. They fascinate me. Here's a poor, demon possessed man, and everybody knows him. "Watch out for him," they cry. "Put him in chains. Keep him away from respectable society." Then one day he gets cured, and you'd think everybody would say, "Wow! What a story. Let's put it in *Newsweek*."

Mark 4:35–5:42

Miracle	Realm	People	Means	Results	Faith
Stilling of the Storm	Physical	Disciples Jesus			
Demoniac	Mental	Jesus Man Townspeople			
Woman with the Hemorrhage	Physical/ Emotional	Jesus Woman Disciples			
Jairus' Daughter	Physical/ Emotional/ Spiritual	Jesus Jairus Daughter Disciples Mourners			

But the townspeople are anything but excited—particularly when they find out that the demons have gone into their pigs, causing them to stampede off a cliff and drown. As a result they lose all of their economic investment. And are they mad! They are more concerned about the local economy than they are about the cure of a fellow human being.

How about the woman with the hemorrhage? We looked at her in chapter 22. Here the disciples become very important. They set up the atmosphere in verse 31: "You see the multitude pressing in on You, and You say, 'Who touched Me?'" In other words, "How in the world do we know who touched You?" Of course, there's also the woman herself. The text says she had been ill for twelve years. That's a long time and indicates a serious problem. And there is also Jesus.

Let's move to Jairus's daughter. There's Jairus, his daughter, and the mother. There's Christ, who takes Peter, James, and John. That's instructive. There's also a collection of professional mourners. Isn't that fascinating? Jesus comes on the scene and declares, "She's not dead. She's just asleep." And they roar. Probably the first time they'd ever laughed at a funeral.

The Means

Let's observe the means Jesus uses in each of the miracles. There are some phenomenal things taking place here. In the storm, all He does is speak. "Be quiet," He says. Or, it can be translated, "Be muzzled." And the tempest shuts down. The sea becomes completely calm.

With the demoniac, again all He needs to do is speak.

As for the woman, He doesn't even need words. He uses touch; actually, she touches Him.

And then in the Jairus experience, He uses both touch and words. He takes the little girl by the hand, and He also calls her by name.

The Results

Now let's link the means with the results. The result in the stilling of the storm was "a great calm," the text says. I don't know if you've ever been in a storm at sea. But every fisherman and sailor knows that just because a storm stops, the sea does not stop. It churns, sometimes for days to come. But this was a miracle, and there was an immediate calm.

With the demoniac, the spirits come out, and the man returns to normalcy. In fact, the text says he was sitting "clothed and in his right mind." He wasn't doing that prior to the miracle.

For the bleeding woman, the result of touching Jesus is immediate healing. That's significant because her problem has been twelve years in duration. But it doesn't take twelve days or even twelve minutes for her to recover.

Finally, Jairus's daughter. She immediately stands up, which indicates instant restoration. She also starts to walk, and she takes some food.

Faith

The component of faith is critical in each of these miracles. In the storm, the disciples lose all faith. They are scared to death. Even after Jesus calms things down, they are still afraid. No faith, but lots of fear.

And yet the disciples have just heard Jesus' lectures on faith in the first part of chapter 4. They've sat under the greatest Teacher in

Mark 4:35–5:42

Miracle	Realm	People	Means	Results	Faith
Stilling of the Storm	Physical	Disciples Jesus	Speaks	A Great Calm	No Faith / Only Fear
Demoniac	Mental	Jesus Man Townspeople	Speaks	Normalcy (Sitting Clothed Rt Mind)	Recognition Desire to Follow
Woman with the Hemorrhage	Physical / Emotional	Jesus Woman Disciples	Touch	Immediate Healing	Her Faith Healed Her
Jairus' Daughter	Physical / Emotional / Spiritual	Jesus Jairus Daughter Disciples Mourners	Touch Speaks	Stands Walks Eats	Great Faith

the world. But when they take an exam on the lake, their blue books come back with a big, fat "F" on them. And that isn't for "Faith." They've flunked. In fact, Jesus asks them, "How is it that you [you, of all people!] have no faith?" (v. 40).

As for the demoniac, his faith begins with a recognition of who Jesus is. He has come to the right Person. And he wants to follow Him—a clear expression of commitment. But Jesus says, "No, you need to go home and give your testimony."

The woman is perhaps the star of this section when it comes to faith. She takes initiative on the basis of what she has heard about Jesus. And Jesus says that her faith has healed her. That's impressive.

Jairus demonstrates faith in Christ through a two-stage process. First he comes and says, "My daughter is at the point of death." That's a start. But then his friends rush in and tell him that his little girl has died. Can you imagine his feelings? As long as there's life, there's hope. But once she was dead, I'm sure he just wanted to give up. He must have been crushed.

But Jesus says, "No, keep on believing." And he does. Not only does he begin in faith, he follows through with it. And guess who sees that? The disciples. Remember, the ones who had no faith? They are right there watching this man who has no reason to hope anymore. He hasn't been to the lectures. Yet he has great faith because the Lord has said, "Just hang in there. Trust Me. Follow Me." And he does.

USING THE CHART

Look over the grid chart. We've got an incredible volume of material, but it is summarized in a way that we can grasp. We can study the chart in two ways. First, we can study it compositely by moving across from left to right. That is, we can take each of the miracles and evaluate it in terms of the realm, the people, the means, the result, and the element of faith.

On the other hand, we can study it comparatively by moving from top to bottom. For instance: What kind of faith did the disciples have? What kind of faith did the demoniac have? What kind of faith did the woman have? And what kind of faith did Jairus have?

A chart such as this is invaluable, because it gives you a maximum return on your investment in the Bible study process. Every time you come back to this passage, you can pull out your chart and quickly review what this section is all about. You don't have to start from scratch every time. Neither do you have to rely on your memory. In fact, charting is so valuable to the step of Observation that we're going to look at it in more detail in the next chapter.

HOW TO STUDY A SECTION

But first, let me offer a few suggestions on how you can glean the most out of a section of Scripture.

1. Read the entire section completely. In fact, try reading it two or three times, perhaps in different translations.

2. Identify the paragraphs, and put a label or title on each paragraph. In the section we looked at above, I labeled the

four miracles as shown on the left-hand column of the chart. Remember that the paragraph is the basic unit of study. So it's important to grasp the main idea or theme of each paragraph, and then state that in a word or two.

3. Evaluate each paragraph in light of the other paragraphs. Use the six clues I gave you earlier in the book to look for relationships. In the grid chart above, I compared and contrasted the four miracles according to the realm, the people, the means, the result, and the element of faith.

4. Evaluate how the section as a whole relates to the rest of the book, using the same principles (things emphasized, repeated, and so on).

5. Try to state the main point of the section. See if you can boil it down to one word or a short phrase that summarizes the content. For instance, I could call it Mark 4-5 "the lectures and the laboratory of faith."

6. Keep a list of observations on the section. Better yet, record them in your Bible, using brief, descriptive words.

7. Study the persons and places mentioned. See what you can learn about them that throws light on the section as a whole.

8. Keep a list of your unanswered questions and unresolved problems. Those become avenues for further investigation.

9. Ask yourself: What have I seen in this section that challenges the way I live? What practical issues does this passage address? What change do I need to consider in light of this study? What prayer do I need to pray as a result of what I've seen?

10. Share the results of your study with someone else.

You Try It

I've got a passage for you to try out, now that I've shown you how to observe a section. It's the the parable of the soils in Matthew 13:1-23. Here's a grid chart to help you get started. It considers four questions for each of the four kinds of soil: How does Jesus describe the soil? What sort of growth took place? What were the hindrances to growth? What was the outcome, or result, of the planting?

SOILS	DESCRIPTION	GROWTH	HINDRANCES	RESULTS

25

SUMMARIZE YOUR OBSERVATIONS

O ne of the most fascinating stories of the last decade is the emergence of *USA Today*. It remains to be seen whether the paper will succeed financially, but without question it has succeeded conceptually. Readers seem to like its summarization of news in a way that makes for quick reading. And simple, colorful graphics are one of the primary means to that end. In fact, no matter what the future of *USA Today* turns out to be, it has permanently altered the look of the newspaper medium in this country.

There's a lesson here for the student of Scripture. Bible study is information-intensive. If you do the job of observation as I've described it in the previous chapters, you'll have more data than you can possibly handle. And that's a problem, because what good is information if you can't access it? One solution is the strategy of *USA Today*: Show rather than tell. Summarize your findings in a chart.

THE VALUE OF CHARTS

A chart is to the Bible student what a map is to a mariner. It aids him or her in navigating an ocean of words, pages, books, ideas, characters, events, and other information. Without a chart or some similar device, he is liable to founder on the shoals of mental overload. There are just too many details to keep track of.

But a good chart can keep you on course in several ways. First, it uses the power of the picture. This is especially helpful in our culture.

As I pointed out in a previous chapter, we live in a visually-oriented society. We've come to prefer images rather than text. Charts make use of that. They can show the relationships between verses, paragraphs, sections, and even books. Using a chart, you can comprehend the purpose and structure of a portion of Scripture at a glance.

A well-constructed chart also tends to be memorable. Again, this is largely a function of its visual appeal. For instance, suppose you've never memorized the names of the books of the Bible. If I handed you a list of them, it would probably take you quite a while to memorize that list perfectly. But if I showed you a chart of the books arranged by categories, you could memorize their names much more quickly. (See page 29.) That's because a chart gives you some visual landmarks.

One final benefit worth mentioning is the way charts can illustrate your observations. For example, I mentioned the six clues to look for: things emphasized, things repeated, things related, and so on. A chart can show those findings. It can illustrate the parts in light of the whole. It can highlight the important ideas or characters. It can demonstrate contrasts and comparisons. It can point out key terms and phrases. Most important, it can sketch out the structure, which is crucial to the author's purpose.

THE ART OF THE CHART

The chart is an incredibly useful tool in Bible study, but keep in mind that it is only a means to an end. Your ultimate goal in studying God's Word is not to produce a chart but to produce change in your life. The chart is simply a way to handle the information that you cull from the text.

Let me discuss the examples of charts shown here, and then I'll list some suggestions for how you can get started in effective charting.

Mark

The first chart (next page) shows the gospel by Mark, the whole book at a glance, on one piece of paper. The person who made it observed that the key verse, the one that actually summarizes the book's structure, is 10:45: "For even the Son of Man did not come to be served, but to serve, and to give His life a ransom for many."

That helped him observe that the book is divided into two major sections: the first half deals with Jesus' service, and the last half deals

The Gospel of Mark

"Came to Serve"		and	"Give His Life"	
PROLOGUE	SERVICE		SACRIFICE	EPILOGUE
Jesus Came	Who Is He?	Who Do People Say That I Am ?	Where's He Going?	Jesus... Received Up
1:1–45	2:1 8:26	8:27 30	8:31 15:47	16:1–20
His Person		and	His Purpose	

with His sacrifice. You can see how he charted these and other observations, so that both visually and verbally he could understand the book at a glance.

I particularly like this chart because it is simple. If we were to enlarge it to the size of a full page, we could add all kinds of detail. But as it stands, we have the basics. We know immediately what Mark is all about.

1 Peter

The chart at the top of the next page is one that I developed for 1 Peter, the book I call a "Syllabus for Suffering Saints." (Second Peter is the "Syllabus for Significant Saints.")

As I've studied 1 Peter, I've noticed that there are three major divisions to the book, three major issues addressed: salvation, submission, and suffering. It's interesting to think of them in reverse order: Suffering will never make sense until you have submitted yourself to the Father's will; and submission will never make sense until you understand what salvation is all about. That's how the writer unfolds his argument through the five chapters of the book.

1 PETER
SYLLABUS FOR SUFFERING SAINTS
How to Hold Up—Not Fold Up

SALVATION	SUBMISSION	SUFFERING
privileges of salvation 1:2–12 products of salvation 1:13–25 process of salvation 2:1–10	in the state 2:13–17; civil in the household 2:18–25; social in the family 3:1–7; domestic	as a citizen 3:13 – 4:6 as a saint 4:7–19 as a shepherd 5:1–7 as a soldier 5:8–11
DOCTRINE IS DYNAMIC!	THE CHRISTIAN'S LIFESTYLE!	THE CHISEL TO SHAPE THE SOUL!
1:3 2:10	2:11 3:12	3:13 5:11
The DESTINY of the Christian	The DUTY of the Christian	The DISCIPLINE of the Christian

Malachi

The next example shows Malachi. I've titled this "The Wail of Wounded Love." Do you want to study an Old Testament book? This is it. Remember we talked about using the question-and-answer approach (chapter 11)? Well, Malachi was the prophet with a question mark for a brain. Over and over he asks the question, "Who, me?"

You see, in Malachi God is rebuking the nation of Israel for its sins. And every time He does, the people respond, "Prove it." They are like a little kid with his hand in the cookie jar and crumbs all down the front of him. His mom says, "Son, I told you not to take the cookies."

And he says, "What cookies?"

That's exactly what you have in this book.

MALACHI
"The Wail of Wounded Love"

	REBUKE	WARNING	APPEAL	
Intro 1:1–5	Priests 1:6 - 2:9	Accusation 2:17	Response 3:7 - 18	Concl. 4:4–6
	People 2:10 - 16	Announcement 2:17　3:6	Reason 3 :7　4:3	
	1:6　2:16	2:17　3:6	3:7　4:3	

Luke

You need to think of charts as more than just a final, polished product of your study. They are actually powerful tools to help you investigate the text.

For instance, here's an overview of the gospel by Luke that shows what I call the law of proportion. We talked about looking for things that are emphasized by the amount of space devoted to them. The law of proportion says that the importance of material to an author's meaning is in direct proportion to the amount of space he gives to it. A chart such as this one illustrates that principle.

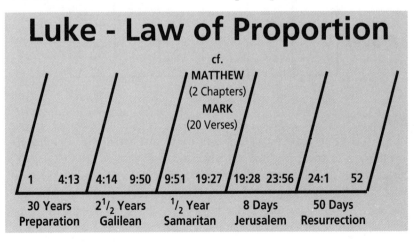

Luke - Law of Proportion

cf.
MATTHEW
(2 Chapters)
MARK
(20 Verses)

| 1 | 4:13 | 4:14 | 9:50 | 9:51 | 19:27 | 19:28 | 23:56 | 24:1 | 52 |

| 30 Years Preparation | 2½ Years Galilean | ½ Year Samaritan | 8 Days Jerusalem | 50 Days Resurrection |

Ephesians

Notice the grid chart of Ephesians below. Remember, I used a grid chart in the last chapter to study Mark 4-5.

Let's say I've been observing the epistle to the Ephesians, and I notice that there are four themes that keep popping up: the grace of God, the activity of Satan, the believer's lifestyle, or "walk," and prayer. So I need to ask: Are there any relationships between these themes? Is one of them more dominant than the others? How much space is devoted to each one? How do they relate to the overall theme and structure of the book?

A grid chart can help me follow these four themes through the letter so that when I'm done I can see the relationships.

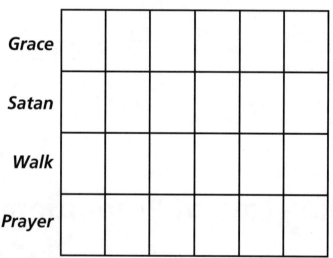

EPHESIANS

Love

The final chart, on page 187, is different from the others. It summarizes a topical study on love. Topical studies are fascinating because they look at one subject that appears in many passages, and then correlate the results. Here, the study revealed that two key passages in Matthew are central texts on the subject of love. One

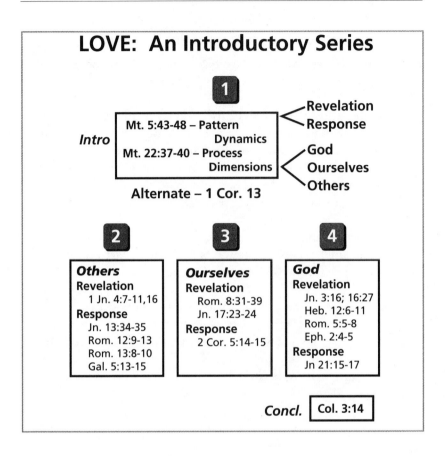

LOVE: An Introductory Series

1

Intro Mt. 5:43-48 – Pattern
                Dynamics
         Mt. 22:37-40 – Process
                Dimensions

         Alternate – 1 Cor. 13

Revelation
Response

God
Ourselves
Others

2

Others
Revelation
  1 Jn. 4:7-11,16
Response
  Jn. 13:34-35
  Rom. 12:9-13
  Rom. 13:8-10
  Gal. 5:13-15

3

Ourselves
Revelation
  Rom. 8:31-39
  Jn. 17:23-24
Response
  2 Cor. 5:14-15

4

God
Revelation
  Jn. 3:16; 16:27
  Heb. 12:6-11
  Rom. 5:5-8
  Eph. 2:4-5
Response
  Jn 21:15-17

Concl. Col. 3:14

gives the pattern for love, which is God's love, and the other describes the process of love, which is to love others as you love yourself. Notice that a related text is 1 Corinthians 13, the love chapter.

The study also discovered that when it comes to practicing love, there are three domains—loving God, loving ourselves, and loving others. In each case, there is revealed truth to consider and a response to that truth.

There are obviously other ways to organize this material and show the relationships. What matters is that the chart makes sense to the person who constructs it. It needs to show what he has found in the text. It's his tool, his way of owning the text.

MAKING A START WITH YOUR CHART

Are you ready to try your hand at making a chart? Let me give you a few suggestions.

1. As you study a text, assign titles and labels to the content in a way that summarizes the material. Be creative. I talked about acquisitive Bible reading, making the text your own. Placing your own titles on the verses, paragraphs, sections, and books of the Bible is one way to do that. They help you retain your insights in neat packages.

2. As you visualize your chart, ask: What are the relationships? What am I trying to show? What's this chart all about? When I've finished it, how am I going to use it?

3. Keep your charts simple. You can always add detail; the challenge is to trim away the clutter. What key ideas, characters, themes, verses, terms, and other data from the text ought to take priority? What is the big idea? What structure needs to be shown? What material do you want to see at a glance?

4. If you find that you've got too much material to include in a chart, chop it up and make several charts. By the way, too much unrelated data is a clue that you need to go back to the text and do some more observing.

5. Be creative. I've only shown a handful of possibilities above. There are dozens of other ways to show relationships in the text. Let your imagination flow. Draw illustrations or symbols if they help. It's your chart, so make it work for you.

6. Revise your charts in light of your study. No chart can summarize everything. As you continue to study a passage, you'll gain new insights that should cause you to revise or even redo your chart. Remember, charts are a means to an end, not an end in themselves. They are useful to the extent that they accurately represent what is in the biblical text.

You Try It

Now that you've seen several illustrations of how to make a chart, try to construct your own chart of the book of Acts, using the suggestions given in this chapter. To get started, review chapter 6 where we looked at Acts 1:8. I pointed out that the four places mentioned—Jerusalem, Judea, Samaria, and the uttermost part of the earth—form an outline for the book. You might want to use that observation in organizing your material. Or, come up with your own overview. But develop a chart that summarizes the account in a way that helps you quickly grasp what is going on in Luke's book.

26

"FACTS ARE STUPID THINGS UNTIL..."

R emember the story of Louis Agassiz and his method for teaching students to observe the fish? He left his students in front of their specimens for days and weeks, giving them only one instruction: "Look! Look! Look!"

If I could give students of Scripture only one instruction, it would be the same: "Look! Look! Look!" The truth of God is in the Bible, but most people miss it primarily because they don't look for it. They never put forth the time and effort required to answer the fundamental question of Observation, What do I see? As a result, they have no basis for understanding what God has revealed.

In this section of the book, I've given you an introduction to the process of seeing. As I've pointed out, Observation is only the first step in Bible study method. But it's an absolutely critical step, and unfortunately one to which most people pay scant attention.

We've seen that in order to observe Scripture, we first must learn to read. We have to learn to read better and faster, as for the first time, and as though the Bible were a love letter. And we looked at ten strategies that can help us become first-rate readers of God's Word.

Then we learned what to look for in the biblical record. We discovered six clues that unlock the text for our understanding: things emphasized, things repeated, things related, things alike, things unlike, and things that are true to life.

We practiced these skills on three kinds of biblical material—a verse, a paragraph, and a section. We saw that there is no end to the amount of detail that the observant person can uncover. And all of it leads to greater insight.

Finally, we looked at the value of charts in summarizing the fruits of our study. We saw that charts are efficient tools for visualizing data so that we can use it in understanding the text.

Now we need to move on in the process. Professor Agassiz trained his students in the method of discovering facts and their orderly arrangement, but he was never content to leave it there. "Facts are stupid things," he would say, "until brought into connection with some general law."

That brings us to the second step in Bible study method. Once we've seen what the text says, we're ready to ask, What does it mean? So let's shift into second gear and look at the second stage in the process, Interpretation.

You Try It

A student of mine showed me the following exercise in observing the account of the Fall in Genesis 3:1-7. It's an excellent opportunity to use all of the skills that you've learned in this section.

Monday
Read Genesis 3:1-7 from the perspective of the heavenly Father witnessing the sin of His children from heaven.

Tuesday
Read the account with the goal in mind of finding the most important verse in the paragraph.

Wednesday
Read it from Satan's perspective as he tempts God's children.

Thursday
Read with the goal in mind of determining how this passage affects your understanding of what Jesus did on the cross.

Friday
Read from the perspective of Adam and Eve as they are sinning. What was going through their minds?

Saturday
Read from the perspective of someone who knows nothing of the Bible or "religious" things and who is reading this passage for the first time.

The Scientist and the Flea

A scientist was using the inductive method to observe the characteristics of a flea. Plucking a leg off the flea, he ordered, "Jump!"

The flea promptly jumped.

Taking another leg off, the scientist again commanded, "Jump!"

The flea jumped again.

The scientist continued this process until he came to the sixth and final leg. By now the flea was having a little more difficulty jumping, but it was still trying.

The scientist pulled the final leg off and again ordered the flea to jump. But the flea didn't respond.

The scientist raised his voice and demanded, "Jump!" Again the flea failed to respond.

For a third time the scientist shouted at the top of his lungs, "Jump!" But the hapless flea lay motionless.

The scientist then made the following observation in his notebook: "When you remove the legs from a flea, it loses its sense of hearing."

STEP 2
Interpretation

What does it mean?

27

THE VALUE OF
INTERPRETATION

One time I heard a speaker give a brilliant presentation of a passage of Scripture. On the way out of the auditorium, I overheard two people talking.

"Well," one of them was asking, "what did you think of that?"

The other person shrugged. "Not very much. He didn't do a blessed thing but explain the Bible."

Nothing but explain the Bible? Why, that's the highest compliment I can imagine. After all, the primary task of any teacher of Scripture is to explain what the text means. You see, it is impossible to apply the Word of God until you understand it. In fact, the better you understand it, the better you can apply it. That's why David prayed, "Give me understanding, and I will keep your law and obey it with all my heart" (Psalm 119:34, NIV).

Acting on what God has said assumes that you understand what He has said. That's why the second major step in firsthand Bible study is the step of Interpretation. Here you ask and answer the question, What does it mean?

"DO YOU UNDERSTAND WHAT YOU ARE READING?"

Acts 8 records the story of Philip. Philip was the Billy Graham of his day. He preached the gospel in Samaria, and the entire region responded. But one day the Spirit of God said to him, "Go south on the road—the desert road—from Jerusalem to Gaza" (v. 26).

"What?" he could have argued. "I'm a metropolitan man. I only do big crusades. I don't go in for any one-on-one stuff."

But instead he heads south, and en route he meets a man, an Ethiopian eunuch. Actually, he is the secretary of the treasury for his country. And they get involved in a conversation. The official has been reading a passage of Scripture.

So Philip asks him, "Do you understand what you are reading?"

Imagine boarding a plane, sitting down next to someone reading *Time* magazine, and asking, "Hey, do you understand what you're reading?" I suspect the person would give you a portion of his mind that he couldn't afford to lose.

But Philip must have known how to ask that question, because the man answers, "Well, how could I, unless someone guides me?" (v. 31).

Mark it well: this man had a copy of the Scriptures, but he needed help in understanding them. He was deeply involved in the process of Interpretation. That's clear from the perceptive question he asks after reading the passage: "Tell me please, who is the prophet talking about? Himself, or someone else?" (v. 34).

Philip helped the man gain insight into what the text meant. And after he understood it, he was able to respond in faith. Verse 39 says he went home rejoicing. So in a real sense, the step of Interpretation helped to open Africa to the gospel.

WHAT DO WE MEAN BY INTERPRETATION?

Every book of Scripture has a message, and that message can be understood. Do you ever wonder sometimes whether the Bible is just a giant riddle? God intended it as a revelation. Second Timothy 3:16 says, "All Scripture is *profitable*" (italics added). That is, it has purpose, it has meaning. God is not playing a game of hide-and-seek with you. He doesn't invite you into His Word only to puzzle and confound you. He's far more interested that you understand it than you are.

But the question is, what do we mean by "meaning"? Let me give you an illustration. I happen to be partially color-blind, so I can't easily distinguish between greens and blues. Suppose you showed me a sweater and said, "Prof, I just love this blue sweater." We would both be looking at the same sweater, but the color you see would not be the same as the color I see.

That happens all the time in biblical interpretation. Two people will look at the same verse and come up with two completely different interpretations. In fact, they may be opposing interpretations. Can they both be correct? Not if the laws of logic apply to Scripture.

But unfortunately, many people today have decided that the laws of logic do not apply to Scripture. To them, it doesn't really matter whether you see the text as blue and I see it as green. In fact, it doesn't really matter what color the text actually is. For them, the meaning of the text is not in the text, it's in their response to the text. And everyone is free to have his or her own response. Meaning becomes purely subjective.

Now there are good reasons Christians may disagree on the interpretation of a passage. We'll come back to that in the next chapter. But if we're to have any hope of interpreting God's Word accurately, we've got to start with a fundamental premise: "Meaning" is not our subjective thoughts read into the text but God's objective truth read out of the text. As someone has well said, the task of Bible study is to "think God's thoughts after Him." He has a mind, and He has revealed it in His Word.

The miracle is that He used human authors to do so. Working through their personalities, their circumstances, and their concerns, the Holy Spirit superintended the crafting of a document. And each of the human authors—God's coauthors, we might call them—had a specific message in mind as he recorded his portion of the text.

That's why I like to refer to the step of Interpretation as the re-creation process. We're attempting to stand in the author's shoes and re-create his experience—to think as he thought, to feel as he felt, and to decide as he decided. We're asking, What did this mean to him? before we ever ask, What does it mean to us?

THE CONSTRUCTION OF MEANING

So how does Interpretation relate to Observation? Recall that in Observation we asked and answered the question, What do I see? That was the foundational phase of Bible study, the laying of the cornerstone. Having done that, we need to move on to Interpretation, where we develop the superstructure.

You see, in Observation we excavate. In Interpretation we erect. And buildings are always determined by their foundations. The more substantial the foundation, the more substantial the superstructure.

Imagine that we went downtown in your city and saw workers digging a foundation. In fact, they'd been at for two and a half years. Then they pour a slab across it, and invite the public to a dedication ceremony. We show up—only to find a chicken coop in the middle of the slab. We would automatically ask, "What gives? Why such a massive foundation for such a miniscule building?"

In the same way, the quality of your interpretation will always depend on the quality of your observation. It is impossible to understand what a writer means until you notice what the writer says. Therefore, to observe well is to interpret well. You always need to observe with a view to interpreting (and eventually to applying) the Scripture. Observation is never an end in itself but always a means to an end.

WHY INTERPRETATION?

But the question remains, why must we interpret Scripture? Why can't we just open the Word, read what we're supposed to do, and then do it? Why do we have to go to so much trouble to understand the text? The answer is that time and distance have thrown up barriers between us and the biblical writers, which block our understanding. We need to appreciate what those roadblocks are. They are not insurmountable, but they are substantial.

Language barriers

Have you ever learned a foreign language? If so, you know that learning the words is not enough. You have to learn the mind-set, the culture, the worldview of those who speak it if you really want to understand what they are saying.

In the same way, when it comes to the Bible, we have some excellent translations from the Hebrew, Greek, and Aramaic languages in which it was originally written. Even so, the English text leaves us a long way from a complete understanding. That's why the process of Interpretation involves the use of a Bible dictionary and similar resources. We have to go back and recover the shades of meaning that translated words alone cannot convey.

Cultural barriers

These are closely related to the problems of language because language is always culture-bound. The Bible is the product and presentation of cultures that are dramatically different from our own—and also different from each other. To appreciate what is going on in Scripture, we have to reconstruct the cultural context in areas of communication, transportation, trade, agriculture, occupations, religion, perceptions of time, and so on.

This is where archaeology proves helpful. I'll suggest some sources to consult in chapter 34.

Literary barriers

Another problem we run into in interpreting Scripture is the variety of the terrain. If it were all mountains or desert or ocean, we could outfit ourselves appropriately and have at it. But the literary genres of the Bible are quite diverse and demand vastly different approaches. We can't read the Song of Solomon with the same cold logic that we bring to Romans. We won't get the point of the parables through the same exhaustive word studies that might unlock truths in Galatians.

In chapter 29, I'll talk about the different types of literature in the Bible, along with suggestions for interpreting each one.

Communication barriers

Perhaps you've seen the Far Side cartoon in which the first panel shows a man lecturing his dog, saying "OK, Ginger! I've had it! You stay out of the garbage! Understand, Ginger? Stay out of the garbage, or else!" The caption reads, "What people say." The next panel shows the situation from the dog's point of view, captioned, "What dogs hear." What do dogs hear? "Blah, blah, blah, blah...!"

Sometimes I feel that way as a teacher. I wonder what my students are hearing. And frankly, they're probably wondering what in the world I'm talking about.

It's the age-old problem of communication. And even though God Himself is speaking through Scripture, we still must contend with breakdowns in the communication process. As finite creatures, we can never know what is going on in someone else's mind completely. As a result, we have to settle for limited objectives in our interpretation of Scripture.

So can we interpret anything? Is it possible to interpret the Bible? Of course. But you need to know that you will always encounter problems. You can never answer every question—as a seasoned old preacher wisely perceived. He was dining in a restaurant when in walked the local atheist, who thought he'd have a little sport with him. The skeptic sat down, pointed at the minister's Bible, and asked, "Reverend, you still believe that book?"

"Absolutely," the old gentleman replied.

"You mean you believe everything in it?"

"Every word."

"Well," he said, "is there anything you can't explain?"

"Oh, there are lots of things I can't explain," the preacher responded. He opened his Bible and showed the fellow all the question marks in the margins.

Surprised, the man asked, "Well, what do you do with all of the things you can't explain?"

He said, "Very simple. I do the same thing I'm doing with this fish I'm eating. I eat the meat and push all the bones to the side of the plate, and then let any fool that wants to choke over them."

I run into people who are really blown away that I and other faculty of a theological seminary can't explain everything in the Bible. So I usually provoke their thinking with a question: Does it really bother you that I as a finite person cannot fully understand an infinite Person? Does that really bother you? It would bother me more if I could, because then I wouldn't need God. I'd be as smart as He is.

Don't get tied up in knots over the problems and unanswerable questions that come up in your study of the Bible. The miracle is that you can understand all of the essential things that God wants you to understand for your eternal salvation and for your daily living.

That brings us to what is really a fifth barrier to understanding the biblical text—the problem of faulty interpretation. I want to warn you of some of the dangers in the next chapter.

"I Don't Know Greek or Hebrew!"

Have you ever felt shut out of understanding the Bible because you don't know the languages in which they were originally written? You don't have to feel that way any longer, thanks to the many extrabiblical resources that have been developed in recent years. I'm going to discuss a number of these in chapter 34. But here's a preview of what is available to help you interpret Scripture accurately.

TYPE OF RESOURCE	DESCRIPTION	USE IT TO OVERCOME...
Atlases	Collections of maps showing places mentioned in the text, and perhaps some description of their history and significance	Geographic barriers
Bible dictionaries	Explain the origin, meaning, and use of key words and terms in the text	Language barriers
Bible handbooks	Present helpful information on subjects in the text	Cultural barriers
Commentaries	Present a biblical scholar's study of the text	Language, cultural, and literary barriers
Interlinear texts	Translations with the Greek or Hebrew text positioned in between the lines for comparison	Language barriers

28

HANDLE WITH CARE!

O ne Sunday morning I was home recovering from surgery, when two men showed up at my house, one older, one younger man, both nicely dressed. "We're visiting in the neighborhood today to talk with folks about God and religion," they told me. "Could we come in?"

Curious, I said, "Sure, come on in."

So we got involved in a conversation. They kept talking about a particular passage, and I kept saying "But that's not what the Bible says."

"Oh, yes it is," the younger man insisted. "It's in the Greek." He didn't know that I teach at a seminary.

So I asked, "What's Greek got to do with it?"

"Well, Mr. Hendricks, apparently you don't know that the New Testament was written in Greek."

"Really," I replied. "That fascinates me. Do you study Greek?"

He said, "Yes, it's a part of our training program."

"Good," I replied, and handed him my Greek New Testament. I'd have given anything to have captured on tape what happened next. He fumbled with the text, trying to make sense out of it. The older man jumped in to try and bail him out. Finally I said, "Wait a minute," and I read the passage to them, first in Greek, then in English, and said, "You see, it doesn't say that. And it doesn't mean that."

The younger guy found that very interesting, but his older companion quickly hustled him out of there. (I've never been visited by that group since. No doubt they put the word out to stay away from Hendricks.) But that kind of thing goes on every day of the week, all over the world. The problem is not with the Word of God. It's with misinterpretation of the text.

HAZARDS TO AVOID

Let me mention six pitfalls of interpretation. Watch out for them as you read and study the Scriptures.

Misreading the text

You'll never gain a proper understanding of Scripture if you don't or can't read the text properly. If Jesus says, "I am the way" (John 14:6), but you read it as, "I am a way," you are misreading the text. If Paul writes, "For the love of money is a root of all sorts of evil" (1 Timothy 6:10), but you read it as, "Money is the root of all evil," you are misreading the text. If the psalmist cries, "Delight yourself in the Lord; and He will give you the desires of your heart" (Psalm 37:4), but all you pay attention to is, "He will give you the desires of your heart," you are misreading the text.

That's why I said at the beginning of this book that if you want to study God's Word, you've got to learn to read. There is no other way. Ignorance of what the text says is the unpardonable sin of interpretation. It shows that you really haven't done your homework. You've skipped the first step in Bible study method—Observation.

Distorting the text

The two men who visited me on that Sunday morning were guilty of distorting the text. They were making it say what they wanted, not what it actually said.

Apparently Peter ran into the same problem in the early church, because in 2 Peter 3:16 he writes, "There are some points in [Paul's] letters which are difficult to understand" (Phillips). (I've always derived a great deal of comfort from that. If Peter couldn't figure them out, I guess I'm not too bad off.) "And which ill-informed and unbalanced people distort (as they do the other scriptures), and bring disaster on their own heads."

You see, it's one thing to struggle with difficulties in interpretation; it's another thing to distort the meaning of God's Word. That's serious. That's something He will bring to judgment. So we need to be careful to learn how to interpret Scripture accurately, practically, and profitably.

Contradicting the text

Contradicting the text is even worse than textual distortion. It amounts to calling God a liar. The classic illustration is Satan in the Garden of Eden:

> He said to the woman, "Did God really say, 'You must not eat from any tree in the garden'?"
> The woman said to the serpent, "We may eat from the trees in the garden, but God did say, 'You must not eat fruit from the tree that is in the middle of the garden, and you must not touch it, or you will die.'"
> "You will not surely die," the serpent said to the woman.
>
> (Genesis 3:1-4, NIV)

That's a direct contradiction of God's express Word (Genesis 2:16-17). No wonder Jesus called Satan a liar and the father of lies (John 8:44). Satan has been lying from the beginning of history, and he's still lying today by encouraging people to contradict the biblical text.

One of his favorite strategies is to use the words of God to authorize a belief or practice that goes against the character of God. Is God a killjoy who delights in human guilt and self-flagellation? Does God reward faith and good behavior with material prosperity? Is God for wild, sexual orgies and similar immoralities? Is God for the genocide of blacks, Jews, Orientals, Native Americans, Moslems, the elderly, the unborn, the insane, the mentally handicapped, or the "genetically inferior"? Of course not. Yet people have used Scripture to argue for these very kinds of things.

Subjectivism

Many Christians tolerate a form of mysticism in reading their Bibles that they would allow in no other realm. They violate every tenet of reason and common sense. Their Bible study is totally subjective. They wander around the Scriptures, waiting for a liver-quiver to tell them when they've struck pay dirt.

Now there's nothing wrong with having an emotional reaction to the Word of God. But as I mentioned in the last chapter, the meaning of the text is in the text, not in our subjective response to the text.

In Lewis Carroll's classic, *Through the Looking-Glass* (the second part of *Alice in Wonderland*), the White Queen engages Alice in an instructive dialogue:

> "How old are you?"
> "I'm seven and a half exactly."
> "You needn't say 'exactly,'" the Queen remarked: "I can believe it without that. Now I'll give you something to believe. I'm just one hundred and one, five months and a day."
> "I can't believe that," said Alice.
> "Can't you?" the Queen said, in a pitying tone. "Try again: draw a long breath, and shut your eyes."
> Alice laughed. "There's no use trying," she said: "one can't believe impossible things."
> "I daresay you haven't had much practice," said the Queen. "When I was your age, I always did it for half an hour a day. Why, sometimes I've believed as many as six impossible things before breakfast."[1]

I'm afraid that's the condition of many people today. They think our faith means taking a deep breath, shutting our eyes, and believing what we know deep down is absolutely incredible. Christianity has even been caricatured as the nonthinking man's religion.

But nothing could be further from the truth. Jesus said that the greatest commandment is to love the Lord with all your heart, soul, strength, and *mind*. When you become a Christian, you don't throw your brain into neutral. You don't put your head in a bucket of water and fire a .45 into it! You don't commit intellectual suicide.

So let me ask, Do you love the Lord with all of your mind? As we turn to the step of Interpretation, I can assure you that if you want to interpret Scripture accurately and perceptively, you're going to have to use your mind. As I've said before, the Bible does not yield its fruit to the lazy—and that includes the intellectually lazy. So get ready to exercise some mental muscle.

Relativism

Some people approach Scripture assuming that the Bible changes meaning over time. The text meant one thing when it was written but something else today. Its meaning is relative.

1. Lewis Carroll, *Alice in Wonderland* (Philadelphia: John C. Winston, 1923), p. 198.

Take the resurrection of Jesus. As Frank Morison found (chapter 8), there is no other credible explanation for the behavior of Jesus' disciples after His departure than that they sincerely believed in a bodily resurrection. That's what Paul talks about in 1 Corinthians 15. But today, some teachers have changed Paul's meaning. Yes, he's talking about a resurrection, they say; but now it means a spiritual resurrection, a "newness of life." It doesn't matter to them whether Jesus actually got up and walked out of that tomb—just so long as He "lives in your heart." That's a relativistic interpretation of Scripture.

When we get to Application we will see that a passage can have numerous practical implications. But it can have only one proper interpretation, one meaning—ultimately, the meaning it had to the original writer. We must reconstruct his message if we want an accurate understanding.

Overconfidence

In Bible study, as in life, pride goes before a fall. The minute you think that you've mastered a portion of Scripture, you are setting yourself up for a tumble. Why? Because knowledge puffs up (1 Corinthians 8:1). It can make you arrogant and unteachable. Some of the worst abuses of doctrine occur when someone sets himself up as the ultimate authority on the text.

Some of us have been studying Scripture all of our lives. Yet no human being can ever master more than one book of the Bible, even in an entire life of full-time study. So don't expect that when you come to the Bible and spend a half hour or forty-five minutes, you're going to walk away with the ultimate answers.

That's not to say that you shouldn't come to conclusions about what the text means, or that you cannot feel confident in what you believe. Just keep in mind that Interpretation never ends. You can never come to the end of your study and say, "Well, I've got that one. I know that passage."

THE RIGHT TO DISAGREE

In light of all these dangers, is it really possible to come up with an accurate interpretation of the biblical text? Yes, it is. In the next few chapters, I'm going to show you how.

But let me stress one final point before we launch into the process. Even though a Bible passage ultimately has only one correct interpretation, you'll always find two Christians who disagree about what that interpretation ought to be. That can be frustrating, but it's inevitable. Two people may watch the exact same bank robbery, but in court they'll describe it in completely different terms.

Differences in interpretation are fine as long we keep in mind that the conflict is not in the text, but in our limited understanding of the text. God is not confused about what He has said, even if we are.

We also need to preserve the right to disagree with each other, along with the responsibility to be as faithful and accurate to the text as we know how. In 2 Timothy 2:15, Paul encourages us, "Do your best to present yourself to God as one approved, a workman who does not need to be ashamed and who correctly handles the word of truth" (NIV).

This verse hangs a big sign on the Bible that says, "Handle with care!" That's a good motto for the step of Interpretation. So let's get started. I want to show you how to avoid pitfalls and reap the benefits of an accurate understanding of God's Word.

What Does the Bible Really Say?

Nearly every major heresy begins with a misreading of the biblical text. Here are a handful of common misstatements, as well as what the Bible actually says.

WHAT SOME PEOPLE SAY	WHAT THE BIBLE SAYS
"Money is the root of all evil."	"The love of money is a root of all sorts of evil" (1 Tim. 6:10).
"Jesus never claimed to be God."	"[Jesus] also was calling God His own Father, making Himself equal with God"(John 5:18). "I and the Father are one" (John 10:30).
"We are all gods or part of God."	"The Lord, He is God; there is no other besides him" (Deut. 4:35). "Is there any God besides me? No, there is no other Rock; I know not one" (Isa. 44:8, NIV).
"Jesus was just a great moral teacher."	"But these have been written that you may believe that Jesus is the Christ, the Son of God" (John 21:31).
"The Bible says that Christians should give away their possessions."	"Command those who are rich...not to be arrogant nor to put their hope in wealth, which is so uncertain, but to put their hope in God" (1 Tim. 6:17, NIV). "Work with your hands...so that you will not be dependent on anybody" (1 Thess. 4:11-12, NIV).
"The Bible says that work is a curse."	"Cursed is the ground" (Gen. 3:17). "Do your work heartily....It is the Lord Christ whom you serve" (Col. 3:23-24).
"All religions lead to the same end. No one religion is right."	"There is salvation in no one else" (Acts 4:12).

29

WHAT TYPE OF
LITERATURE IS THIS?

In *A Preface to Paradise Lost*, C. S. Lewis writes:

> The first qualification for judging any piece of workmanship
> from a corkscrew to a cathedral is to know *what* it is—what it
> was intended to do and how it is meant to be used. After that
> has been discovered the temperance reformer may decide that
> the corkscrew was made for a bad purpose, and the communist
> may think the same about the cathedral. But such questions
> come later. The first thing is to understand the object before
> you: as long as you think the corkscrew was meant for opening
> tins or the cathedral for entertaining tourists you can say
> nothing to the purpose about them. The first thing the reader
> needs to know about *Paradise Lost* is what Milton meant it to
> be.[1]

The same could be said for the Word of God. Before ever
launching into a study of a book in the Bible, the first thing a reader
needs to know is what that book's author meant it to be. In other
words, what kind of literature was he writing? What literary form
did he employ?

You see, literary genre is crucial to interpretation. Suppose I
randomly pick a text from the Scripture: "O that Thou wouldst slay

1. C. S. Lewis, *A Preface to Paradise Lost* (London: Oxford, 1942), p. 1.

the wicked, O God" (Psalm 139:19). Or, "Whatever you devise against the Lord, He will make a complete end of it" (Nahum 1:9). Or, "Father Abraham, have mercy on me, and send Lazarus" (Luke 16:24). Or, "After these things I looked, and behold, a door standing open in heaven" (Revelation 4:1). Unless you know what types of literature those are taken from, you are in no position to determine their meaning.

BIBLICAL GENRES

In this chapter I want to give a brief introduction to six kinds of writing that appear in the Bible and how they influence our understanding. There are more, to be sure, as well as subsets of the ones I'm going to mention, and many of these overlap. But here are the major literary genres that God used to communicate His message.

Exposition

An exposition is a straightforward argument or explanation of a body of objective truth. It is a form of writing that appeals primarily to the mind. The argument usually has a tight structure that moves from point to point in logical fashion.

Paul's letters are outstanding examples of the expositional form in Scripture. The book of Romans is a tightly reasoned explanation of the gospel. Paul argues like a lawyer presenting a case before a court, which is no surprise because we know that as a young man Paul had extensive rabbinical training, including the oratorical arts.

For instance, he links his paragraphs and chapters together with transitional, connective words such as *for, therefore, and,* and *but.* He makes extensive use of the rhetorical question (for example, 2:17-21, 26; 3:1, 3, 5; 4:1, 3, 9). He uses long, elaborate sentences (for example, 1:28-32; 9:3-5). On the other hand, he also employs short, rapid-fire passages that buffet the mind (for example, 7:7-25; 12:9-21).

Expositional books are ideal if you're just getting started in Bible study. Their meaning lies close to the surface. They appeal to the average person's preference for logic, structure, and order. And their purposes are easy to grasp; they practically outline themselves. Yet they also make for exciting in-depth analysis because their truths are inexhaustible.

The key to understanding a work of exposition is to pay attention to its structure and the terms it employs. We'll look at an example from Romans when we get to chapter 37.

Narrative and biography

Narrative means story. The Bible is full of stories, which is one reason it is so popular.

For example, Genesis relates the story of God's creation of the world, the story of the Flood, the story of the tower at Babel, and the story of the patriarchs, Abraham, Isaac, Jacob, and Joseph. Exodus continues the story by recounting Israel's departure from Egypt, led by Moses. Ruth tells the story of Ruth, the great-grandmother of King David.

In the New Testament, the four gospels tell the story of Jesus from four different points of view. One of them, Luke, continues the narrative in the Acts of the Apostles, as we have seen. Within the accounts of Jesus, we find stories that He told to His followers (more on that in a moment).

So the Bible is heavily composed of stories. That makes for interesting reading, but it also makes for interesting interpretation. What are we to make of the stories in the Bible? How do we determine their meaning and significance?

"There is no method except to be very intelligent," remarked T. S. Eliot. Perhaps, but let me suggest three things to pay attention to.

First, what is the plot? In other words, what movement is there in the story? This could be physical, as in the case of the Israelites moving across the Sinai peninsula in Exodus; it could be spiritual, as in the case of Samson in Judges, or Jonah in the book of Jonah; it could also be relational, as in Ruth, or political, as in 1 and 2 Kings. The question is, what development is there in the story? What is different at the end of the book, and why?

Another thing to study is characterization. Who is in the cast of characters? How are they presented? What roles do they play? What decisions do they make? How do they relate to each other, and to God? What progress or regress do they make? Do they fail? If so, why? Why are they in the story? In what ways are they individuals, and in what ways are they representative of others? What do we like or dislike about them? What would we do in their place?

A third element to consider is, in what ways is this story true to life? Remember, that was one of the clues to look for under Observation. It's also a doorway to understanding. The stories of Scripture show us life as God wants us to see it. So we can ask: What questions does this story raise? What problems do the characters have to deal with? What lessons do they learn or not learn? What things do they encounter that we should be sure to avoid? Or how do they deal with things in life that are unavoidable? What do they discover about God?

There is much more to the narratives in Scripture. But if you start by asking yourself these kinds of questions, you'll go a long way toward understanding what the stories are all about.

Parables

Closely related to narrative is the parable and its cousin, the allegory. A parable is a brief tale that illustrates a moral principle. Most of the parables in Scripture come from the teaching of Jesus. In fact, we can infer from Matthew's account that the parable may have been His preferred method of communication (Matthew 13:34).

It's easy to see why. Parables are simple, memorable, and entertaining. Most are rather easy to understand. They deal with everyday matters such as farming, fishing, travel, money, and human dynamics. Parables can have a powerful impact. They make use of basic ethical principles such as right and wrong (the sower and the three kinds of seed), love and compassion (the prodigal son, the good Samaritan), justice and mercy (the Pharisee and the tax collector).

Poetry

The Bible contains some of the finest lines of verse ever composed. Indeed, some have become icons in our culture: "The Lord is my shepherd,/I shall not want" (Psalm 23:1); "God is our refuge and strength,/A very present help in trouble" (Psalm 46:1); "To every thing there is a season, and a time to every purpose under heaven" (Ecclesiastes 3:1, KJV); "Our Father, which art in heaven, Hallowed be thy name" (Matthew 6:9, KJV).

The distinctive feature of poetry is its appeal to the emotions, as well as the imagination. That's why the psalms are so popular. They express some of the deepest feelings, longings, rapture, and pain of the human heart.

But when you study biblical verse, make sure you understand the dynamics of Hebrew poetry. In the first place, most of the psalms were meant to be sung, not read. They were composed for worship, and many include prefatory notes on what kinds of instruments were to accompany them. So even though we no longer have the music to which they were sung, you should still listen for how they sound (which is true of all poetry).

One of the main features of Hebrew poetry is its extensive use of "parallelism." If you look through the psalms, for instance, you'll notice that the majority of the verses have two lines. The two lines work off of each other to communicate meaning. Sometimes the second line will reinforce what the first line says by repeating its thought. For instance, Psalm 103:15 says,

As for man, his days are like grass;
As a flower of the field, so he flourishes.

Sometimes it will extend the thought by adding new information, as in Psalm 32:2:

How blessed is the man to whom the Lord does not impute
    iniquity,
And in whose spirit there is no deceit!

And sometimes the second line will oppose the first with an alternative thought:

How blessed is the man who has made the Lord his trust,
And has not turned to the proud, nor to those who lapse into
    falsehood.

(Psalm 40:4)

Another key to appreciating Hebrew poetry is to recognize "hyperbole," extreme or exaggerated language that makes its point through overkill. Earlier I cited a line from Psalm 139. Here's the larger context:

O that Thou wouldst slay the wicked, O God;

Depart from me, therefore, men of bloodshed.
For they speak against Thee wickedly,
And thine enemies take Thy name in vain.
Do I not hate those who hate Thee, O Lord?
And do I not loathe those who rise up against Thee?
I hate them with the utmost hatred;
They have become my enemies.

(vv. 19-22)

This is strange language to find in the Bible. What's going on here? The answer is to notice who David is talking about—"the wicked," people who have shed blood, spoken against God, taken His name in vain, (all violations of the Ten Commandments), and otherwise demonstrated that they hate the Lord. In becoming God's enemies they have become David's enemies. In a formal, ritualized way, he denounces them with the strongest language he can find.

Here are some other interpretive questions to consider as you approach the poetry of the Bible: Who composed this material? Can you determine why? What is the central theme of the poem? What emotions does the verse convey, and what response does it produce? What questions does it ask? Which ones does it answer, and which does it leave unanswered? What does the poem say about God? About people? What images does the poet use to spark the imagination? Are there references to people, places, or events that you are unfamiliar with? If so, what can you find out about them elsewhere in Scripture or through secondary sources?

The Proverbs and wisdom literature

One of the richest quarries to mine in the biblical material is the broad category known as wisdom literature. In this genre, the writer assumes the role of a wizened veteran of life prepared to share his insights with a younger, inexperienced, but teachable reader.

The book of Proverbs obviously belongs to this category. A proverb is a short, poignant nugget of truth, typically practical, and often concerned with the consequences of a course of behavior. Like the poetry of the psalms that we saw above, proverbs make strategic use of parallelism, especially the pairing of opposites. For instance, Proverbs 15:27:

He who profits illicitly troubles his own house,
But he who hates bribes will live. (Italics added)

And Proverbs 20:3:

Keeping away from strife is an honor for a man
But any fool will quarrel. (Italics added)

The Proverbs come right to the point. Of all the biblical material, they are perhaps the easiest to understand, though sometimes the hardest to apply. If you need a "spiritual vitamin" to perk up your way of life, chow down on the Proverbs. It will be a feast for your soul.

Prophecy and apocalyptic
The final and perhaps most challenging type of literature in the Bible is the prophetic. We tend to think of prophecy as a prediction for the future. And certainly the prophetic books look ahead. But a more striking feature is their tone of warning and judgment and the use of a formula to denote direct words from God: "Thus saith the Lord!"

The role of the prophet in Scripture was not to tell futures but to proclaim the words of the Lord; not to foretell but to "forth-tell," as someone has well put it. God raised up prophets in Israel when it became clear that the people were determined to resist Him. Their thankless task was to warn the nation of the dire consequences of continued disobedience, in hopes of sparking repentance and a return to the Lord.

In reading the prophets, it is critical that you re-create the situation. It is absolutely critical that you bombard the text with the six questions of selective Bible reading—who, what, where, when, why, and wherefore. Answering them will give you an invaluable database for considering these additional issues: What is the main problem that the prophet is addressing? What images does he use to describe it? What is the response of the people? What does this prophet's message tell you about God? What happens after this prophet delivers his message? Why do you think God included this book in His Word?

A special category of prophetic literature is apocalyptic, of which Revelation is the primary example. As the term implies, apocalyptic literature deals with cataclysmic events of global proportions having to do with the end of the world. The language of apocalyptic literature is highly symbolic, and the events unfold in quick, dazzling displays of light, noise, and power.

This makes the genre fertile ground for speculation and subjective interpretation. To avoid that, I suggest that when you study Revelation, pay close attention to the structure of the book. What movement is there from the opening to the close? What changes come about? Also, who is the material written to? What was the historical and cultural context in which the writer was working? How might that have influenced his method of communication? In terms of understanding the book's symbols, look carefully at the Old Testament for insight into what the author is describing. Rather than worry about a time line for future events, ask what implications this book would have had for Christians in the early church.

Literary Genres of the Bible

GENRE	CHARACTERISTICS	BIBLICAL BOOKS AND EXAMPLES
Apocalyptic	Dramatic, highly symbolic material; vivid imagery; stark contrasts; events take place on a global scale; frequently narrated in the first-person as an eyewitness account; portrays a cosmic struggle between good and evil.	Revelation
Biography	Close-up view of an individual's life; subject is often portrayed in contrast to someone else; selected events reveal character development, either positively (comedy) or negatively (tragedy).	Abraham, Isaac, Jacob, Joseph, Moses, Saul, David, Elijah, Jesus
Encomium	Sings high praise of someone or something; rehearses in glowing terms the subject's origins, acts, attributes, or superiority; exhorts the reader to incorporate the same features into his own life.	1 Sam. 2:1-10 Psalm 19 Psalm 119 Prov. 8:22-36 Prov. 31:10-31 Song of Solomon John 1:1-18 1 Corinthians 13 Col. 1:15-20 Hebrews 1-3
Exposition	Carefully reasoned argument or explanation; well-organized; logical flow; terms are crucial; builds to a logical, compelling climax; the aim is agreement and action.	Paul's letters Hebrews James 1 and 2 Peter 1, 2, and 3 John Jude
Narrative	A broad category in which story is prominent; includes historical accounts; structure is conveyed through plot; characters undergo psychological and spiritual development; selected events used to convey meaning; events juxtaposed for contrast and comparison.	Genesis–Ezra The gospels Acts

GENRE	CHARACTERISTICS	BIBLICAL BOOKS AND EXAMPLES
Oratory	Stylized oral presentation of an argument; uses formal conventions of rhetoric and oratory; frequently quotes from authorities well known to listeners; usually intended to exhort and persuade.	John 13-17 Acts 7 Acts 17:22-31 Acts 22:1-21 Acts 24:10-21 Acts 26:1-23
Parable	Brief oral story illustrating moral ; truth frequently relies on stock characters and stereotypes; presents scenes and activities common to everyday life; encourages reflection and self-evaluation.	2 Sam. 12:1-6 Eccles. 9:14-16 Matt. 13:1-53 Mark 4:1-34 Luke 15:1-16:31
Pastoral	Literature dealing with rural, rustic themes, especially shepherds; heavy on description, lean on action; often meditative and quiet; emphasis on the bond between a shepherd and his sheep; idealized presentation of life away from urban evils.	Psalm 23 Isa. 40:11 John 10:1-18
Poetry	Verse intended to be spoken or sung rather then read; emphasis on cadence and the sounds of words; vivid images and symbols; appeals to the emotions; may employ features of encomium, pastoral, and other literary styles; in O.T., heavy use of parallelism.	Job Psalms Proverbs Ecclesiastes Song of Solomon
Prophecy	Strident, authoritative presentation of God's will and words; frequently intended as a corrective; intended to motivatechange through warnings; foretells God's plans in response to human choices.	Isaiah–Malachi

GENRE	CHARACTERISTICS	BIBLICAL BOOKS AND EXAMPLES
Proverb	Short, pithy statement of a moral truth; reduces life to black-and-white categories; often addressed to youth; frequently employs parallelism; points readers toward the right and away from evil; heavy use of metaphors and similes.	Proverbs
Satire	Exposes and ridicules human vice and foolishness; is employed by various literary styles, especially narrative, biography, and proverb; warns readers through a negative example.	Prov. 24:30-34 Ezekiel 34 Luke 18:1-8 2 Cor. 11:1-12:1
Tragedy	Relates the downfall of a person; uses selected events to show the path toward ruin; problems usually revolve around a critical flaw in the person's character and moral choices; warns readers through a negative example.	Lot Samson Saul Acts 5:1-11
Wisdom Literature	A broad category in which an older, seasoned person relates wisdom to a younger; may use parable; gives observations on fundamental areas of life—birth, death, work, money, power, time, the earth, and so on; appeals on the basis of human experience.	Job Proverbs Psalm 37 Psalm 90 Ecclesiastes

For additional help with the literary types of the Bible, see Leland Ryken's excellent book *The Literature of the Bible* (Grand Rapids: Zondervan, 1974).

FIVE KEYS TO INTERPRETATION

Content
Context
Comparison
Culture
Consultation

30

CONTENT

When the psalmist prayed to God, "Give me understanding, that I may observe Thy law, and keep it with all my heart" (Psalm 119:34), he was knocking on the door of interpretation. He realized that apart from understanding the meaning of the text, there could be no application of the Word to his life. Conversely, once the Spirit opened the door of insight, he was prepared to act on what God had said.

Are you? Is that your aim in coming to the Scriptures—life-change? If so, then get ready for action, because God always opens the door to the one who knocks for that reason.

In this chapter I want to offer the first of five keys that will help you unlock the biblical text, five basic principles of Interpretation. The first key is one you already possess:

CONTENT

There is a direct cause-effect relationship between content and meaning. The content of a passage is the raw material, the database, with which you will interpret the text. And because of your work in Observation, you already know quite a bit about how to determine the content of a passage.

Remember, you looked for terms, structure, literary form, and atmosphere. You asked a series of penetrating questions: who, what, Where, when, why, wherefore. You looked for things that are emphasized, repeated, related, alike, unlike, and true to life.

In short, you have barraged the text with a variety of strategies aimed at answering the question, What do I see? If you have done your homework well, you have uncovered the content of the passage. In other words, you've answered the question; you know what the author is saying.

That is why I say: The more time you spend in Observation, the less time you will have to spend in Interpretation, and the more accurate will be your result. The less time you spend in Observation, the more time you will have to spend in Interpretation, and the less accurate will be your result.

So whatever you do in Observation will provide the basic content out of which you will interpret the meaning of the text.

But don't stop there. God has provided four more keys to help you unlock His Word.

You Try It

In this chapter we've looked at the first of five keys of interpretation, content. So I want to get you started on an interpretive study that will continue through the next five chapters. The section I want you to consider is Daniel 1-2, one of the most instructive passages for a believer today, especially if you work in the marketplace.

Begin by observing the content of Daniel 1-2. Use all of the tools that I discussed earlier in the book. Remember that your work at this stage is determinative for what you will interpret later. Your observations will form the database from which you will construct the meaning of the text.

In this first look at Daniel 1-2, invest as much time as you can answering the six questions of selective reading: Who? What? Where? When? Why? and Wherefore?

31

CONTEXT

Remember the old spiritual:

The knee bone's connected to the thigh bone,
The thigh bone's connected to the hip bone,
The hip bone's connected to the tail bone,
Now hear the word of the Lord!

That's primitive physiology but good methodology. It recognizes the connectedness of the body, that it all hangs together. There's unity.

So it is with Scripture. The Bible is a sixty-six-book collection, but it hangs together as one Book. It's a unified whole. And that's the principle on which the second key of biblical interpretation depends:

CONTEXT

What do I mean by context? Context refers to that which goes before and that which follows after.

I suppose anyone who has had to face the press can appreciate the importance of context. When I was chaplain for the Dallas Cowboys, I was visiting one day at their old training site in Thousand Oaks, California. Quarterback Roger Staubach had agreed to an interview with *Sports Illustrated*, and I was sitting in the room with him during the session.

I heard every word that Roger said. But when I read the article in the next month's issue, I couldn't believe it. A number of his statements had been ripped out of their context and presented in a way that completely distorted their original meaning. It made Roger appear to say things he had never actually said.

A person can do the same thing with the Word of God. In fact, every major cult is built on a violation of the principle of context. I mentioned the two men who came to see me about their religious persuasion (chapter 31). They were distorting the text of Scripture. But a great deal of that sort of doctrinal error could be corrected by simply asking, "Would you please read the previous verses or the ones that follow?"

I wish I had known that as a boy. I used to visit the home of a little girl that I loved to play with because she was so easily scared. (Little boys thrill to scare little girls.) Her house had an ancient parlor where the shades were always down, and her family rarely used it. I liked to hide there, especially behind the couch, while she looked for me. When she finally came in there, I would jump out and shout, "Boo!" and she'd go through the ceiling.

But while hiding in that parlor, I occasionally stuck my head out to look around. And there on the wall was a placard with the motto: "Work out your own salvation with fear and trembling." I had a vague sense that it was a quote from the Bible. But it scared me to death. I thought, *If that's true, there's no hope for me. I'll never make it.*

I was correct in thinking that it came from the Bible. It's the last part of Philippians 2:12. But I was incorrect in my understanding of it, that salvation is basically by works. Unfortunately, many people read that verse the way I did, and come to the same erroneous conclusion. It was not until years later that I discovered what the next verse says: "For it is God who worketh in you both to will and to do of his good pleasure" (v. 13, KJV). That puts verse 12 in an altogether different light.

Likewise, remember our observation of Acts 1:8? We broke into a paragraph at verse 8, and because the verse begins with "but," a contrast, we were forced to look back at the preceding context. There we discovered the disciples asking Jesus a question about the kingdom. Verse 8 turned out to be part of His answer.

But we also discovered that immediately following verse 8 is the ascension. And that ended up having a profound effect on verse 8. What Jesus said there turned out to be the last words of His life. And of course, last words are lasting words. So given the context, His listeners would have never forgotten what happened and what Jesus said. His words must have galvanized them into action.

So whenever you study a verse, a paragraph, a section, even an entire book—always consult the neighbors of that verse, that paragraph, that section, that book. Whenever you get lost, climb a contextual tree and gain some perspective.

SEVERAL KINDS OF CONTEXT

There are several kinds of context. Each one gives a different slant on whatever passage you are considering.

Literary context

In the Acts 1:8 example in chapter 6, we saw an illustration of literary context, that is, the words before and after verse 8. The literary context of any verse is the paragraph of which it is a part, the section of which that paragraph is a part, and the book of which that section is a part. And, given the unity of Scripture, the ultimate context of any book is the entire Bible.

Historical context

In other words, when is this taking place? Where does this passage fit in history? What else was taking place in the world at this time? What were some of the social, political, and technological influences on the writer and on those to whom he was writing?

Cultural context

Culture has a powerful influence on all forms of communication, and the cultures in biblical times had a profound effect on the creation of the Bible. So the more you know about ancient cultures, the more insight you'll have into the text. Because this is so important, I'll come back to it, as well as the matter of historical context, in chapter 33.

Geographic context

Geography is a fascinating subject that is incredibly relevant to the interpretation of Scripture.

For instance, in Mark 4 we saw the miracle of the stilling of the storm. I pointed out the geographic features around the Sea of Galilee that bring about storms like that. Knowing that information lends tremendous relevance and realism to Mark's account. It also offers a clue as to how violent that particular storm must have been; it terrified the fishermen who had seen a lifetime of storms on that lake.

Investigating the geographical context answers questions such as: What was the terrain like? What topographic features made this region unique? What was the weather like? How far was this town from places mentioned in the text? What were the transportation routes for these people? What size city was this? What was the layout of this town? What was this location known for?

In chapter 34 I'll mention some resources, such as atlases, that you can consult when you look into the geographical context.

Theological context

The question here is, what did this author know about God? What was the relationship of his readers to God? How did people worship Him at that point? How much Scripture did the writer and his audience have access to? What other religions and worldviews were competing for influence?

A central issue here is, where does this passage fit in the unfolding of Scripture? You see, the Bible was not dropped out of the sky as a finished piece of work. It took thousands of years to put it all together. And during that time, God revealed more and more of His message to the authors.

Have you ever held a progressive dinner with a group of friends? You go to one person's house and have appetizers. Then you go to someone else's house for the salad. Then you go somewhere else for the main course. You work your way around until you've eaten the whole meal. Well, that's the sort of process the Bible went through, only we call it "progressive revelation." Over time, God slowly unveiled the truth of His Word.

So it's important to locate your passage in the flow of Scripture. If you're studying Noah in Genesis, then you're before the Ten Commandments, before the Sermon on the Mount, before John 3:16. In fact, Noah didn't have a scrap of biblical text to work with. So what does that tell you when you read that "Noah found favor in the eyes of the Lord" (Genesis 6:8)?

One of the helpful resources you'll want to turn to as you investigate theological context is a commentary. I'll say more about commentaries in chapter 34.

You Try It

In the last chapter you began a study of Daniel 1-2 by observing the content, paying particular attention to the questions, Who? What? Where? When? Why? and Wherefore? Your observations from that exercise will give you a base of information from which you will be able to interpret the text.

Now it's time to move on to context. Since Daniel 1 begins the book, you will have to go back and read 2 Kings 24-25 and 2 Chronicles 36 to get the preceding context. Then look at the later chapters of Daniel to see what follows this section.

32

COMPARISON

W e're all familiar with the Protestant Reformation. One of its rallying cries was *sola scriptura*—Scripture alone is our final authority for faith and practice. That led to a crucial development in the history of Christianity, the right to private interpretation. The Reformation, coupled with the Gutenberg Bible, put Scripture back into the hands of laypeople. However, as R. C. Sproul says so perceptively,

> Private interpretation never meant that individuals have the right to distort the Scriptures. With the right of private interpretation comes the sober responsibility of accurate interpretation. Private interpretation gives us license to interpret, not to distort.[1]

How can you avoid distorting God's message? We've already seen two keys to help you unlock the door of accurate understanding— content and context. Now we come to a third key, which is perhaps the best insurance against distortion:

COMPARISON

In comparison we compare Scripture with Scripture. And that offers a great safety net, because the greatest interpreter of Scripture is Scripture itself.

1. R. C. Sproul, *Knowing Scripture* (Downers Grove, Ill.: InterVarsity, 1977), pp. 35-36.

Donald Grey Barnhouse used to put it so clearly: "You very rarely have to go outside of the Bible to explain anything in the Bible." That's very instructive coming from an individual who was incredibly well-read and who knew how to use a wide variety of secondary sources. But he understood the priority of the Word of God. He realized that the more you compare Scripture with Scripture, the more the meaning of the Bible becomes apparent. The parts take on meaning in light of the whole.

Remember, although we have about forty different human authors, the sixty-six books are ultimately the result of one primary Author, the Holy Spirit, who coordinated the entire message. His Book is integrated. It hangs together.

THE VALUE OF A CONCORDANCE

Comparison points out the great need you have for a concordance. A concordance is a tool that enables you to chase down terms and concepts from one book of the Bible to the next. Using a concordance, you can put together things that appear isolated in the text; and they take on greater meaning in relation to each other. Let me give you several illustrations.

"Belief"

The word *belief* is one of the most determinative terms in the Bible. But it is used in a variety of ways. If you look it up in a concordance, you'll find that it is especially prominent in the gospel by John (see page 245). For example, in John 2:23 we read:

> Now while [Jesus] was in Jerusalem at the Passover Feast, many people saw the miraculous signs he was doing and *believed* in his name. But Jesus would not entrust himself to [or *believe in*] them, for he knew all men. He did not need man's testimony about man, for he knew what was in a man. (NIV, italics added)

You see, they "believed" superficially, on the basis of the miracles. It was obvious He had done them; the facts were known to all. But facts do not save. They are an essential basis for salvation, but one must *believe*, that is, embrace the truth, use those facts on a personal basis.

Let me illustrate how John uses believe here. Suppose you come to me and say, "Prof, I hate to tell you this, but I'm suffering from a terminal disease."

We talk about it for a while, and after learning more about your situation, I say, "Hey, I've got fantastic news. I've got a doctor friend in Houston who's just come up with a proven cure for that disease. If you go see him, I guarantee you'll be fully cured."

You say, "That's wonderful."

"Do you believe it?" I ask.

"Oh, certainly."

So I reach out and shake your hand and say, "You're cured."

Naturally, you'd think I was one brick shy of a load! No amount of information concerning a doctor in Houston who has a cure for your disease will do anything to bring healing to your body. You've got to go there. You've got to submit yourself to his treatment. You've got to benefit from the medicine that he prescribes.

That's the connection between facts and faith in John's gospel. Jesus knows that, which is why John says in verse 24, "He knew what was in a man." In fact, John goes on in chapters 3 and 4 to give three interesting exhibits of the Lord's omniscience concerning what is "in a man": Nicodemus (3:1-21); the woman at the well in Samaria (4:1-42); and the nobleman (4:46-54).

"Equip"

A second illustration of comparative Bible study comes from Ephesians, which is a fascinating book that tells you how to live a heavenly life in a hell-like world. When you read it you come across two remarkable verses:

> And He [that is, the risen Christ, vv. 7-10] gave some as apostles, and some as prophets, and some as evangelists, and some as pastors and teachers, for the *equipping* of the saints for the work of service, to the building up of the body of Christ. (4:11-12, italics added)

Are there any terms to chase down in this passage? Yes, a crucial one, *equip*. How is it used? Again, turn to your concordance and look it up. And you discover three things.

First, the word *equip* is used of the mending of broken nets. Fishermen such as the disciples would be out fishing all day, and their nets would become torn and broken. So in the evening they would repair (literally, "equip") them, so that the next morning they'd be ready to go. What a beautiful expression of what a pastor-teacher is called to do. Living in this world, people's nets get broken. A pastor's job is to help repair, or "equip," them.

But the same word is used for the setting of broken bones. It's a medical term. Two bones get out of joint. So what does a doctor do? He sets them, he mends them, he "equips" them. He brings them back together so that they can heal and return to their former strength. Again, that's exactly what happens in life. There's no such thing as living in this world without getting broken up. Ours is a broken society. So we need to be under the Word of God with someone who is "equipping" us, healing the broken bones.

Third, the word is also used of outfitting a ship for a journey. Imagine a ship being prepared to cross the Mediterranean. No shopping malls out there. So the crew must load on board everything they will need until they arrive at their destination. That image grabs me, because good preaching and teaching of the Word should outfit people for their journey through life. It should "equip" them so that when they're out in the marketplace, when they're in a crisis, when they really need to know God's mind, they know it. Somebody has "equipped" them to be and to do what God wants them to be and to do.

Moses
Comparative study goes beyond studying terms. Let's suppose you want to study a character in Scripture. I highly recommend it. Biographical study is fascinating beyond words. Say you get captivated by the life of Moses. I suggest you get out a concordance and look him up.

The first thing that becomes obvious is that the bulk of his life story can be found in Exodus. That means you'll need to do a concerted study of the book of Exodus to find out how he got started. You'll want to study his remarkable parents, who hid him from the king, so that ultimately he became the quintessential leader of Israel.

You'll also discover from your concordance that there's something about Moses in Acts 7. In fact, you'll find there some of the most insightful material on this man, editorialized by the Spirit. So anyone who wants to study Moses and doesn't read Acts 7 is really out of it.

Moses can also be found in Hebrews 11. In fact, he takes up more space in God's Hall of Fame than any other character. You'll find his life described from God's perspective in that passage. What does He think of him? What does He call significant in Moses' life?

I'll talk more about concordances in chapters 34 and 35. But whenever you study the Word of God, pull out the key of comparison. Keep putting things together so that you come up with a fully-orbed understanding of Scripture.

You Try It

By now you should have looked at the content and the context of Daniel 1-2. Are you beginning to get some sense of what's going on in this story? What questions do you have as a result of your study?

Perhaps you'll answer some of them by doing a little comparison of this text with other portions of Scripture. Using a concordance, look up the following four items, each of which is crucial to understanding the passage. See how much you can learn about them from other places in Scripture:

- Daniel
- Nebuchadnezzar
- Babylon
- dreams

The Cow

I ran across a touching essay by a ten-year-old pupil. It has some correct observation, but incorrect interpretation. It also has some correct interpretation, with incorrect observation. Here's what the child wrote:

> The cow is a mammal. It has six sides. Right, left, an upper and below. At the back it has a tail on which hangs a brush. With this it sends the flies away so that they do not fall into the milk. The head is for the purpose of growing horns and so that the mouth can be somewhere. The horns are to butt with and the mouth is to moo with. Under the cow hangs the milk. It is arranged for milking. When people milk the milk comes and there is never an end to the supply. How the cow does it I have not yet realized. But it makes more and more. The man cow is called an ox. It is not a mammal. The cow does not each much, but what it eats, it eats twice so that it gets enough. When it is hungry it moos, and when it says nothing it is because its inside is all filled up with grass.

As you can see, we need to be very precise in how we go about this process of interpretation. We must make sure our observations are accurate so that we have a basis for accurate interpretation.

33

Culture

I was once the guest of a man who lived in San Francisco. He was an importer of exquisite oriental lace. One evening as we were leaving his house, a little end table in the vestibule by the front door caught my eye. What attracted me was not the table but a piece of lace laying on it.

I said, "My, that's beautiful."

My host grimaced and cried, "That's a piece of junk. I keep telling my wife to take that thing out of here."

Surprised, I asked him, "How can you tell good lace from junk?"

He winked and said, "When we get back, I'll show you."

Believe me, I didn't forget. So when we returned he took me into a room with a large black table that had a brilliant light over it. He threw a massive piece of oriental lace over the table, and proceeded to give me a lesson in how to tell the difference between fine lace and junk material. In the process, he commented, "You'll never understand the exquisiteness of good lace until you see it against a dark background with bright light shining on it."

Later I thought, *That's a clue to studying the Bible.* You have to see it against the right background, with the right light shining on it, to capture its meaning. In chapter 31 we saw the importance of context in terms of the text of Scripture—paying attention to what comes before and what comes after the passage you are studying. In the same way, you have to pay attention to the cultural and historical context—to the factors that led to the writing of the passage, the influences they had on the text, and what happened as a result of the message. That's the fourth key in making accurate interpretation of the Scriptures:

CULTURE

Let me illustrate what I mean by the cultural context with several examples.

Ruth

The Old Testament book of Ruth, for example, is a beautiful story of love and courage. But most people overlook the fact that it takes place during the period of the judges, Israel's Dark Ages. That's because they fail to observe Judges 21:25, which sets up the context for Ruth 1:1. It shows that the nation was mired in a cesspool of iniquity. It was a time in the culture when they couldn't tell the difference between Chanel No. 5 and Sewer Gas No. 9. Reading the account, you have to wonder, was anyone faithful to God during this period?

Answer? Look in the book of Ruth. It's a shaft of light in the midst of a dark period. It's a brilliant lily in a putrid pond. Here's a dear family, faithful to Jehovah, even in the midst of apostasy.

And yet, because of a few events in the story, I've heard people make snide remarks about it. One guy said to me with a snicker, "Hey, that's kind of a saucy book, isn't it? A little sexy."

I thought, *My friend, that's a greater commentary on you than it is on the book of Ruth.*

You see, that fellow was tipping his hand. He was showing me that he didn't know the front end from the back end of the culture in which Ruth took place. When you go back and study the customs involved, you discover that in context they are of the highest moral standard. Nothing cheap about them. This is no trashy novel you are reading. It's the highest form of literature, both in terms of content and morality.

But here as elsewhere, we read the Bible according to our own culture, as through a pair of glasses that distorts the context. No wonder we can't make sense of the passage.

The Last Supper

A classic illustration of this tendency is Leonardo da Vinci's masterpiece, *The Last Supper* (see page 239). It's an incredible work of art, no doubt. Yet that would not be the place to go if you wanted to find out what the Last Supper was really like. It gives a rather distorted picture of the setting—actually a fifteenth-century interpretation of it.

In the first place, Leonardo has Jesus and His disciples sitting at a table. But people didn't sit at tables to eat in the time of Christ; they reclined. They lay on couch-like furniture, leaning on an elbow, which left the other hand free to eat. That's important, because remember that Peter asked John, "Who is Jesus talking about when He says that one of us is going to betray Him?" (John 13:24). The rest of the disciples could not hear Peter. Why? Because he was able to lean back, John could come forward, and the two could communicate.

Leonardo also has them all seated on the same side of the table, as at a speaker's table. It's a careful arrangement, as if someone had said, "Hey guys, let's all gather around and take a company picture. One last shot before the Lord goes." But of course, in reading the account you realize that that was not the seating involved.

Another interesting feature of *The Last Supper* is that Leonardo has painted a fifteenth-century frieze on the back wall. That obviously reflects Leonardo's time, not the first century. And if you observe carefully, you'll notice that in Leonardo's painting, it is daylight outside. But according to the biblical account, the actual Last Supper took place in the evening, and probably well into the night.

Now don't misunderstand. As a painting, *The Last Supper* has great value. But the unfortunate thing is that by looking at a beautiful piece of art, people often get a rather flawed interpretation of a passage of Scripture. (Actually, if they knew better how to look at art, they would gain insight into the situation. That's one of the marks of good art.) Accuracy demands that one go back to that period and culture to find out what was really going on. Indeed, unless you understand the original context of the Last Supper, you can't fully appreciate Leonardo's masterpiece.

Psalm 24

Let me give you another illustration. When I was a boy in Philadelphia, we were allowed to read the Bible in school—but only five of the psalms. Psalm 24 was one of them. I can still remember the words:

Lift up your heads, O ye gates;
and be ye lifted up, ye everlasting doors;

and the King of glory shall come in.
Who is this King of glory?
The Lord strong and mighty,
the Lord mighty in battle.
Lift up your heads, O ye gates;
even lift them up, ye everlasting doors;
and the King of glory shall come in.
Who is this King of glory?
The Lord of hosts,
he is the King of glory.
(vv. 7-10, KJV)

I used to hear that and think, *What in the world is this talking about?* It made no sense to me. (That's why they didn't mind our reading this psalm; nobody had a clue as to what it meant.)

But years I later I was studying the life of David, and I looked at a map of Palestine. The story says that before he became king, whenever he wanted to go from the southern part of the country to the north, he had to pass a city by the name of Jebus. Jebus was an ancient fortress—a hangout (and hangover) from the days of Joshua, when the Israelites never took the Promised Land as God had commanded them.

So whenever David went by Jebus, its defenders appeared on the wall and taunted him. "Hey, David," they yelled, "When you become king, don't try to take this place. We'll put cripples at the gate. We'll put blind men on the watchtowers. But you still won't conquer us."

When David became king, he didn't forget those words. He said to his warriors, "The first thing we're going to do is to clean out Jebus."

It turns out that is what Psalm 24 is talking about. David defeated Jebus and made it his capital (which we know as Jerusalem, 2 Samuel 5:3-10). One of his first acts as king was to bring the Ark of the Covenant to Jebus. Psalm 24 is the processional hymn that he and the people sang as they brought it up the incline to the city: "Lift up your heads, O gates! Tear down the walls! Enlarge the breeches!"

And the walls, as if sharing the ancient antipathy of their defenders, ask, "Who is this king who demands that we enlarge the gates?"

The answer comes back: "The Lord of hosts. He is the King of glory."

So you see, once you understand the historical background, Psalm 24 suddenly comes alive.

1 Corinthians 8

One final illustration comes from 1 Corinthians 8, where Paul discusses the problem of eating meat offered to idols—not exactly one of the critical problems we face today. Yet when I came out of seminary, I think I knew more about Corinth and eating meat offered to idols than just about any other human being. Today, after forty years of teaching, I'm still looking for somebody who's got that problem. If I ever find them, believe me, I'm loaded for bear.

Does that render 1 Corinthians 8 irrelevant for today? It does if you have no idea of the cultural background involved. Notice verse 1: "Now concerning things sacrificed to idols, we know that we have all knowledge." Again, in verse 4 he writes, "Therefore concerning the eating of things sacrificed to idols, we know that there is no such thing as an idol in the world."

But verse 7 declares, "Not all men have this knowledge." So Paul warns that you have to be very careful in this matter. Why? Here's where cultural context comes into play. A bit of research reveals that the best meat in town was reserved for offerings to the idols. Not surprisingly, the best meat markets and restaurants were located right next to the temple. So if you wanted to take someone out for a steak dinner, you'd take him there.

But suppose the person was a recent convert. Suppose he had come out of a pagan background of sacrificing and eating meat offered to the idols. Now you're asking him to eat that same meat— in effect, taking him back to his pre-Christian days. How would that feel to him?

Paul says clearly that "we know that there is no such thing as an idol," that is, that idols have no real power; they are false gods. But that's not the issue. The issue is doing what is best for a brother or sister in Christ. Even harmless practices can be a source of offense to a weaker brother who still has an uneducated conscience.

Given that cultural perspective, does 1 Corinthians 8 have anything to say to us today? Well, are there any "gray" areas in modern life? Are there any matters of conscience that some Christians practice freely, whereas others take offense? I'll let you answer that. But if you want my advice, 1 Corinthians 8 ought to be on your required reading list.

When you study it—or any portion of the Word of God—make sure you study the background. Re-create the culture. Because then and only then will the text come alive.

You Try It

How are you doing in your study of Daniel 1-2? Did you learn some useful background from your concordance study of Daniel, Nebuchadnezzar, Babylon, and dreams?

Now you are ready to look outside the biblical text to some extrabiblical resources, such as a Bible dictionary and a Bible handbook. You may have to check the library at your church or in your community to locate one of these. Several are listed in the back of this book under "Additional Resources."

Using either or both of these tools, look up the four items that you've already studied within the biblical text—Daniel, Nebuchadnezzar, Babylon, and dreams. See what additional information you can find that shed light on Daniel 1-2.

34

CONSULTATION

I have a good friend who is a carpenter. He's actually a craftsman, incredibly gifted at working with wood. I love to kid him whenever he comes to my house, because he always brings so many tools.

One day when I was riding him, he responded, "Well, you know, Prof, the more tools a guy has, the better a carpenter he's likely to be."

The same thing is true in Bible study. You can go a long way with just your own eyes and the English text. But you can go even farther if you add some tools to the process. That's why the fifth and final key to interpretation is:

CONSULTATION

Consultation involves the use of secondary resources. They can shed light on the text that will help you make more sense out of what you're looking at.

You see, we never want to become arrogant in the study process by thinking that we've got all of the answers, that the Holy Spirit speaks to us, but He's never spoken to anyone else. The truth of the matter is, thousands of people have walked this road before us. And some of them have left behind valuable helps. They are like some mountain climbers who leave their pitons wedged into the rock, so that others can climb up after them. Using secondary sources, you can leverage yourself against the contributions of others.

But one word of caution: Never forget the order. First the text of Scripture; then secondary sources. To go to secondary helps without even consulting the text gives small place to the Word of God. That's why the first thing you need, before you ever obtain any of the resources mentioned below, is a good study Bible (see "How to Select a Bible," pages 32-33). Start with that. Then you can add to your library as you go.

And there are five especially helpful tools that I want to describe. Many more could be mentioned, so be sure to check the section at the back of the book called "Additional Resources." But these five will get you started on building a valuable tool chest to use in your interpretational work.

Concordances

I've mentioned concordances several times already. Next to a study Bible, it's probably the one tool you can't do without. A concordance is somewhat like an index to the Bible. It lists all of the words of the text alphabetically, with references for where they appear, along with a few of the surrounding words to give some context.

There are many profitable uses for a concordance. A common one is to do word studies. We saw some of that when we talked about comparison in chapter 32, and we'll see more in the next chapter.

A concordance can also help you locate a passage when you can't remember its reference. This happens all the time. Say you are studying 1 Peter and you read: "For you were continually straying like sheep, but now you have returned to the Shepherd and Guardian of your souls" (2:25). This is an obvious reference to Christ. And somewhere in the back of your bean you remember that Jesus was called the Good Shepherd. But you can't remember where. So you look up "shepherd" in your concordance, and find a reference to John 10:11, "I am the good shepherd." Bingo! You've found your passage.

Whatever you do, make sure you get an *exhaustive concordance* rather than an abridged one. An exhaustive concordance is one that lists each and every instance of each and every word of the text. Two well-regarded ones are Strong's and Young's. But every major translation of the Bible has its own concordance, and you want to make sure that you get one that corresponds to your translation. Otherwise, you'll be looking up words that are translated a bit differently from those in your Bible.

CONCORDANCE — BEINGS-BELIEVE 145

days, *b* tempted by the devil.	Lk 4:2	
with unclean spirits were *b* cured.	Lk 6:18	
a dead man was *b* carried out,	Lk 7:12	
And *b* aroused, He rebuked the wind	Lk 8:24	
"If you then, *b* evil, know how to	Lk 11:13	*5225*
"And which of you by *b* anxious	Lk 12:25	
His opponents were *b* humiliated;	Lk 13:17	
the glorious things *b* done by Him.	Lk 13:17	*1096*
just a few who are *b* saved?"	Lk 13:23	
of God, but yourselves *b* cast out.	Lk 13:28	
lifted up his eyes, *b* in torment,	Lk 16:23	*5225*
but now he is *b* comforted here,	Lk 16:25	
they were *b* given in marriage,	Lk 17:27	
God, *b* sons of the resurrection.	Lk 20:36	*1510*
And *b* in agony He was praying very	Lk 22:44	*1096*
were *b* led away to be put to death	Lk 23:32	
the sun *b* obscured;	Lk 23:45	
All things came into *b* by Him,	Jn 1:3	*1096*
into *b* that has come into being.	Jn 1:3	*1096*
into being that has come into *b*.	Jn 1:3	*1096*
were coming and were *b* baptized.	Jn 3:23	
b wearied from His journey,	Jn 4:6	
"How is it that You, *b* a Jew,	Jn 4:9	*1510*
'From his innermost *b* shall flow	Jn 7:38	*2836*
to Him before, *b* one of them),	Jn 7:50	*1510*
and because You, *b* a man,	Jn 10:33	*1510*
again *b* deeply moved within,	Jn 11:38	
but *b* high priest that year, he	Jn 11:51	*1510*
b a relative of the one whose ear	Jn 18:26	*1510*
Arimathea, *b* a disciple of Jesus,	Jn 19:38	*1510*
day by day those who were *b* saved.	Ac 2:47	
mother's womb was *b* carried along,	Ac 3:2	
were taking note of him as *b* the one	Ac 3:10	*1510*
b greatly disturbed because they	Ac 4:2	
and they were all *b* healed.	Ac 5:16	
their widows were *b* overlooked	Ac 6:1	
one *of them* *b* treated unjustly,	Ac 7:24	
But *b* full of the Holy Spirit, he	Ac 7:55	*5225*
Christ, they were *b* baptized,	Ac 8:12	
and after *b* baptized, he continued	Ac 8:13	
prevents me from *b* baptized?"	Ac 8:36	
Samaria enjoyed peace, *b* built up;	Ac 9:31	
gaze upon him and *b* much alarmed,	Ac 10:4	*1096*
but prayer for him was *b* made	Ac 12:5	*1096*
was *b* done by the angel was real,	Ac 12:9	*1096*
So, *b* sent out by the Holy Spirit,	Ac 13:4	
b amazed at the teaching of the	Ac 13:12	
the word of the Lord was *b* spread	Ac 13:49	
b sent on their way by the church,	Ac 15:3	
Silas, also *b* prophets themselves,	Ac 15:32	*1510*
b committed by the brethren to the	Ac 15:40	
were *b* strengthened in the faith,	Ac 16:5	
our city into confusion, *b* Jews,	Ac 16:20	*5225*
accept or to observe, *b* Romans."	Ac 16:21	*1510*
his spirit was *b* provoked within	Ac 17:16	
"*B* then the offspring of God, we	Ac 17:29	*5225*
were believing and *b* baptized.	Ac 18:8	
and *b* fervent in spirit, he was	Ac 18:25	*2204*
b acquainted only with the baptism	Ac 18:25	2204
of the Lord Jesus was *b* magnified.	Ac 19:17	
indeed we are in danger of *b* accused	Ac 19:40	
of our fathers, *b* zealous for God,	Ac 22:3	*5225*
of Thy witness Stephen was *b* shed,	Ac 22:20	
are *b* carried out for this nation,	Ac 24:2	*1096*
Paul was *b* kept in custody at Caesarea	Ac 25:4	
"And *b* at a loss how to	Ac 25:20	*639*
O King, I am *b* accused by Jews.	Ac 26:7	
also when they were *b* put to death	Ac 26:10	
and *b* furiously enraged at them, I	Ac 26:11	
than by what was *b* said by Paul.	Ac 27:11	
we were *b* violently storm-tossed,	Ac 27:18	
b saved was gradually abandoned.	Ac 27:20	
as we were *b* driven about in the	Ac 27:27	
And some were *b* persuaded by the	Ac 28:24	
because your faith is *b* proclaimed	Ro 1:8	
b understood through what has been	Ro 1:20	
b filled with all unrighteousness,	Ro 1:29	
b instructed out of the Law,	Ro 2:18	
I also still *b* judged as a sinner?	Ro 3:7	
b witnessed by the Law and the	Ro 3:21	
b justified as a gift by His grace	Ro 3:24	
who believe without *b* circumcised,	Ro 4:11	*203*
calls into *b* that which does not exist.	Ro 4:17	*1510*
and *b* fully assured that what He	Ro 4:21	
are *b* led by the Spirit of God,	Ro 8:14	
ARE *B* PUT TO DEATH ALL DAY LONG;	Ro 8:36	
off, and you, *b* a wild olive,	Ro 11:17	*1510*
b saved it is the power of God.	1Co 1:18	
his heart, *b* under no constraint,	1Co 7:37	*2192*
b accustomed to the idol until	1Co 8:7	
conscience *b* weak is defiled.	1Co 8:7	*1510*
though not *b* myself under the Law,	1Co 9:20	*1510*
though not *b* without the law of	1Co 9:21	*1510*
to God among those who are *b* saved	2Co 2:15	
b manifested that you are a letter	2Co 3:3	
are *b* transformed into the same	2Co 3:18	
we who live are constantly *b* delivered	2Co 4:11	
inner man is *b* renewed day by day.	2Co 4:16	
this tent, we groan, *b* burdened,	2Co 5:4	
b always of good courage,	2Co 5:6	
but *b* himself very earnest,	2Co 8:17	*5225*
which is *b* administered by us for	2Co 8:19	
myself from *b* a burden to you,	2Co 11:9	*4*
For you, *b so* wise, bear with the	2Co 11:19	*1510*
Who is weak without my *b* weak?	2Co 11:29	
b more extremely zealous for my	Ga 1:14	*5225*
"If you, *b* a Jew, live like the	Ga 2:14	*5225*
you now *b* perfected by the flesh?	Ga 3:3	
b shut up to the faith which was	Ga 3:23	
But God, *b* rich in mercy, because	Eph 2:4	*1510*
Jesus Himself *b* the corner *stone*,	Eph 2:20	*1510*
b fitted together is growing into	Eph 2:21	
in whom you also are *b* built	Eph 2:22	
b rooted and grounded in love,	Eph 3:17	
b diligent to preserve the unity	Eph 4:3	
b fitted and held together by that	Eph 4:16	
b darkened in their understanding,	Eph 4:18	*1510*
which is *b* corrupted in accordance	Eph 4:22	
complete by *b* of the same mind,	Php 2:2	
and *b* made in the likeness of men.	Php 2:7	*1096*
b found in appearance as a man,	Php 2:8	
But even if I am *b* poured out as a	Php 2:17	
b conformed to His death;	Php 3:10	
the secret of *b* filled and going hungry,	Php 4:12	
been firmly rooted *and now* *b* built up	Col 2:7	
b supplied and held together by	Col 2:19	
put on the new self who is *b* renewed	Col 3:10	
God, displaying himself as *b* God.	2Th 2:4	*1510*
but the woman *b* quite deceived,	1Tm 2:14	
worse, deceiving and *b* deceived.	2Tm 3:13	
For I am already *b* poured out as a	2Tm 4:6	
Him, *b* detestable and disobedient,	Ti 1:16	*1510*
b subject to their own husbands,	Ti 2:5	
that *b* justified by His grace we	Ti 3:7	
and is sinning, *b* self-condemned.	Ti 3:11	*1510*
b designated by God as a high	Heb 5:10	
worthless and close to *b* cursed,	Heb 6:8	
cursed, and it ends up *b* burned.	Heb 6:8	
days, when, after *b* enlightened,	Heb 10:32	
by *b* made a public spectacle	Heb 10:33	
his *b* taken up he was pleasing to God.	Heb 11:5	*3331*
b warned *by God* about things not	Heb 11:7	
in goatskins, *b* destitute,	Heb 11:37	
b content with what you have;	Heb 13:5	
"I am *b* tempted by God";	Jas 1:13	
of the soil, *b* patient about it,	Jas 5:7	
are *b* built up as a spiritual	1Pe 2:5	
and while *b* reviled, He did not	1Pe 2:23	
b submissive to their own husbands.	1Pe 3:5	
without *b* frightened by any fear.	1Pe 3:6	
are *b* accomplished by your brethren	1Pe 5:9	
destroyed, *b* flooded with water.	2Pe 3:6	
His word are *b* reserved for fire,	2Pe 3:7	
b carried away by the error of	2Pe 3:17	
b in labor and in pain to give	Rv 12:2	*2192*
BEINGS		
and of human *b*, of the women who	Nu 31:35	5315
And the human *b* were 16,000, from	Nu 31:40	5315
and the human *b* were 16,000—	Nu 31:46	5315
figures resembling four living *b*.	Ezk 1:5	2421b
In the midst of the living *b* there	Ezk 1:13	2421b
back and forth among the living *b*.	Ezk 1:13	2421b
And the living *b* ran to and fro	Ezk 1:14	2421b
Now as I looked at the living *b*,	Ezk 1:15	2421b
on the earth beside the living *b*,	Ezk 1:15	2421b
And whenever the living *b* moved,	Ezk 1:19	2421b
the living *b* rose from the earth,	Ezk 1:19	2421b
of the living *b was* in the wheels.	Ezk 1:20	2421b
of the living *b was* in the wheels.	Ezk 1:21	2421b
over the heads of the living *b there was*	Ezk 1:22	2421b
the living *b* touching one another,	Ezk 3:13	2421b
They are the living *b* that I saw	Ezk 10:15	2421b
of the living *b was* in them.	Ezk 10:17	2421b
These are the living *b* that I saw	Ezk 10:20	2421b
BEKA		
a *b* a head (*that is*, half a shekel	Ex 38:26	1235
BEL		
B has bowed down, Nebo stoops over;	Is 46:1	1078
captured, *B* has been put to shame,	Jer 50:2	1078
"And I shall punish *B* in Babylon,	Jer 51:44	1078
BELA		
of Zeboiim, and the king of *B*	Gn 14:2	1106b
king of Zeboiim and the king of *B*	Gn 14:8	1106b
B the son of Beor reigned in Edom,	Gn 36:32	1106a
Then *B* died, and Jobab the son of	Gn 36:33	1106a
B and Becher and Ashbel, Gera and	Gn 46:21	1106a
of *B*, the family of the Belaites;	Nu 26:38	1106a
the sons of *B* were Ard and Naaman:	Nu 26:40	1106a
B was the son of Beor, and the	1Ch 1:43	1106a
When *B* died, Jobab the son of	1Ch 1:44	1106a
and *B* the son of Azaz, the son of	1Ch 5:8	1106a
B and Becher and Jediael.	1Ch 7:6	1106a
And the sons of *B* were five:	1Ch 7:7	1106a
the father of *B* his first-born,	1Ch 8:1	1106a
B had sons: Addar, Gera, Abihud,	1Ch 8:3	1106a
BELAITES		
of Bela, the family of the *B*;	Nu 26:38	1108
BELCH		
they *b* forth with their mouth;	Ps 59:7	5042
BELIAL		
Or what harmony has Christ with *B*,	2Co 6:15	*955*
BELIEVE		
stunned, for he did not *b* them.	Gn 45:26	539
"What if they will not *b* me,	Ex 4:1	539
"that they may *b* that the LORD,	Ex 4:5	539
that if they will not *b* you or heed	Ex 4:8	539
b the witness of the last sign.	Ex 4:8	539
if they will not *b* even these two signs	Ex 4:9	539
and may also *b* in you forever."	Ex 19:9	539
how long will they not *b* in Me,	Nu 14:11	539
I did not *b* the reports,	1Ki 10:7	539
did not *b* in the LORD their God.	2Ki 17:14	539
"Nevertheless I did not *b* their	2Ch 9:6	539
you like this, and do not *b* him,	2Ch 32:15	539
I could not *b* that He was	Jb 9:16	539
"He does not *b* that he will	Jb 15:22	539
on them when they did not *b*,	Jb 29:24	539
Because they did not *b* in God,	Ps 78:22	539
did not *b* in His wonderful works.	Ps 78:32	539
They did not *b* in His word,	Ps 106:24	539
For I *b* in Thy commandments.	Ps 119:66	539
speaks graciously, do not *b* him,	Pr 26:25	539
If you will not *b*, you surely	Is 7:9	539
order that you may know and *b* Me,	Is 43:10	539
Do not *b* them, although they may	Jer 12:6	539
the son of Ahikam did not *b* them.	Jer 40:14	539
The kings of the earth did not *b*,	La 4:12	539
You would not *b* if you were told.	Hab 1:5	539
you *b* that I am able to do this?"	Mt 9:28	*4100*
ones who *b* in Me to stumble,	Mt 18:6	*4100*
'Then why did you not *b* him?'	Mt 21:25	*4100*
and you did not *b* him;	Mt 21:32	*4100*
and harlots did *b* him;	Mt 21:32	*4100*
remorse afterward so as to *b* him.	Mt 21:32	*4100*
'There *He is*,' do not *b him*.	Mt 24:23	*4100*
in the inner rooms,' do not *b them*.	Mt 24:26	*4100*
the cross, and we shall *b* in Him.	Mt 27:42	*4100*
repent and *b* in the gospel."	Mk 1:15	*4100*
be afraid *any longer*, only *b*."	Mk 5:36	*4100*
saying, "I do *b*; help my unbelief."	Mk 9:24	*4100*
little ones who *b* to stumble,	Mk 9:42	*4100*
b that you have received them,	Mk 11:24	*4100*
'Then why did you not *b* him?'	Mk 11:31	*4100*
'Behold, *He is* there'; do not *b him*;	Mk 13:21	*4100*
cross, so that we may see and *b*!"	Mk 15:32	*4100*
seen by her, they refused to *b* it.	Mk 16:11	*569*
but they did not *b* them either.	Mk 16:13	*4100*
because you did not *b* my words,	Lk 1:20	*4100*
that they may not *b* and be saved.	Lk 8:12	*4100*
they *b* for a while, and in time of	Lk 8:13	*4100*
only *b*, and she shall be made well."	Lk 8:50	*4100*
'Why did you not *b* him?'	Lk 20:5	*4100*
"If I tell you, you will not *b*;	Lk 22:67	*4100*
and they would not *b* them.	Lk 24:11	*569*
"O foolish men and slow of heart to *b*	Lk 24:25	*4100*
while they still could not *b it* for joy	Lk 24:41	*569*
that all might *b* through him.	Jn 1:7	*4100*
even to those who *b* in His name,	Jn 1:12	*4100*
you under the fig tree, do you *b*?	Jn 1:50	*4100*
earthly things and you do not *b*,	Jn 3:12	*4100*
b if I tell you heavenly things?	Jn 3:12	*4100*
not *b* has been judged already,	Jn 3:18	*4100*
"Woman, *b* Me, an hour is coming	Jn 4:21	*4100*
of what you said that we *b*,	Jn 4:42	*4100*
wonders, you *simply* will not *b*."	Jn 4:48	*4100*
for you do not *b* Him whom He sent.	Jn 5:38	*4100*
"How can you *b*, when you receive	Jn 5:44	*4100*
believed Moses, you would *b* Me;	Jn 5:46	*4100*
"But if you do not *b* his writings,	Jn 5:47	*4100*
how will you *b* My words?"	Jn 5:47	*4100*
you *b* in Him whom He has sent."	Jn 6:29	*4100*
sign, that we may see, and *b* You?	Jn 6:30	*4100*
have seen Me, and yet do not *b*.	Jn 6:36	*4100*
are some of you who do not *b*."	Jn 6:64	*4100*
who they were who did not *b*,	Jn 6:64	*4100*
for unless you *b* that I am *He*, you	Jn 8:24	*4100*
things, many came to *b* in Him.	Jn 8:30	*4100*
speak the truth, you do not *b* Me.	Jn 8:45	*4100*
speak truth, why do you not *b* Me?	Jn 8:46	*4100*
therefore did not *b it* of him,	Jn 9:18	*4100*
"Do you *b* in the Son of Man?"	Jn 9:35	*4100*
He, Lord, that I may *b* in Him?"	Jn 9:36	*4100*
"Lord, I *b*." And he worshiped Him.	Jn 9:38	*4100*
"I told you, and you do not *b*;	Jn 10:25	*4100*
"But you do not *b*, because you	Jn 10:26	*4100*
works of My Father, do not *b* Me;	Jn 10:37	*4100*
I do them, though you do not *b* Me,	Jn 10:38	*4100*
do not believe Me, *b* the works,	Jn 10:38	*4100*
was not there, so that you may *b*;	Jn 11:15	*4100*
in Me shall never die. Do you *b* this?	Jn 11:26	*4100*
"Did I not say to you, if you *b*,	Jn 11:40	*4100*
may *b* that Thou didst send Me."	Jn 11:42	*4100*

This is a page from the *New American Standard Exhaustive Concordance*, © 1981 by The Lockman Foundation. Used by permission.

As I say, a concordance is probably the most essential tool to have for Bible study. If you don't have anything else, get yourself a good concordance. It is well worth the investment.

Bible dictionaries

I'm amazed at how many people use a Webster's dictionary to look up words from a book or magazine article but never dream of consulting a Bible dictionary when they run into a strange word in the Bible. Bible dictionaries provide loads of helpful information on subjects in the text. There are some excellent ones on the market.

You see, in recent years a great deal of light has been shed on biblical studies, particularly as a result of archaeological discoveries. In fact, we know more about the Bible now than in all of the history of interpretation. Much of this knowledge is available to you in Bible dictionaries.

A classic is *An Expository Dictionary of New Testament Words*, the life work of a scholar named W. E. Vine. Thanks to him, you don't have to know Greek to study the New Testament, because he gives you the background of the words. He tells you what they mean, how they are used, and all of their variations. We're going to use Vine in the next chapter when we talk about word studies.

Another more recent work, and one that I use extensively, is *The New Bible Dictionary*, edited by J. D. Douglas. It is cram packed with helpful material. Suppose I come across the name, "Babylon," and I don't know anything about Babylon. I look it up and discover all kinds of information. The book even has an illustration of a ziggurat, which was a worship center. It also has a street map showing what the city was like. That kind of input becomes enormously valuable in interpreting passages such as Genesis 11 (the Tower of Babel), and books such as Nehemiah, Daniel, and Revelation.

Again, suppose I run across the term "Ark of the Covenant." What was that? Consulting a Bible dictionary, I learn that it was a box that was used in the Hebrew worship, in a place called the Holy of Holies. There is a lot more to the story. But the term "ark" is also used of Noah's ark, the vessel that carried Noah and his family and all of the animals through the Flood. Yet I've known people to see a picture of the box—the Ark of the Covenant—and say, "No way. You couldn't get all of the animals in that thing." But if they had looked it up, they would know that there were two different arks.

Bible handbooks

A related resource to the Bible dictionary is a Bible handbook. It is sort of a one-volume encyclopedia.

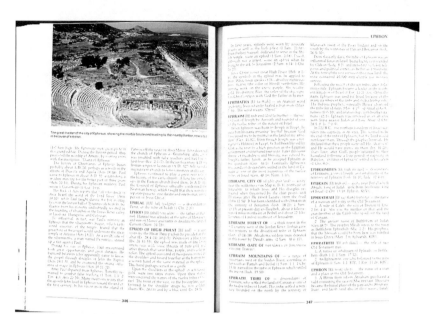

Nelson's Illustrated Bible Dictionary, © 1986 by Thomas Nelson Publishers. Used by permission.

I frequently use *Eerdman's Handbook to the Bible.* It is beautifully done with four-color photography and covers more than three hundred important biblical events. It goes book by book through the entire Bible, providing all kinds of background material.

For instance, maybe you want to know something about coins and money. The biblical text mentions the drachma and the denarius. What were these units of exchange? You can look them up and discover their modern equivalents.

Or maybe you want to know about clothing and shoes. What did the biblical characters wear? What did their clothes look like? What were they made of? You can consult *The Handbook of Life in Bible Times* and find out.

How about food? There are many passages in which food is mentioned, but it was altogether different than the food we have today. You can look it up and find a whole section on food and drink, on food and its preparation.

After you consult a resource such as this and get the background, you start to find all kinds of insights into the Scriptures that eluded you before. This kind of detail makes the Word of God come alive.

Atlases

Geography is one of the most helpful sciences to Bible study. Yet most people completely bypass the significance of place in the account. For instance, the cities that Paul visited—Antioch, Corinth, Ephesus, Rome—are just dots on a page to most readers. Yet these were major metropolitan centers with populations in the hundreds of thousands, as cosmopolitan and sophisticated as any city in our country today.

I spoke with a professor at an Ivy League school recently. "What do you teach?" I asked him.

"English literature."

"Fantastic," I said, "How are you making out?"

He said, "It's the worst assignment I've ever had."

"Why?"

"Because my students come with no knowledge of the Bible," he explained. "How in the world can you study English lit without a background in the English Bible?"

Good question. In an earlier generation, that was considered basic knowledge. Today, we're without it. That's why you need to have a good atlas. It fills in the story behind the places mentioned in Scripture.

One of my favorites is the *Moody Atlas of Bible Lands*. It's a beautiful presentation, with pictures and diagrams. It tells about things various gems found in Palestine, or the soils. It gives you some idea of the topography. For instance, when we looked at the stilling of the storm in Mark 4, we said that the Sea of Galilee was 690 feet or more below sea level. Where do you learn that? In a resource such as the *Moody Atlas*.

Another useful one is the *Zondervan Pictorial Bible Atlas*. In the center it has transparent overlays for the maps that add information to the basic geography. There's also the *Macmillan Bible Atlas*, which is probably the most accurate, based on up-to-date discoveries.

A good study Bible will have maps included in the back. But if you really want to investigate the geographical context, invest in a comprehensive atlas.

Bible commentaries

Have you ever sat under the teaching of someone who has mastered a portion of the Word and thought, *Wow, wouldn't I like to have him sitting beside me next time I come to the Scriptures.* Well, a commentary does essentially that. It offers you the insights of someone who has perhaps spent his whole life studying the text. A commentary can't do your study for you, but it certainly is an excellent means of evaluating your own study.

There is no end to the number of commentaries available, especially on popular books such as the Psalms, the gospels, Romans, and so forth. The question is, how do you know where to begin? I suggest that if you are just starting out in the process and just starting to build your library of tools, get a good, single-volume, general commentary—one that covers one or both of the testaments in one, or at the most, two volumes.

A helpful one with which I'm familiar is the *Bible Knowledge Commentary*, produced by several members of the faculty at Dallas Theological Seminary, where I teach. It comes in two volumes, one on the Old Testament and one on the New. It covers every book of the Bible, from Genesis to Revelation. For every book it presents the background in terms of the author and purpose, an outline, and a discussion of the text, particularly the difficult passages.

In addition to a general commentary, you may want to consult a specific commentary on an individual book of the Bible. For instance, a series called the *Tyndale Old Testament Commentaries* includes a volume on Ecclesiastes. Did you ever bump your head on the ceiling of that book? Maybe you've even been asked to teach it, but you didn't know enough about it to teach it. A little commentary such as that one can help you get your bearings.

Perhaps, though, you're ready for something a little deeper, with a little more detail. You might try the *Expositor's Bible Commentary*, a twelve-volume series by Dr. Frank Gabelein. You can start with one volume to suit your study needs at the moment, and then add to the collection as you work your way through the books of the Bible.

Commentaries can be a blessing and a curse. The downside is the tendency to start depending on them rather than familiarizing yourself with the biblical text. There's nothing wrong with commentaries, but remember that ultimately they are just one person's opinion. They are certainly not inspired.

At the same time, a scholar who has spent a lifetime investigating the biblical text can frequently get you past the barriers to understanding. His comments can also help you evaluate your own personal study.

Additional resources

I could go on and on listing secondary resources and study helps. For instance, there are several periodicals on archaeology available, such as *Biblical Archaeology Review*. They are written at the popular level and have invaluable information on research affecting biblical studies.

Another fruitful area for secondary study is the vast collection of literature that survives from the biblical era. Contemporaneous histories, political theory, law, poetry, and drama fill in a lot of detail about the cultures of the day. In this connection, you might also want to consult historical studies by more recent scholars, such as Will Durant's studies of Rome and Greece, or Alfred Edersheim's classic, *The Life and Times of Jesus the Messiah*. Another fascinating look at comparative history is Bernard Grun's *The Timetables of History*, which is a giant time line spanning the centuries.

You can find more tools listed in the back of the book under "Additional Resources."

GETTING STARTED

An absolute ocean of valuable resources is available to you. So where do you get started? Which ones should you obtain first?

I suggest you start with a good study Bible and a companion concordance. For my money, those are crucial. If those were all you had, you would already be in good shape. You would have the text of Scripture and a list of all the words. So you could navigate freely among the passages, using the skills you've learned in Observation and Interpretation.

Then, if you obtained a good Bible dictionary, a Bible handbook, an atlas, and a simple, one-volume commentary, you'd be in business. You'd have the basic tools of the trade, a basic library with which to work. You could add to it as time goes by. But at least you'd have some good resources to start with.

A word of warning, though, as you power up these tools: Beware of relying too much on secondhand information. The use of extrabiblical resources should never be a substitute for personal Bible study, but rather a stimulus for it. The order is always the same: First the Word of God; then secondary sources.

You Try It

Earlier you worked with a concordance in your study of Daniel 1-2, and in the last installment you consulted a Bible dictionary and a Bible handbook. Now you have two additional resources to consider—atlases and commentaries.

Find an atlas that shows Babylon at the time of Nebuchadnezzar. Where was it in relation to Israel? What modern-day country now occupies this area?

Also consult a general commentary on the Old Testament and perhaps a single-volume commentary on the book of Daniel. What questions do these resources answer for you? What additional information do they supply?

By the way, you might also want to go back to the Bible dictionary and Bible handbook to look up some additional items related to this text, such as: government in Babylon, the Chaldeans, ziggurats, Cyrus, and foods in the ancient world.

35

COMING TO TERMS

I n one of Gary Larson's *Far Side* cartoons, a French horn player is sitting in the middle of a symphony orchestra during a concert. Pointing at the sheet music on his stand, he says, "Gee, look at all the little black dots!"

The words in the biblical text are just little black dots on a page to many readers, strange hieroglyphics that remain inscrutable. These folks may own a Bible, but they don't own the words in the Bible because they don't know how to determine their meaning. Tragically, they are missing out on the very words of life that God has spoken.

But that need not be the case for you. If you've been practicing the process outlined in this book, you've already discovered a number of strategies to make sense out of Scripture. The most important thing you've learned to do is to look for terms. In this chapter, I want to help you investigate biblical terms in order to discern their meaning.

A "term" is a key word or phrase that an author uses to make his point. He may use the word repeatedly to give it emphasis. He may place it on display in some prominent verse. He may build a story around it to illustrate its significance. Or he may put it in the mouth of a central character in his narrative. However he signals them, an author wants you to pay attention to his terms, because they are freighted with meaning. Unless you "come to terms with the terms," you'll never understand his message.

Two secondary resources mentioned in the last chapter are especially helpful in this process—the concordance and the Bible dictionary. Let me show you how you can use them to advantage.

USING A CONCORDANCE FOR A WORD STUDY

Say you run across the word *joy* in Paul's letter to the Philippians. *Joy* and *rejoice* appear to be key terms for that book. So you open your concordance and look up *joy*. (Let's assume you are working with the *New American Standard* translation and its concordance; see page 245.)

The first thing you notice is that there are scores of references, in both the Old and New Testaments. That's significant: *joy* is not an obscure term; it is very common. If you want to launch an exhaustive study of the term, you need to look up each and every passage where it is used. You want to evaluate what light the various contexts shed on the meaning and significance of *joy*.

But since you are concentrating on Philippians, pay special attention to its usage there. Here's what the listing shows:

always offering prayer with j in	Php 1:4	5479
your progress and j in the faith	Php 1:25	5479
make my j complete by being of the	Php 2:2	5479
and share my j with you all.	Php 2:17	4796
same way and share your j with me.	Php 2:18	4796
receive him in the Lord with all j	Php 2:29	5479
I long to see, my j and crown,	Php 4:1	5479

So the word *joy* appears seven times in the letter. You need to do a little observing to compare and contrast these different uses. You might even want to expand your study to the use of joy in Paul's other letters.

One thing to be sure to notice is the little number to the right of each entry. At Philippians 1:4, it is 5479. Likewise at 1:25 and 2:2. But at 2:17, it changes to 4796. Those numbers refer to the Greek words which are translated "joy." In the back of the NAS concordance, you'll find that 5479 is the word *chara*, which means "joy" or "delight." It comes from the Greek verb *chairo*, "to rejoice" or "be glad."

What about 4796? That's the word *sugchairo*—obviously related to *chairo*, but with a prefix, *sug*, that shades the meaning. The concordance tells you that *sugchairo* means "to rejoice with." So in the two instances of *joy* in Philippians 2:17-18, Paul is talking about a shared experience. That's obvious enough from the English text. But a good concordance will help you when something is not so obvious. So even though you don't know the original languages, you do not have to be at a disadvantage.

USING A CONCORDANCE TO STUDY OBSCURE WORDS

Another use for a concordance is to chase down obscure references. For example, suppose you are studying the books of 1 and 2 Kings, and you come across the name *Molech* in 1 Kings 11:7:

> Then Solomon built a high place for Chemosh the detestable idol of Moab, on the mountain which is east of Jerusalem, and for Molech the detestable idol of the sons of Ammon.

Who or what was Molech? The text tells you that it was a detestable idol and that Solomon was apparently building a center of worship for it. But you decide to do a little comparative study. So you look up Molech in your concordance and find that the name appears eight times in the Old Testament and never in the New. That tells you something about the time span for Molech.

You also notice that of the eight references, five are in Leviticus, one in 1 Kings, one in 2 Kings, and one more in Jeremiah. That ought to draw your attention to Leviticus. Just looking at the concordance entries, you read in four of the five cases about offspring being offered to Molech. So already you have a clue as to why the author calls Molech "the detestable idol." People were sacrificing their own children to it. And apparently that's what Solomon was getting into.

Of all the tools of Bible study, a concordance is the one you will use most frequently. It's ideal for word studies because it locates terms in the text. It also gets you started in the task of comparing Scripture with Scripture, which is the best way to understand the meaning of biblical terms. If you buy only one secondary resource for your Bible study program, make sure it is an exhaustive concordance for the translation of your study Bible. The investment will pay for itself many times over.

USING A BIBLE DICTIONARY

The other tool to use when investigating terms in Scripture is a Bible dictionary. I mentioned Vine's *Expository Dictionary of New Testament Words*. Let's use it to investigate the word *earth*.

Remember our observation of Acts 1:8 (chapter 6)? Jesus told the apostles that they were to take the gospel "even to the remotest part of the earth." I said that the word *earth* meant the inhabited earth. How did I know that? I looked it up in Vine.

Vine gives a comprehensive overview of the word *earth*. He shows that there were two Greek words that we commonly translate "earth": *gé* (pronounced "gay"), and *oikouméne* (pronounced "oi-koo-men-nay").

Gé was used to describe five main ideas: earth as arable land; the earth as a whole, the world (as opposed to the heavens); the inhabited earth; a country or territory; the ground; and land. Based on his extensive knowledge of ancient Greek, Vine lists verses in the New Testament for each of these usages. Acts 1:8 is listed with the third meaning, "the inhabited earth."

It's interesting to notice that all of the references in Luke and Acts fall under this third meaning, and none under the other five. And of the nine references listed with "the inhabited earth," six are from the book of Acts. So *earth* is a crucial term for Luke. And every time he uses it he is referring to "the inhabited earth." Its prominence in Acts adds weight to our conjecture that Acts 1:8 is something of an outline for the book. Jesus tells His followers to go to the inhabited earth, and that's exactly where they go.

Another piece of information that Vine gives you is that the other word for earth, *oikouméne*, also denotes the inhabited earth. And he adds this note (italics added): "It is translated 'world' in every place where it has this significance, *save in Luke 21:26...where it is translated 'earth.'*" Very interesting. Again, Luke always has in mind the inhabited earth. What do you suppose that suggests about the purpose of his two-volume account?

Words are the basic building blocks of language. To understand any piece of literature, you have to come to terms with the author; you have to interpret his words. Concordances and Bible dictionaries are invaluable in helping you do that. However, some words have a meaning that lies beneath the surface. We call them figures of speech, and we'll look at how they work in the next chapter.

You Try It

In this last part of your study of Daniel 1-2, I want you to do two word studies that have important implications for the interpretation of this passage. The first is the word *defile*, found in Daniel 1:8:

> But Daniel made up his mind that he would not *defile* himself with the king's choice food or with the wine which he drank; so he sought permission from the commander of the officials that he might not *defile* himself. (Italics added)

The second term is *latter days*, found in Daniel 2:28:

> However, there is a God in heaven who reveals mysteries, and He has made known to King Nebuchadnezzar what will take place in the *latter days*. This was your dream and the visions in your mind while on your bed. (Italics added)

Use a concordance to locate other uses of these words in the Bible. What can you learn from these additional texts? Then look up *defile* and *latter days* in a Bible dictionary to see what else you can discover about the meaning and significance of these terms.

36

FIGURING OUT THE FIGURATIVE

A n old, old man sat before his twelve sons. His eyes had failed, but his insight had not. Knowing that his time was drawing near, he wished to pronounce his vision of each man's future. They stood waiting, respectful in their silence. Finally the ancient one spoke: "Come close, my sons. Listen carefully to what your father tells you."

The gathered successors leaned closer, straining to hear. Robert, the oldest, occupied a central position. It was to him that the wheezing voice spoke first.

"Robert, you were the first, my pride and joy. But you are boiling water. You shall be first no longer."

The younger man's face fell, fighting back shame and rage. But he dared not reply. The old man was continuing without a pause.

"Stephen and Lawrence. You are thieves and murderers. To you I leave no blessing, only a curse.

"John, you are a lion's cub, and so you will rule. But someday you will wash your clothes in wine.

"Zachary is a seaport where ships will find harbor.

"Ian is nothing but a wild mule. Satisfied with anyone who feeds him, he will spend his days in forced labor.

"Daniel, you are a snake lying in the road. You will strike at your brothers and be their judge.

"George, you are a bandit. You will rob and be robbed, and live in uncertainty.

"Allen loves the choicest of meats. But he will spend his days cooking, not eating.

"Nathan is a deer on the run. His words will leap and dance.

"Jonathan, you are my tree along the cool river bank. You will grow and prosper and shade all your brothers. To you will come the blessings of my fathers, and through you will pass the blessings to my descendants.

"Bradley, my last, is a vicious wolf, hungry and wild. All day you will kill, an all night you will devour."

He finished abruptly, and no sound could be heard but the droning of flies. No one moved. Each son brooded on the words given to him. They failed to notice that the rattling patriarch, his words at an end, had dropped his head on his chest and sighed his last.

A WAY OF SPEAKING

What are we to make of this biblical tale? Oh, did I forget to tell you? This is a loose reconstruction of Genesis 49, where Jacob summons his twelve sons and prophesies the future of each one's lineage.

If you read the account, you'll notice the odd descriptions assigned to several of them: Judah is called a "lion's welp" (v. 9); Zebulun is a "haven for ships" (v. 13); Issachar is "a strong donkey" (v. 14); Dan is a "serpent in the way, a horned snake in the path" (v. 17); Naphtali is a "doe let loose" (v. 21); Joseph is a "fruitful bough by a spring" (v. 22); and Benjamin is a "ravenous wolf" (v. 27).

Again, what are we to make of these descriptions? We might expect Noah to talk to his sons like this after being cooped up on the ark, but what are these words doing in the mouth of Jacob? Are we to take them literally? If not, why not? How do we know when Scripture is actually representing reality and when it merely describes reality?

The issue here is figurative language. We're all familiar with figures of speech. We use them all the time: "I could have died of embarrassment." "I guess I'll have to face the music." "So-and-so is as mad as a hornet." "He was bored to tears." "Don't let the cat out of the bag." "She has a green thumb."

The biblical writers and characters were no different. They laced their material with vivid images, and peculiar ways of speaking. David says that the person who follows God's Word will be like a tree, but the wicked are like chaff (Psalm 1:3-4). The bride in Song of Solomon 2:1 says she is "the rose of Sharon, the lily of the valleys." She calls her lover a gazelle or young stag "climbing on the mountains, leaping on the hills" (2:8-9). Jesus called Herod a fox (Luke 13:32), the Pharisees whitewashed tombs (Matthew 23:27), and James and John the Sons of Thunder (Mark 3:17). Paul called certain false teachers dogs (Philippians 3:2).

Of course, the Bible's figurative language can be far more elaborate, even going beyond the spoken word to graphic object lessons. God told Jeremiah to buy a clay pitcher, take it to the leaders, prophesy against them, and then break the pitcher as a picture of what God was going to do to the nation (Jeremiah 19). Hosea was told to marry an adulteress as a symbol of God's faithful love for His people, and their faithlessness toward Him (Hosea 1:2-9; 3:1-5).

When we come to John's Revelation, we run into some very unusual language. A ruler in heaven appears as a jaspar stone surrounded by a rainbow (4:3). He sees a lamb with seven horns and seven eyes (5:6). He also sees a beast rising up out of the sea, with ten horns and seven heads (13:1). And at the end of the book, an entire city covering more than two million square miles drops out of heaven (21:16).

These things make for interesting reading. But what do they mean? How are we to interpret them in our Bible study process? How do we know when to read the Bible literally and when to read it figuratively?

I'm going to give you ten principles for figuring out the figurative. But first, let's make sure we understand the difference between "literal" and "figurative." People talk about a "literal interpretation of Scripture." Does that mean that in Genesis 49, they see Judah as a real, live lion's cub? Or Joseph standing by a creek with roots going down into the soil? Or Benjamin as some sort of uncontrollable werewolf? If so, I've got a good psychiatrist I can recommend.

When we speak of "literal interpretation," we mean taking the language in its normal sense, accepting it at face value as if the writer is communicating in ways that people normally communicate. As one person has put it, "When the plain sense of Scripture makes common sense, seek no other sense."

So, according to this principle, when Jesus tells us to "render to Caesar the things that are Caesar's" (Luke 20:25), we don't need to look for some hidden meaning or elaborate interpretation. It's quite plain that He is telling us to pay our taxes. On the other hand, when He calls Herod a fox, He obviously is not saying that the man is a roving carnivore. He's speaking figuratively, comparing Herod to that sly, dog-like creature.

FIGURING OUT THE FIGURATIVE

What happens when the "plain sense" does not make common sense? Are there any rules that govern when we should interpret odd expressions figuratively and when we should take them literally? I'm afraid there are no foolproof means for that. But here are ten principles that will keep you out of the worst kinds of trouble.

1. Use the literal sense unless there is some good reason not to

This is clear from what we have just talked about. In reading the Bible, we have to assume that the writers were normal, rational people who communicated in the same basic ways that we do. And yet time and time again, people "spiritualize" the text, trying to make it say everything but what it plainly says.

A classic illustration is the Song of Solomon. For years, interpreters have said that this is an allegory of the relationship between Christ and His church. But how can that possibly fit with the text? The poem was written centuries before Christ. It has a definite lyric form and needs to be read according to the conventions of that genre. Moreover, there's a simpler, more sensible interpretation: this is a book that celebrates erotic love in marriage as God intended it to be.

2. Use the figurative sense when the passage tells you to do so

Some passages tell you up front that they involve figurative imagery. For instance, whenever you come across a dream or a vision, you can expect to find symbolic language because that's the language of dreams. In Genesis 37, it's clear from the context that Joseph's dreams are talking about things that are going to happen in the future. The same is true of the Pharaoh's dreams in Genesis 41 and of Daniel's prophetic visions in Daniel 7-12.

3. Use the figurative sense if a literal meaning is impossible or absurd

This is where we need some sanctified common sense. God does not shroud Himself in unknowable mysticism. When He wants to tell us something, He tells us. He doesn't confound us with nonsense. However, He often uses symbolism to make His points. Yet He expects us to read them as symbols, not absurdities.

Consider Revelation 1:16, where the Lord appears: "Out of His mouth came a sharp, two-edged sword." What does this mean? Is it likely that our Lord would have a literal sword sticking out of His mouth? Hardly. The most likely explanation is a figurative one, so we need to search the text for what this picture represents.

It's probably not what you think. You may be thinking of Hebrews 4:12, which says that the Word of God is "sharper than any two-edged sword." On that basis, you might assume that the Revelation image is about Christ and His Word. But a word study rules otherwise.

The word for "sword" in Revelation 1:16 is not the same as the word used in Hebrews 4:12. In Hebrews, the sword is a short, fighting sword like those used by Roman soldiers. But the sword in Revelation is a large, ceremonial sword of victory and judgment. Carried by a conquering king, it would be used to execute the vanquished after a triumphal procession. Consider how that fits with the theme and imagery of Revelation.

So figurative language can be both descriptive and precise.

4. Use the figurative sense if a literal meaning would involve something immoral

In John 6:53-55, Jesus confounds certain Jews who opposed Him with these words:

> Truly, truly, I say to you, unless you eat the flesh of the Son of Man and drink His blood, you have no life in yourselves. He who eats My flesh and drinks My blood has eternal life; and I will raise him up on the last day. For My flesh is true food, and My blood is true drink.

That's a rather strange way of talking, to say the least. Was He suggesting that His followers become cannibals? No, that would have been a repulsive violation of the Old Testament law. And none of His listeners took it that way. They were puzzled by His words, to be sure: "How can this man give us his flesh to eat?" cried the Pharisees (6:57, NIV). You see, they were grappling with the problem of interpretation. Others said, "This is a hard teaching. Who can accept it?" (6:60, NIV). But they recognized that the Lord was speaking figuratively.

. God never violates His character. And since He bases His Word on His character, we can be sure that His commandments are consistent with who He is. He never asks us to do something that He would not do or has not done Himself.

5. Use the figurative sense if the expression is an obvious figure of speech

The biblical text often signals its use of figures of speech. Similes, for instance, use the words *like* or *as* to make comparisons: "*Like* a gold ring in a pig's snout is a beautiful woman who shows no discretion" (Proverbs 11:22, italics added, NIV). "[The Lord] makes Lebanon skip *like* a calf" (Psalm 29:6, italics added).

Scripture uses other figures of speech that make sense only when read figuratively. When Isaiah predicts that "the moon will be abashed and the sun ashamed" (24:23), he is using an obvious personification. When Paul quotes Hosea, "O death, where is your victory? O death, where is your sting?" (1 Corinthians 15:55), he is using a form called apostrophe, addressing a thing as if it were a person. Expressions such as "he was gathered to his people," a man "knew" his wife, the Lord gave the people "into the hands of" their enemies, or that someone "fell asleep" are common euphemisms and idioms.

6. Use the figurative sense if a literal interpretation goes contrary to the context and scope of the passage

Revelation 5:1-5 describes a fascinating scene before the throne of God. We read about "the Lion of the tribe of Judah." Is the writer talking about a literal beast? Obviously not, as that would make no sense in the context. A bit of comparative study shows that he is using a title given to the Messiah. So we need to determine what that title represents and why he uses it.

Remember that in figuring out the figurative one of your best guides is the context.

7. Use the figurative if a literal interpretation goes contrary to the general character and style of the book

This is really an extension of what we just looked at. Remember, the context of any verse is the paragraph, the section, and ultimately the book of which it is a part.

This principle applies especially to two types of literature: the prophetic, which often makes sense only if read figuratively; and the poetic, which employs imaginative language as matter of routine.

For instance, the psalmist says, "In the shadow of Thy wings I sing for joy" (Psalm 63:7). That does not mean that God has feathers. But He does protect His children with the same watchful concern as a mother eagle for her chirping nestlings. That image fits with the general atmosphere and style of this psalm.

8. Use the figurative sense if a literal interpretation goes contrary to the plan and purpose of the author

Again, 'context is crucial. Have you ever heard someone come up with an interpretation of a verse that sounds plausible in isolation but heretical in comparison with the neighboring verses? It's a case of the ugly duckling. It doesn't fit. Something's out of place. In fact, a good habit to get into whenever you interpret a passage is to step back, look at the interpretation, and ask, what's wrong with this picture? Or does everything fall into place?

We saw in Psalm 1 that the person who delights in God's law will be like a well-watered tree. And verse 3 adds, "In whatever he does he prospers." Now some people come to that and claim that it guarantees material prosperity to every faithful believer. But does that really fit the context or the purpose of the author?

Hardly. Looking at Psalm 1 and the rest of the psalms, it's clear that the psalmists were far·more concerned about people's walk with God than they were with their financial well-being. Psalm 1:3 makes the most sense if we understand it to describe the quality of a person's outcome, not the quantity of blessings he enjoys.

9. Use the figurative sense if a literal interpretation involves a contradiction of other Scripture

The great interpreter of Scripture is Scripture. The Bible is unified in its message. Although it sometimes presents us with paradox, it never confounds us with contradiction.

Jesus told His followers, "It is easier for a camel to go through the eye of a needle than for a rich man to enter the kingdom of God" (Mark 10:25). What an intriguing image. People have gone to incredible lengths to try and explain what Jesus is talking about.

But one thing we know for certain: He is not saying that there can be no salvation for the rich. That's what the disciples wondered (v. 26). But not only does He respond to that question (v. 27); the rest of Scripture teaches otherwise. For instance, Paul warns against the dangers of wealth (1 Timothy 6:17-19), but he never says that the wealthy are categorically excluded from the kingdom.

So if Mark 10 were all we had on the subject, we might have reason to wonder as the disciples did. But by comparing Scripture with Scripture, we can put it in perspective.

10. Use the figurative sense if a literal interpretation would involve a contradiction in doctrine

This follows from the point just made. We need to be consistent in our interpretation of Scripture and in the systems of belief that we build using Scripture.

In 1 Corinthians 3:16-17, Paul writes,

Do you not know that you are a temple of God, and that the Spirit of God dwells in you? If any man destroys the temple of God, God will destroy him, for the temple of God is holy, and that is what you are.

That is rather severe language. What does Paul mean by, "If any man destroys the temple of God, God will destroy him"? Is this a threat that if a person commits suicide, he forfeits his salvation? Some have taken it that way. But not only does that compromise the context, it conflicts with the doctrine of eternal security, the teaching that God will preserve His children. Furthermore, Paul encourages us to read this passage and its context figuratively (4:6). A literal interpretation would make no sense.

You Try It

Here's a chance to try your hand at "figuring out the figurative." Read and study Psalm 139, one of the most profound and intimate of all the psalms. It is filled with figurative language. Use the principles covered in this chapter to interpret what David is talking about. Refer to the list on the next page, "Figures of Speech," for additional help in recognizing and understanding David's imagery. (By the way, don't forget to start with the step of Observation.)

Figures of Speech

Anthropomorphism
The attribution of human features or actions to God.

"The Lord's hand is not so short that it cannot save; neither is His ear so dull that it cannot hear" (Isaiah 59:1).

Apostrophe
Addressing a thing as if it were a person, or an absent or imaginary person as if he were present.

"O death, where is your victory? O death, where is your sting?" (1 Corinthians 15:55).

Euphemism
The use of a less offensive expression to indicate a more offensive one.

"Would that those who are troubling you would even mutilate themselves" (Galatians 5:12).

Hyperbole
Exaggeration to say more than is literally meant.

"I robbed other churches, taking wages from them to serve you" (2 Corinthians 11:8).

Hypocatastasis
A comparison in which likeness is implied rather than stated directly.

"Beware of the leaven of the Pharisees, which is hypocrisy" (Luke 12:1).

Idiom
An expression peculiar to a particular people.

"And [Samson] said, 'I will go in to my wife in her room'" (Judges 15:1).

Merism
A substitution of two contrasting or opposite parts for the whole.

"Thou dost know when I sit down and when I rise up" (Psalm 39:2).

Metaphor

A comparison in which one thing represents another.

> "You are the light of the world" (Matthew 5:14).

Paradox

A statement that seems absurd, self-contradictory, or contrary to logical thought.

> "Whoever wishes to save his life shall lose it; but whoever loses his life for My sake shall find it" (Matthew 16:25).

Personification

Ascribing human characteristics or actions to inanimate objects or animals.

> "The moon will be abashed and the sun ashamed" (Isaiah 24:23).

Rhetorical question

A question that requires no response, yet forces one to answer mentally and consider its ramifications.

> "In God I have put my trust, I shall not be afraid. What can man do to me?" (Psalm 56:11).

Simile

A comparison using "like" or "as."

> "He will be like a tree firmly planted by streams of water" (Psalm 1:3).

37

PUTTING IT ALL
TOGETHER

S o far in this section I've given you a lot of input on the
interpretation of Scripture. I've pointed out some of the
obstacles to understanding the text, along with some of the
dangers to avoid. I've discussed the importance of genre and how
that influences what we read. I've handed you five keys to unlocking
the meaning of the text—content, context, comparison, culture, and
consultation.

In terms of consultation, I reviewed some of the many kinds of
secondary sources that can assist you in the process. Then I focused
on the use of the concordance in investigating terms. And finally I
listed ten principles for figuring out the figurative passages in the
biblical account.

Now let's get some involvement. In this chapter I want to
demonstrate how to put these parts of the process together by
looking at a specific passage, the first two verses of Romans 12. They
form a paragraph, which is helpful. Remember that the paragraph
forms the basic unit of Bible study. (See page 270 for the textual re-
creation.)

WHAT IS "THEREFORE" THERE FOR?

We said that the first key to accurately interpreting Scripture is
content. That is based on observation of the text. So let's start with
that.

The first thing that grabs me about this text is its sense of urgency. "I urge you," verse 1 begins. "I beseech you." "I implore you." I love J. B. Phillips's rendering: "With eyes wide open to the mercies of God." So Paul comes at his readers with a sense of urgency.

The first word in the paragraph is that key word, *therefore*. That's essential. Remember our motto: whenever you see a therefore, stop to see what it's there for. Here, it compels us to go back and check out the preceding context. So let's take the suggestion of the writer and step back to get the big picture of Romans.

Investigation shows that the book of Romans finds its theme in chapter 1 verse 17, where the writer tells us that he is talking about a "righteousness from God"—not our own righteousness, but one that He provides.

Moreover, there are three major divisions to the book. The first eight chapters deal with a righteousness that God has revealed but we must receive. Then chapters 9-11 turn to the subject of Israel. Paul says that the righteousness from God was rejected by His people. Finally, beginning in chapter 12 (where we find our passage, beginning with *therefore*), we come to the practical section of the book that talks about a righteousness reproduced in the believer's life.

So, on the basis of one connective, we've already got a good overview of the book.

But there's an additional phrase that forces us to see the connection: "by the mercies of God." In other words, the mercies of God become the basis for Paul's urgent appeal. In effect, that phrase summarizes the first eleven chapters of the book. Paul is saying, essentially, "On the basis of what God has done for you, I want you to do something."

That's an important spiritual truth. God never asks us to do anything for Him until He fully informs us of what He has done for us.

What is it that He wants us to do? Verse 1 states it plainly: "to present your bodies." What does that mean? The word *present* is a key term, and we need to make an effort to understand it. Actually, it's a technical term. It was used of the presentation of a sacrifice to God in the Old Testament Temple. It has the idea of giving something over to another, to relinquish one's grip on it. To "present" something means you can't give it and then later take it back. There's an element of decisiveness involved.

¹I urge you therefore, brethren,

> **by the mercies of God,**

to present your bodies

> **a living and holy sacrifice,**

> > **acceptable to God,**

> > **which is your spiritual service of worship.**

²And do not be conformed to this world,

> **but be transformed**

> > **by the renewing of your mind,**

> > **that you may prove what the will of God is,**

> > > **that which is good**

> > > > **and acceptable**

> > > > **and perfect.**

INVESTIGATING TERMS

Now as we've seen, whenever we find a term like that, we need to make extensive use of a concordance. So let's do that. A concordance tells us that the same word, *present*, is used in Luke 2:22:

> And when the days for their purification according to the law of Moses were completed, they [that is, Mary and Joseph]

brought Him [the baby Jesus] up to Jerusalem to *present* Him to the Lord. (Italics added)

So Jesus was presented to God in the Temple by His parents. This gives us a little insight into the life of our Lord, given the meaning of *present*. His parents were giving Him to God, with no thought of taking Him back.

The concordance also tells us that *present* is used elsewhere in the book of Romans. That's helpful, since the same term used by the same author in the same book provides a lot of insight. It's like having brothers and sisters in the same town, as opposed to distant relatives far away. In Romans 6:13 this is what we find,

And do not go on *presenting* the members of your body to sin as instruments of unrighteousness; but *present* yourselves to God as those alive from the dead, and your members as instruments of righteousness to God. (Italics added)

In other words, he's giving you an option: You can either present your body as an instrument of righteousness, or you can present your body as an instrument of sin.

Let me illustrate. Consider a surgeon's scalpel. It is sharper than a razor, light to the touch, and sterile. In short, it is perfect for the purpose for which it was designed. But the real question is, in whose hand is it placed? In my hand it would mean butchery. But in the hand of a skilled surgeon, it brings healing and health to the patient. That's what Paul describes in Romans 6: Present your body to the right hands, to the Person who is going to use it skillfully to accomplish His purposes.

But notice: Paul is talking about the presentation of your body—the same as in Romans 12. What is "the body"? A word study reveals that it stands for the total person, the total being. It also represents the instrument for sacrifice. In fact, it's really the only instrument of sacrifice that we have, the only thing we can give to God. (You'll find two other uses of *present* in that same section of Romans [6:16 and 19]. I'll let you investigate those on your own.)

Present also appears in Ephesians 5, in the passage about husbands and wives:

Husbands, love your wives, just as Christ also loved the church and gave Himself up for her; that He might sanctify her, having cleansed her by the washing of water with the word, that He might *present* to Himself the church in all her glory. (Vv. 25-27, Italics added)

Again we find the same word. If you are a husband, the Bible charges you with the responsibility to present your wife to God. You are accountable for the relationship with the woman God gives you.

There are several more passages we could look at, but let's take just one of them, Colossians 1:28:

And we proclaim [Christ], admonishing every man and teaching every man with all wisdom, that we may *present* every man complete in Christ. (Italics added)

What was Paul's purpose in building into the lives of others? To present every one of them to the Lord, so that they might come to full maturity.

INSIGHTS THROUGH CONSULTATION

Back in Romans 12, we need to notice several things about the presentation of our bodies to God. First, we are presenting a "living sacrifice." That's a contradiction in terms—except in the spiritual realm. You see, we're talking not about offering a dead body but a very alive body. It is to be sacrificed to God. And it must be both holy and acceptable.

Paul gives a conclusion about doing this in the expression, "which is your spiritual service of worship." What does that convey? It shows the expectation that presenting ourselves to God is really the least we could do, the most logical thing we could do, in light of what He has done for us.

Now we come to verse 2: "And do not be conformed to this world." We've used the interpretational principle of comparing Scripture with Scripture to investigate the meaning of *present*. Here we can use it to learn something about being "conformed" to the world.

If we look up *conform* in a Bible dictionary, we discover that it has the idea of pouring something into a mold. We're all familiar with the process of dissolving Jell-O in some boiling water and pouring it into a Jell-O mold. When it cools, it retains the shape of the mold.

That's the idea Paul uses here. "Don't let the world around you squeeze you into its own mold," Phillips paraphrases it. Don't take on the shape of the world. Don't allow the world to do the opposite of what God wants to do.

You see, we have an option, according to this passage. The little word *but* indicates a contrast, and we've learned to pay close attention to things that are unlike. Our option—the alternative to conforming to the world's pattern—is to "be transformed." That, too, is a grabbing term. It actually indicates a metamorphosis, a complete makeover. It's like the little caterpillar that builds itself a cocoon. After a time, it begins to wiggle and gradually work its way out, revealing a completely changed form as a butterfly.

But note: the transformation of the chrysalis comes from within. So it is in Romans 8. Paul indicates that by saying, "Be conformed *by the renewing of your mind.*"

Another principle we looked at was consultation. That is, having made our own exhaustive study of the text, we can then go to secondary sources, perhaps to a commentary, to find out what light they might throw on the passage. Consulting a commentary on this passage, we gain some profound insight. We learn that the word for "be transformed" is actually the passive form of a verb, whereas the word for "renewing" is active.

Now we may have to go back to our high school English and dust off the cobwebs. Anything passive is being acted upon; if it's active, it is doing the acting. So Paul is saying that we don't do the transformation; God does that. We can't do it, so He does what we can't do. Is there anything we can do? Yes, we can renew our minds. That's our job. In fact, the overhauling of our thinking is what allows God to effect the transformation.

In my early days as a believer, I was heavily influenced by Donald Grey Barnhouse, the pastor of Tenth Presbyterian Church in Philadelphia. In effect, he served as a mentor for me. I spent a lot of time with him, and I remember asking him once, "Dr. B., how can I find the will of God?"

URGENCY!   *THEME (1:17)*   *1 8 9 11 12 16*

¹I urge you therefore, brethren,

 by the mercies of God, *BASIS — SUMMARY of CH (1-11)*

EXCLUSIVENESS
to present your bodies *cf 6:13 & LK 2:22/EPH 5: 25-27*

CONTRADICTION?   *6:16,19*
a living and holy sacrifice,

 acceptable to God, *KEY.*

which is your spiritual service of worship.

THE LEAST WE CAN DO!

²And do not be conformed to this world, *NEG*

CONTRAST

PASSIVE
but be transformed *METAMORPHOSIS*   *POS*

 by the renewing of your mind,

   that you may prove what the will of God is,

     that which is good

       and acceptable

       and perfect.

I'll never forget his response. In his typical, brusque way, he whipped around and said, "Hendricks, ninety percent of the will of God will be found from your neck up!" And he turned around and walked off. I was a bit stunned. But all of a sudden it dawned on me why it was that Dr. Barnhouse spent so much of his time "brainwashing" my mind with the Word of God. That's where God begins to do His work of conforming me to Christ—in my mind.

Unfortunately, most of us are conformed to this world. For the most part, we do not sit down, think through all of our options, and then make an informed decision. No, we act because our culture does it. Our society squeezes us into its mold. How? By working on our minds. That's why it's so dangerous to throw our minds into neutral and just go with the flow.

"PROVING" GOD'S WILL

What is the purpose of God's transforming work? What is it going to do for us? Paul writes, "That you may prove what the will of God is." Word study reveals that *prove* means to test or approve. For example, a person takes a piece of jewelry to an appraiser, who evaluates it and assesses its value. "That's genuine silver," he says, "and it's worth this much." In the same way, Paul says we are going to prove three things about the will of God.

First, we're going to assess it as "good." The term *good* has been devalued by our culture. Suppose I advertise a car for sale, and a prospective buyer asks, "What's the condition?"

"It's good," I tell him.

His tendency will be to wonder, "What's the matter with it?" We've so corrupted the word *good* that unless something is "fantastic," we think it's a piece of junk.

But the word used in Romans 12 is the same word used of God elsewhere in Scripture. You want to know how "good" it is? It's as good as God is.

Moreover, Paul says it's "acceptable," not only in prospect but also in retrospect. We couldn't add anything to the will of God and in any way improve it. We couldn't take anything away from it or in any way make it better. His will is totally, absolutely acceptable.

And if that's not enough, it's also "perfect." Again, it's as perfect as God is. It matches His character, His holiness.

Such is the will of God. That's what He wants us to test in our lives. Unfortunately, most people spend the bulk of their lives trying to find the will of God, when all the while they've never presented their bodies as a living sacrifice.

An additional discovery that we make from a commentary is that the key verb in this passage, "to present," happens to be in a form called an "aorist" tense. The aorist form of this verb indicates

URGENCY! *THEME (1:17)* / *1 8 9 11 12 16* /

¹I urge you therefore, brethren,

by the mercies of God, *BASIS — SUMMARY of CH (1-11)*

DECISIVENESS

to present your bodies *cf 6:13 & LK 2:22/EPH 5: 25-27*

CONTRADICTION? *6:16,19*

a living and holy sacrifice,

acceptable to God, *KEY.*

which is your spiritual service of worship.
THE LEAST WE CAN DO!

²And do not be conformed to this world, *NEG*

CONTRAST

PASSIVE

but be transformed *METAMORPHOSIS*   *POS.*

ACTIVE   *COMES*

by the renewing of your mind, *FROM WITHIN*

PURPOSE   *TEST/APPROVE*

³ that you may prove what the will of God is,

that which is good *AS GOOD AS GOD IS.*

PROSPECT

and acceptable *{ RETROSPECT*

and perfect. *AS PERFECT AS HE IS!*

---

decisiveness. This is a major division in our lives, a point at which we present ourselves to God, just as Jesus was presented. There's no turning back. It describes a complete commitment to God, for Him to do with us whatever He desires.

Imagine a notebook full of pages that represent the will of God for particular aspects of your life. And you say to God, "This is my life as it is right now, as well as I know it. I want to present everything I am to You." And you give that notebook to God; you present it to Him in an act of complete and utter commitment.

But then at a later date, you discover additional material that you weren't able to include in the notebook originally. What then? Well, you already know where the notebook is—you've given it to God. Your life belongs to Him. So as you come across new areas of your life, you can take those and present them to God as well.

Obviously you can't present your wife to God if you are a single person. Nor could you know how many children you might have. But the moment God gives you a marriage or children, then you already know exactly where they belong in terms of God's will. They go in the same notebook that you presented to God in the first place.

That's the idea of "present" in the aorist tense, as it appears in this passage.

Now look back over Romans 12:1-2 as we've discussed it in this chapter. See if this does not flesh out some of the interpretational principles that we've looked at. First we observed the content of the text, which gave us a data base for understanding Paul's message. We also looked at the context. "Therefore" led us to examine the book as a whole. We did some comparison of Scripture, using a concordance. We chased down the verbs "to present" and "be conformed."

Then we did a little consulting. We looked up a few things in a commentary. We discovered that "present" indicates a decisive commitment of ourselves to Jesus Christ. We also found out what the transformation involves. It is something God does; the renewing of our mind is something that we do.

And so, even though we've just gotten our foot in the door of this passage, we've come up with an accurate, perceptive, biblical understanding of what God wants us to do with our bodies as His redeemed people.

38

DON'T STOP NOW!

We live in a society that is drowning in a sea of information. And the tide is rising. One study estimates that 90 percent of what we will know by the year 2000, we haven't even discovered yet. Another goes even further: the amount of information available will double nineteen times by the end of the century. Talk about an information explosion!

This surfeit of data poses a good news-bad news dilemma. On the one hand, we don't have to be enslaved to ignorance. Mention just about any subject, and there's a good probability that someone somewhere has looked into it. That kind of wide-ranging expertise brings about incredible developments the fields such as medicine, physics, biotechnology, agriculture, and transportation.

On the other hand, how do we find the information we're looking for? We're no longer searching for the proverbial needle in a haystack; we're searching for a needle in a haystack made of needles. Furthermore, even though we have a lot of data, much of it is of little practical use. And that's the real issue, isn't it? How to use the information. Yet it seems that more and more careers are built around information-gathering rather than information-productivity.

The same phenomenon holds for Bible study. The majority of people who study the Scriptures get logjammed in the step of Interpretation. In the first place they begin there, which is a major mistake. And furthermore they stop there, which is an even bigger mistake.

The result is that they acquire mountains of information about the text, and lots of speculation about what it means. But what difference does it make in their lives? The Bible becomes little more than a collection of theological brain-teasers, rather than a road map for how to live.

What a tragedy, because the Word of God does not bear fruit when it is understood, only when it is applied. That's why James exhorts us to "receive the word implanted" (1:21). In other words, let God's truth take root in your life. How? By proving yourself to be a doer of the word, not merely a hearer (v. 22).

Imagine plowing a field, dropping seed in the ground, carefully tending the plants that shoot up, pulling out the weeds, waiting for the rains, and then, just as harvesttime arrives, walking off to do something else. A person would starve pretty quickly doing that. Yet that's what happens if you fail to move on to the next step in the Bible study process, Application. You can go to all the trouble of preparing a rich harvest and yet starve spiritually by neglecting to follow through.

I hope by now that you are hungry to see results in your life. If so, I invite you to move on with me to the next section, where we'll explore some ways to turn biblical investigations into practical applications.

STEP 3
Application

How does it work?

39

THE VALUE OF APPLICATION

A reporter was interviewing renowned psychiatrist Karl Menninger at the famous Menninger clinic in Topeka, Kansas. When the conversation turned to the subject of prison reform, the doctor handed his listener a book he had written on the subject. The reporter politely promised to read it.

"No you won't," Dr. Menninger shot back in his acerbic manner. "Besides, what would you do about it if you did? Put the book down and go on to something else?"

That's exactly the situation confronting people in terms of Bible study. They promise to pick up the Word, but it usually amounts to very little. The real question is this: Even if they did read and study God's Word faithfully, what would they do about? What practical difference would they let it make in their lives?

This is a question you need to ponder as we come to the third step in Bible study, Application. Application is the most neglected yet the most needed stage in the process. Too much Bible study begins and ends in the wrong place: It begins with Interpretation, and it also ends there. But we've learned that you don't start with the question, What does this mean? but rather, What does this say? Furthermore, you don't end the process by asking, What does this mean? but rather, How does this work? Again, not does it work— but how?

Understanding, then, is simply a means to a larger end—practicing biblical truth in day-to-day life. Observation plus interpretation without application equals abortion. In other words, every time you observe and interpret but fail to apply, you perform an abortion on the Scriptures in terms of their purpose. The Bible was not written to satisfy your curiosity; it was written to transform your life. The ultimate goal of Bible study, then, is not to do something to the Bible, but to allow the Bible to do something to you, so truth becomes tangent to life.

You see, we frequently come to the Bible to study it, to teach it, to preach it, to outline it—everything except to be changed by it.

MAKE THE TRUTH ATTRACTIVE

Titus 1:1 provides a clear statement of the purpose of Scripture: Paul describes it as "the truth that leads to godliness" (NIV). Then in chapter 2 he gives a specific case in point.

> Teach slaves to be subject to their masters in everything, to try to please them, not to talk back to them, and not to steal from them, but to show that they can be fully trusted, *so that in every way they will make the teaching about God our Savior attractive.* (V. 9, NIV, italics added)

One translation puts it, "that they may adorn the teachings." In other words, that they would put them on, like a set of clothes. Biblical truth is the wardrobe of the soul. It's much more exclusive than anything you can buy from Nordstrom's, it's always in style, it's thoroughly coordinated, and it's perennially attractive.

Attractive truth is applied truth. A man once told me, "You know, Brother Hendricks, I've been through the Bible twelve times." That's wonderful. But the real question is, how many times has the Bible been through him?

You see, there's an inherent danger in Bible study: it can degenerate into a process that's intellectually fascinating but spiritually frustrating. You can get mentally excited by the truth, yet fail to be morally changed by it. If and when that happens, you know there must be something wrong with your study of the Bible.

Our task, then, is two-sided. First, we must get into the Word of God for ourselves. But then we must allow that Word to get into us, to make a permanent difference in our character and conduct.

In this final section of the book, I want to probe into this third area of Bible study. It's very convicting. Fasten your safety belt, because there's liable to be some turbulence ahead. I want this material to provoke your thinking—not paralyze it.

FOUR SUBSTITUTES FOR APPLICATION

What happens when you fail to apply Scripture? Let me suggest four substitutes for application, four routes which, unfortunately, many Christians take in their study of the Word. Every one of them is a dead-end street.

We substitute interpretation for application

How easy it is to settle for knowledge rather than experience. If you've sat through enough sermons, you've probably heard the bromide, "May the Lord bless this truth to your heart." As one who makes his living teaching people how to preach, I've discovered that this frequently means, "I don't have a clue as to how this passage works in your life."

That's an outrage because according to the Bible, to know and not to do is not to know at all.

Do you remember the tragic story of Kitty Genovese? She was a young lady who was brutally attacked, beaten, raped, and ultimately killed in a fashionable New York City neighborhood. In the aftermath of the crime, reporters interviewed countless neighbors to find out if anyone had any clues. Incredibly, they learned that thirty-eight people had heard Kitty's screams. In fact, several of them had witnessed the attack. But none of them came to her rescue. Only one called the police, and that only after the third and fatal attack.

Kitty Genovese's murder was a watershed in American culture, an event on which sociologists have often reflected: How could we develop a society in which a human being could be attacked so viciously and repeatedly, with the public's knowledge, and yet no one respond with help? That's the tragedy of knowledge that does not create responsibility.

Lack of involvement is not the perspective of the Scriptures. From cover to cover the Bible teaches that the moment you know God's truth, the ball is in your court; you are responsible for putting it into action. That's why Jesus so often said that to whom much has been given, much will be required (Matthew 13:12; Luke 12:48). Or, to His disciples, "Why do you call Me 'Lord, Lord,' and do not do what I say?" (Luke 6:46). Implication: either stop calling me "Lord," or start doing what I tell you.

On another occasion, Jesus said, "Many will say to Me in that day [referring to the final judgment], 'Lord, Lord [note the accurate terminology], have we not done many wonderful things in your name?'" (Matthew 7:22). Jesus never denied that they had. But He rejects them nonetheless: "I never knew you, depart from me."

What does that mean? He never knew them cognitively? No, that would be heresy. Jesus Christ was omniscient; He knew everything that was going on. But He was talking about relational knowledge: "I never knew you in terms of a personal relationship."

The classic illustration of interpretation without application is the scribes and Pharisees. These religionists had all of the data. They had mastered the Old Testament, but they were never mastered by the truth. Did they know where the Messiah was to be born? Absolutely. They were authorities on that: Bethlehem of Judea, of course. But when the report came, did they go down to check it out? No, even though the town was only only five miles down the road.

Unfortunately, their knowledge created no responsibility within them. No wonder Jesus said in Matthew 5:20, "Unless your righteousness surpasses that of the scribes and Pharisees, you shall not enter the kingdom." Why not? Because all of their righteousness was external. It was based on facts. It never led to a personal response.

I think the danger is well-expressed in James 4:17: "Anyone, then, who knows the good he ought to do and doesn't do it, sins." How does that grab you? The person who knows the truth but doesn't act on it is not simply making a mistake—making a poor judgment—he is in sin. In God's mind, knowledge without obedience is sin.

We substitute superficial obedience for substantive life-change

This is even more common than the problem we just looked at. Can you identify with it? Here, we apply biblical truth to areas where we're already applying it, not to new areas where we're not applying it. Result: no noticeable change in our lives.

For example, say a man in the business world comes across Ephesians 4:25, which deals with the issue of honesty: "Therefore, laying aside falsehood, speak truth, each one of you, with his neighbor, for we are members of one another."

Pretty clear, isn't it? So what does he do? He thinks of all the areas where he's already honest. For instance, he's honest with his wife; he wouldn't think of lying to her. Likewise, he shoots straight with his children; they can always count on Dad to give them the true story. He's honest with his associates at work; people trust him. When he reads Ephesians 4:25, he thinks of all of these areas in which he is already obeying that truth and pats himself on the back. "Am I speaking the truth with other people?" he asks himself. "You bet."

But meanwhile he overlooks the fact that he's only partially honest with his competitors. He never even thinks of that area. It remains a blind spot for him, with the result that the truth never affects that part of his life.

What would happen if he ever did evaluate his honesty in that regard? He would likely take the third route...

We substitute rationalization for repentance

Most of us have a built-in early-warning system against spiritual change. The moment truth gets too close, too convicting, an alarm goes off, and we start to defend ourselves. Our favorite strategy is to rationalize sin instead of repenting of it.

How would this work for the businessman struggling with the issue of honesty? Well, he rationalizes his lack of integrity. He can't avoid the reality that he lies to get ahead, so he says, "OK, I admit it. I fudge here and there with my competitors. But you've got to understand. They're all non-Christians. They all lie. I mean, you can't expect me to be lily-white when I have to compete against a group like that. I have to work in the real world. I think you should be as honest as you can, but face it—that's just the way the game is played." The bottom line is, he doesn't change. Worst of all, he feels completely comfortable about it.

How do I know? Because one time a man had me to his house for dinner and boasted—in the presence of his children, unfortunately— with how he had ripped off the government for $500 on his taxes. Of course, he didn't get the response from me that he expected. So he pulled out an article he had clipped from the paper on how the government had lost $5 million on some fiasco in Oklahoma.

"Imagine that, five million dollars!" he said. "When the government stops wasting money like that, I'll start paying my extra five hundred."

But that still didn't persuade me. So he changed his approach. "I gave all the money to missions," he said rather piously.

I thought, *I'm sure God must be impressed.*

That's what I call a finely woven system of rationalization.

The older you get, the more experienced you become at doing this. You build up a reservoir of responses so that whenever the truth gets too convicting, you've got sixteen reasons why it applies to everyone but you.

We substitute an emotional experience for a volitional decision

In other words, we study the Word of God, we emote under impact — but we make no real change. There's nothing wrong with responding emotionally to spiritual truth. In fact, believers could stand a lot more of it today. But if that's our only response — if all we do is water our handkerchiefs and sob a few mournful prayers, then go merrily on our way without altering our behavior in the slightest — then our spirituality boils down to nothing more than a vapid emotional experience.

When I speak in a church, I often have to endure what I call the "glorification of the worm" ceremony. That's what takes place at the door of the church after the service. The people come by and shake my hand and say, "Oh, Brother Hendricks, that was a wonderful sermon. It was like listening to Paul." I've had people come by with tears rolling down their cheeks, saying, "You really got to me today. [Sniffle.] I really appreciated that. Thanks a lot." They're really broken up. Yet what do they do? Go home to watch a ball game. There's no change.

The point is, they've had an emotional response to a sermon. But will they ever have a volitional response to God's truth? Will they ever make substantive, fundamental, life-changing decisions based on what the Scriptures say?

Fortunately, every now and then I run into a rare phenomenon — genuine change in response to biblical truth. When that happens, I never forget it.

I was preaching once on the importance of evangelism in one's sphere of influence — developing relationships, cultivating friendships, winning a hearing. Afterward, when I got to the back, I heard all of the usual polite palaver. But finally a young couple came by, and I knew they were for real. They shook my hand warmly and said, "Thanks. Thanks very much. We will never be the same again. Thanks for being the instrument that the Holy Spirit used."

They went home, got lunch for their kids, put them down for a nap, came into their living room, opened up their Bibles to the passage I had expounded that morning, read it over, thought it through in terms of its implications for their lives, got down on their knees, and began to pray, "Lord, give us a burden for our neighbors."

When they got up from their knees, they looked out the front window. They saw their neighbor mowing his lawn, going back and forth, back and forth. The man looked at his wife and said, "Are you getting the same message I am?"

"Yes," she said, "we really need to get to know those people."

So the fellow went over and engaged his neighbor in conversation. Finally he suggested, "Hey, how about coming over to the house for a steak fry this week? Wednesday all right?"

"Sure," the surprised neighbor said. "I'd love to do that."

And that's what they did. In fact, that launched a process that has continued to this day: a steady stream of men, women, and young people have come to Christ through the relationships and impact of that couple. They were not satisfied with just being exposed to the truth of God or convicted by it; they were changed by it. They made a volitional decision in response to what they heard God saying. And that's where real change always begins—in the will.

A LOOK IN THE MIRROR

The apostle James asks a penetrating question in the first chapter of his book: Does the Word work? Answer: Yes, it does, if it is *received* (v. 21). He uses an interesting word. It basically means to put out a welcome mat. Do you welcome the truth into your life? Do you invite it in the door and let it do its work on you?

You see, when we leave church on Sunday morning, the issue is not, what did that preacher say, but rather what are you going to do as a result of what he said? But often we hear a sermon or go to a Bible study and hear a tremendous lesson—very convicting—and what do we do? We walk away from it and say, "When's the next Bible study?"

James says, "Look, you've got to embrace biblical truth." And he offers an interesting illustration to make his point—the analogy of the mirror (vv. 23-25). Most of us spend considerable time in front of a mirror every day, making the most of whatever we've got to work with. James talks about a person who does just the opposite.

"Good night," a guy says, looking in the mirror. "I'd better shave. I'd better rearrange my remaining hairs." But after noticing all of that, he walks off and does nothing.

He goes down to the office, and pretty soon his boss walks in and says, "Hey, man, don't you have any razor blades?"

"Just bought a fresh supply at the Cut-Throat Drugstore," he says.

"Well, you'd better do something about that stubble," the manager warns, "or you won't be long in the employ of this company."

That's the situation James is describing. When you look in the mirror and see that your face is dirty, your hair needs to be combed, and your teeth need to be brushed, yet you walk away and do nothing—that's exactly what you do every time you study the Word of God but are not changed by it.

There's an alternative: "But one who looks intently at the perfect law, the law of liberty and abides by it, not having become a forgetful hearer but an effectual doer, this man shall be blessed in what he does" (v. 25).

All of us want the blessing of God. But are we responding to the revelation of God? Turn with me to the next chapter, and we'll look at four ways to do that.

40

FOUR STEPS IN APPLICATION

Many Christians are like poor photographs—overexposed and underdeveloped. They've had plenty of input from the Word of God, but what difference has it made in their lives? Spiritual growth is a commitment to change. And yet, the human heart resists nothing as strongly as it resists change. We will do anything to avoid it.

In this chapter I want to suggest a means of overcoming the bias toward spiritual inertia. There is a four-step process of Application, four principles that I've reduced to four words, not to oversimplify things but to provide some handles to work with. They will help you apply Scripture in any circumstance.

STEP 1: KNOW

If you want to apply the Bible, you need to know two things.

Know the text

First, you've got to know the interpretation of the biblical text. Application is based on interpretation, so if your interpretation of a passage is erroneous, your application will likely be erroneous. If your interpretation is correct, you have a possibility that your application will be correct.

Here's a statement to keep frontal in your thinking: *Interpretation is one; application is many.* There is only one ultimate interpretation of a passage of Scripture. The text doesn't mean one thing today and something else tomorrow. Whatever it means, it means forever. But you will never cease the process of applying that truth to your life. Implication: Be careful how you interpret. You will only multiply error if you start with a faulty interpretation.

A friend of mine once offered to fly me to Canada in his company's jet. I had a tight schedule to meet, and he wanted to take me. So we climbed into the cockpit, and of course before we could take off we had to set up all the instruments, especially our flight plan.

I asked him, "What happens if you're off a couple of degrees?"

He said, "Remember Korean Airlines 007?" I nodded as I thought back to that chilling incident. A jumbo jet had flown hundreds of miles off its intended course, violating Russian airspace. A Russian fighter intercepted it and shot it out of the sky. "That's what happens," my pilot friend said grimly. "A couple of degrees off here can take us miles away from our destination."

The same is true in Bible study. It's what I call "the error of the fork." Suppose you're coming down the road in biblical interpretation and you come to a thorny interpretational problem. For illustration's sake, let's say that there are two possible interpretations: interpretation A and interpretation B. Suppose that A is actually the correct one; but you choose B. Then the further down the road you go, the more divergent your application becomes from biblical truth.

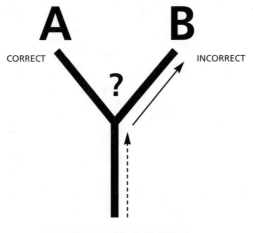

THE ERROR OF THE FORK

In short, the better you understand a passage, the better you'll be able to use it.

Know yourself

Not only must you know the interpretation, you must know yourself. In 1 Timothy 4:16, Paul warns Timothy, "Pay close attention to yourself and to your teaching." Notice the order: Pay attention to yourself, first; then to the communication of that truth to others. Why? Because if you don't know yourself, it's difficult to help other people apply the Bible to their lives.

In fact, one of the main reasons application is not more effective with many people is, frankly, they really don't know themselves. How about you? Let me give you two questions. First, What are your assets? What have you got going for you? Could you write down your three greatest assets on a three-by-five-inch card right now? (In my experience most people have a hard time doing that.) Second, What are your liabilities? What are your limitations? What is your greatest hindrance to growth?

Now put these two together, and you'll see the value in application. If you know your assets, it will develop your confidence. If you know your liabilities, it will develop your faith. Your assets tell you what God has done for you. Your liabilities tell you what God needs to develop in you. The reason most of us don't grow more is that we really don't know what we need.

Romans 12:3 offers insight here: "For by the grace given me I say to every one of you: Do not think of yourself more highly than you ought, but rather think of yourself with sober judgment, in accordance with the measure of faith God has given you" (NIV). Sometimes we have an exaggerated opinion of ourselves. Other times we have a distorted opinion. Paul says, "Don't! Don't get a puffed up idea of who you are. But make sure you don't dump on yourself, either." Every time you dump on yourself, you're doing the devil's work—and he doesn't need your help. He's a specialist in that.

Insight, then, is the first step toward spiritual growth—insight into the passage, and insight into yourself.

STEP 2: RELATE

Once we know the truth of the Word of God, we must relate it to our experience. In fact, Christianity is best understood as a series of new relationships. The biblical pattern for that is 2 Corinthians

Take a Spiritual Inventory

Do you want to apply God's Word to your life? Start by knowing yourself. To help you do that, Doug Sherman of Career Impact Ministries has developed an inventory that reviews your habits and behaviors in light of God's expectations in at least five broad areas of life. Here are few questions to consider.

In your personal life:

- What is the status of your spiritual disciplines—disciplines well-known to correlate with spiritual growth, such as Bible study, Scripture memory, prayer, or the reading of devotional literature?
- What about your physical condition and habits of eating, exercise, sleep, and rest?
- What behaviors do you especially desire to overcome: a temper, or deception, or sexual lust?
- What behaviors do you especially desire to establish: patience, or hospitality, or perseverance?

In your family life:

- Do you have a set come-home time from work that your family can count on?
- Do you "date" your spouse regularly?
- Do you disengage emotionally from work and chores in order to spend unimpeded time involved with your children?
- Are you upholding your responsibilities to your parents? To your spouse's parents? To other relatives?

In your church life:

- How often do you place yourself under the instruction of Scripture?
- Do you faithfully, generously, and joyfully donate money to the cause of Christ?
- Are you praying regularly for your pastor and other church leaders?
- Do you know what your spiritual gift is, and are you using it?

In your work:

- Do you give an honest day's labor to your employer?
- Do you follow through on commitments you make to your customers?
- Do you read and otherwise stay up on new developments, ideas, and methods in your field?
- To the extent that you can, do you hold a steady job by which your needs and those of your family are being adequately met?
- Do you have a family budget? Do you stick within it?

In your community:

- Do you regularly exercise your right and responsibility as a citizen to cast an informed vote?
- Do you pay your fair share of taxes?
- What is the status of your driving record?
- Do you maintain your property within the statutes of your community?
- Are you in any way conscious of and involved with the poor and their needs?

There are scores of other questions that could be asked. The point of such an inventory is to help you evaluate yourself critically to determine areas in which you need to grow spiritually. All of these specific applications flow out of specific Bible passages and biblical principles.

Suggestion: Ask someone who knows you well, such as your spouse or a close friend, to go through this inventory and give their own evaluation of how they think you measure up in each area. Then compare your responses. This is a great way to achieve objectivity and make this exercise more useful.

Adapted from Doug Sherman and William Hendricks, *Your Work Matters to God* (Colorado Springs: Navpress, 1987), pp. 232-33.

5:17: "Therefore if any man is in Christ, he is a new creature; the old things passed away; behold, new things have come."

When you become a Christian, Jesus Christ moves into your life—right to the center. Once there, He affects every area. He improves your home life: you become more sensitive as a partner, as a parent, as a person. He strengthens your thought life: your mind dwells on constructive things, you develop wider interests, and you cultivate more godly values. He renovates your social life: your relationships with friends and associates change as you begin to treat them with Christlikeness.

Christ even affects your sex life. You know, most people don't have a clue that Jesus Christ designed sex, which makes Him the only one who knows how it truly functions. Some may be embarrassed to talk about it, but He was not embarrassed to create it. He wants to create healthy intimacy in your life, to make it new and clean and honorable to God.

What about your business life, your vocational life? People talk about "Christian businesspeople." No, they are not Christian businesspeople; they are businesspeople who happen to be Christians. Unfortunately, many have never related biblical truth to their life in the workplace.

Jesus Christ wants to renew every area of your life. That's why Christian growth is a process—a dynamic process. Every day I wake up and realize that there are still areas of my life over which the Lord does not have control. So a Christian is a person who is maladjusted to the status quo (which has been well defined as "the mess we're currently in"). So I've got to come to the Word of God throughout my lifetime. Spiritual growth is a long-term process. And unless I heed the Word of God, I'll never arrive at the goal of Christlikeness.

The Working Word
Once you realize that Jesus Christ wants to impact your life in a profound way, you need to look for areas in which to relate the Word to life. I like to see these in terms of what I call the "Working Word." In Observation and Interpretation, you come up with new insights—things that you've never seen before. These new insights effect a series of new relationships.

A new relationship to God. He's now your heavenly Father. You have a personal and intimate relationship with Him. He's provided

His Son for your salvation and the Holy Spirit to help you grow and accomplish His purposes.

A new relationship to yourself. You develop a new self-image. Why, if God loves you, if Christ died for you, if the Holy Spirit has gifted and empowered you, that means you have tremendous value and significance. Your life takes on new meaning and purpose.

A new relationship to other people. You discover that other people are not the enemy. They may be victims of the enemy, but they are the people that God has placed in your life. He calls you to treat them with Christlikeness.

A new relationship to the enemy. Please note: Once you come to Christ, you change sides in the battle. Before, you were just a pawn of the enemy. He moved you around wherever he wanted you to go. You had no idea that you were duped by him. But now you discover that you're on God's side. Believe me, the enemy is none too happy about that. That's why your Christian life will remain a constant battle.

The new insights that you gain from Scripture need to be applied in all of these areas of relationships. Notice how that takes place.

The Word exposes your sin. Remember 2 Timothy 3:16? Scripture has a reproving and corrective function. It tells you when you are out-of-bounds in order to clean out the sin from your life.

The Word gives you God's promises. It tells you what you can expect from God and what you can rely on Him to do. That is incredibly comforting when you're facing circumstances that are beyond you.

The Word gives you God's commands. Just as there are promises in Scripture, so there are conditions to be met. Commands and principles are laid down that lead toward health and life.

The Word gives you examples to follow. I like to study the biographies in Scripture, the stories of people who lived their lives before God. That's where the Scripture becomes real. Some offer a positive example, and those are the ones I want to follow. Others present a negative example that I need to avoid.

Using the Working Word, Jesus Christ produces life-change for those who want to apply biblical truth. Is that true of you? A good test is this: Has someone who has known you very, very well over a period of time ever said, "Hey, what makes you so different? I used to know you, but you're not the same person. Something has happened in your life." What explanation could you give? Would it be that Christ has moved into your life?

In short, What is there in your life that you cannot explain on any basis other than the supernatural?

STEP 3: MEDITATE

When I was a younger man, I came to a point in my life where I was the finest candidate for somebody's psychopathic ward that you've ever seen. The boys in the white coats were just about to back up the wagon and take me away, when a friend of mine, an executive, learned of my plight.

He flew to Dallas at his own expense and spent three days with me. Everything I did, he did. Everywhere I went, he went. He listened to every conversation, sat in on every class, even lived in my home. Finally, at the end of that period, he gave me his diagnosis: "Howie, your problem is that you are behind in your think time."

You know, if I had given him $20,000 I don't think I would have paid him enough for that insight. What he was telling me was that I was letting so many things occupy my attention that I wasn't allowing myself time apart to process it all. Eventually I had become overwhelmed.

What my friend was describing is really the habit of meditation. That has become a lost art in contemporary society, except, of course, among adherents of Eastern mysticism. I'm talking about something completely different from mental gymnastics that seek to empty the mind. True meditation is pondering the truth with a view to letting it help and readjust our lives. Since most of us are active, busy people, we're likely to conclude that meditation was a nice thing for an earlier generation of believers, but it really has no relevance in our day and age.

Wrong. We already saw in chapter 14 that meditation is useful in the step of Observation. It is absolutely essential to the step of Application. Remember Joshua 1:8 and Psalm 1:1-2? Both of those passages said that the key to spiritual prosperity is to meditate on the Word *day and night*. In other words, we're to weave Scripture into the fabric of everyday living.

My wife makes a soup that I can hardly resist. It takes her hours to make it. She starts it in the morning, and pretty soon our house is filled with a delightful aroma—and I just drool, ready to gobble it down. But she says, "Not yet. Wait until supper." I call it her Enthusiastic Soup—she throws everything she's got into it. It makes store-bought soup taste like dishwater.

How does the soup become that good? She leaves it on the back burner over a slow, simmering fire, until all of the flavors begin to mingle and make it delightful to the taste. What have you got on the back burner? What's cooking in your mind? Are you taking advantage of the benefits of biblical meditation?

"But I have a hard time thinking," someone will say.

No, the problem is that you're starving your brain. You're not providing it with any fuel. You see, there's a direct link between meditation and memory. Memory provides the mind with the fuel it needs to make meditation profitable.

One of the regrets I have as I reflect back on my spiritual journey is that I did not memorize more Scripture as a young person. Eventually, though, I got into the "Topical Memory System," a set of memory cards produced by the Navigators. It's available in the King James, the NIV, the *New American Standard*, any translation you want. The program helps you memorize two verses a week. That's really not much. But stop to think: do that for fifty weeks during a year and you'll have one hundred verses of Scriptures under your belt.

Can that make a difference in your life? Not long after I began a program of Bible memorization, I had to have surgery. The surgery went fine, but I contracted an infection afterward. And it was the type of thing where I wasn't sure whether I was going to live or die, but I almost wanted to pass on. I found that there was only one thing that sustained me during that period—the Word of God that I had committed to memory. That experience convinced me that memory is the key to meditation. And meditation is the key to changing my outlook.

STEP 4: PRACTICE

The ultimate goal of Bible study is to practice the truth. Scripture was written not to fatten geese but to train athletes and equip soldiers for the realities of life. "Run to win." "Fight to win." That's the message of the Word.

You can't consciously apply every truth you find in your study, but you can consistently apply something. So you always want to ask yourself, *Is there some area of my life for which this truth is needed?*

Let me give you a personal illustration. Philippians 2:14 is a convicting verse: "Do everything without complaining or arguing" (NIV). Maybe that's no problem for you, but for me that's an extremely difficult verse. In fact, I wish I could just skip from verse 13 to verse 15. But there's that little convicting verse right in the middle.

You see, there are many areas in my life where complaining and arguing pose no problem. For instance, teaching. I love to teach. I live to teach. To me, the greatest thing in life is teaching. I'd probably even pay to teach. But the verse says, "Do *everything* without complaining"— not just teaching.

So "everything," for me, includes correspondence. I hate writing letters with about the same passion as I love teaching. But eventually it piles up, and I have little choice but to get after it. So that's an area where I can apply Philippians 2:14. The verse doesn't say I have to like correspondence; it just says I need to learn to do it without complaining and arguing about it.

That may seem to be an inconsequential thing. But there's nothing inconsequential about the changes that God wants to bring about in your life and mine. He's given the Word to transform our experience. And I assure you, your hunger for that Word will be in direct proportion to your obedience to it. In fact, there's a cycle: The more you understand it, the more you use it; and the more you use it, the more you want to understand it. Both are necessary.

In the end, you'll always find two sides to Christian living: you need food, and you need exercise. Too much food leads to obesity. Too little food develops anemia. But food is transformed into energy, and energy enables you to do that which God wants you to do. Yet in the process, you become exhausted and tired. You lose your perspective. So you've got to come back to the Word of God for refreshment. Remember that the Word of God experienced is the Word of God enjoyed.

You Try It

There is a direct correlation between meditation and memorization. The more Scripture you memorize, the more you'll have to meditate on.

Unfortunately, Bible memorization has frequently received a bad press. Actually, memorization itself has received a bad press. Many of us can remember grade school, where we were forced to memorize mindless facts and figures in subjects such as history and arithmetic. Once we graduated from that exercise, we swore we'd never do it again!

But if God promises to bless our lives as the result of meditation (Joshua 1:8; Psalm 1), and if meditation is dependent on memorization, then perhaps we'd better take a second look. I've recommended the "Topical Memory System" published by the Navigators. But here's a little exercise to get you started. Memorize Psalm 100 (NIV):

A psalm. For giving thanks.

^{1}Shout for joy to the Lord, all the earth.
^{2} Worship the Lord with gladness;
   come before him with joyful songs.
^{3}Know that the Lord is God.
   It is he who made us, and we are his;
   we are his people, the sheep of his pasture.
^{4}Enter his gates with thanksgiving
   and his courts with praise;
   give thanks to him and praise his name.
^{5}For the Lord is good and his love endures forever;
   his faithfulness continues through all generations.

This psalm is only five verses long. It's a great psalm to meditate on, because it lifts up your heart in joy before the Lord. It confidently affirms God's faithful character. Here are some suggestionsy:

1. Read and study the psalm using Observation and Interpretation.
2. Read the psalm repeatedly, using the NIV translation above.
3. Concentrate on memorizing one verse at a time, over several days. For instance, the first day, memorize verse 1. Read it several times. Then repeat it to yourself several times. After an hour or so, see if you can remember it. Continue to review it throughout the day. Then the next day, tackle verse 2 in the

same manner, only repeat verse 1 in addition to verse 2. Keep adding verses throughout the week.

4. Repeat what you have memorized out loud to a friend or family member. Have the person check the passage to make sure you have it down word-perfect!

5. If you have the talent, put the psalm to music and sing it. (Most of the psalms were originally sung, not read.)

6. Keep reviewing the psalm in your mind over the next few weeks, until you are certain that it is lodged in your brain.

What is the process of life-change all about? It begins with the Word of God. The Bible is God's divine means of bringing change into our lives. But notice, the Word must first change my life. Then it can begin to change my world. You see, when God's truth changes my life, I can become a change element in my sphere of influence. Have you ever asked yourself, *How can I bring about change in my society?* The only way to bring about permanent and significant change is by changing individuals.

41

NINE QUESTIONS TO ASK

E arlier, when we studied the step of Observation, I said that one of the things to do with any passage of Scripture is to bombard the text with questions. The same is true when it comes to Application. So here are nine applicational questions you can ask whenever you come to the Word:

1. Is there an example for me to follow?

Have you noticed how much of the Bible is biographical? That's not an accident; it's by design. God fills His Word with people because nothing helps the truth come alive the way people do.

The challenge, of course, is to draw parallels between your situation and that of the character you are studying. Consider Abraham in Genesis 18. The Lord reveals to him that He is about to destroy Sodom and Gomorrah, where Abraham's nephew, Lot, lives with his family. So Abraham pleads with the Lord not to destroy Sodom, if he can find enough righteous people living there.

Not too many people have come to me and said, "Hendricks, God told me He's going to destroy such-and-such a city unless we can find ten righteous people living there." If someone did tell me that, I'd be wondering what looney bin he escaped from.

So does that mean there's nothing for me to apply from Genesis 18? No, Abraham is an outstanding model of compassionate prayer on behalf of wicked people. There he is on his knees, begging the Lord to spare them from judgment. So I have to ask, is that the kind of prayer I'm praying for the people around me? Or am I sort of hoping that God will remove all those "evil pagans" out there?

2. Is there a sin to avoid?

One of the values of the Word is that it raises your consciousness in regard to moral issues. Before I became a believer, I did things that if somebody had told me were sin, I'd have said, "You gotta be kidding." I had an altogether different standard of right and wrong.

It was only when I came to Christ and began reading Scripture that I learned what sin really is. It was like my friend who told me, "Man, I didn't even know I had a bad marriage until I became a Christian. I thought that was how everybody lived. Then I read Ephesians five and began to realize how trashed up my marriage really was."

3. Is there a promise to claim?

God's Word is filled with promises—promises that are made by the Person who does not lie and who is totally capable of fulfilling them. Remember our study of Nehemiah 1? Nehemiah claimed God's promise concerning the restoration of the land if the people would confess and repent of their sin. God honored His word. He even used Nehemiah as part of the answer to prayer.

Of course, not all of the promises in Scripture are given to you and me. Some promises God made to certain individuals, not to people in general. Others he made to groups of people, such as the nation of Israel. We can't claim promises that haven't been made to us. But we can certainly claim promises made to the church, as well as those made to "the righteous" in Proverbs and other portions of the wisdom literature.

4. Is there a prayer to repeat?

Abraham teaches us something about prayer in Genesis 18. So does Nehemiah. I encourage you to make a study of the great prayers in Scripture: for example, David's prayer of confession in Psalm 51; Hannah's prayer of thanksgiving after the birth of Samuel (1 Samuel 2:1-10); Jonah's prayer from the belly of the fish (Jonah 2); Mary's prayer in Luke 1:46-55; Paul's prayer for the Ephesians in Ephesians 3:14-21; Jesus' prayer in the Garden of Gethsemane (Matthew 26:36-46; Mark 14:32-42; Luke 22:39-46); and the Lord's Prayer, which is really the Disciples' Prayer, and in fact, our prayer (Matthew 6:5-15).

As you study those passages, ask yourself, *What is there in these prayers that I need to be praying?*

5. Is there a command to obey?

The Bible is filled with potent, clear-cut commands. There are fifty-four in the book of James alone. Likewise, the "applicational" sections of Paul's epistles—Romans 12-15, Galatians 5-6, Ephesians 4-6, Colossians 3-4—are primarily exhortation.

A wise, old scholar was once asked how to determine the will of God. His response was simple: "Ninety-five percent of the will of God is revealed in the commands of Scripture. If you spend your time attending to those, you won't have much trouble working out the other five percent."

6. Is there a condition to meet?

Many of the promises of God are based on conditions set forth in the text. For instance, Jesus said, "If you abide in Me, and My words abide in you, ask whatever you wish, and it shall be done for you" (John 15:7). Do you notice the conditions? "If you abide in Me, and [if] My words abide in you." Jesus makes an incredible promise: "Ask whatever you wish, and it shall be done for you." But the conditions must be met.

7. Is there a verse to memorize?

Obviously, any verse of Scripture can be memorized. But some will carry more significance for you than others. That's why I highly recommend that you launch a Bible memorization program. Perhaps you can use something such as the "Topical Memory System" that I mentioned in the last chapter. After you complete that, you can develop your own list of verses that have become personal and meaningful to you.

I also encourage you to memorize larger portions of the Word. When my sons were just boys, they had a Sunday school teacher who recognized the value of Bible memory. He used to sponsor contests to see how much Scripture they could memorize. Eventually they were memorizing entire chapters of the Bible, such as Psalm 1, Isaiah 53, and even John 14. Word-perfect, too. So it is possible. And the benefits are immeasurable.

8. Is there an error to mark?

One of the positive developments that I've observed among Christians during my lifetime has been a renewed emphasis on people and relationships. That's what the outworking of biblical truth ought to produce—love and concern for people and their needs.

However, during the same period I've observed an unfortunate loss of basic theological and doctrinal knowledge. Many Christians have fuzzy thinking when it comes to fundamental building blocks of the faith such as the resurrection, the virgin birth, the inerrancy of Scripture, and the ministry of the Holy Spirit. As a result, they are sitting ducks for theological error.

Personal Bible study can help to turn that around. As you investigate God's Word, ask yourself: *What doctrines and truths is this passage teaching? What theological errors is it exposing?* And then: *What changes do I need to make in my thinking in order to bring it in line with what the Scriptures teach?*

9. Is there a challenge to face?

Have you ever read a portion of the Bible and felt convicted that you needed to act on the basis of what you've read? The Spirit of God will prompt that. When you read the Word, He'll challenge you to respond in some area of your life, or in some situation that you are facing. Perhaps it's a relationship that needs to be healed. Perhaps it's an apology that needs to be made. Maybe you need to get out of something that is drawing you away from God. Or maybe there's a habit you need to start cultivating. Whatever it is, the Spirit uses Scripture to promote changes in your life.

The question is, are you open to such change? Are you prepared to take on His challenges? I guarantee that if you approach God's Word with any degree of honesty and teachability, the Spirit won't let you go away disappointed.

You Try It

The nine questions listed in this chapter are ones that you should make a habit of asking every time you come to the Word of God. But I want to give you a little practice in using them on a lengthy section from the gospel by Luke.

Beginning in 14:25 and continuing through 17:10, Jesus gives a series of parables and instructions. The key to understanding the context is to observe that three groups of people are listening to Jesus—great multitudes (14:25) that include numerous ne'er-do-wells (15:1), the disciples (16:1; 17:1), and the Pharisees (16:14). Use the skills of Observation and Interpretation that we've looked at to understand this portion of the New Testament. Then answer the nine questions, based on the text:

1. Is there an example for me to follow?
2. Is there a sin to avoid?
3. Is there a promise to claim?
4. Is there a prayer to repeat?
5. Is there a command to obey?
6. Is there a condition to meet?
7. Is there a verse to memorize?
8. Is there an error to mark?
9. Is there a challenge to face?

42

NOW AND THEN

Remember Ken back in chapter 1? Ken has the highest possible regard for the Bible. If you ask him whether it's the revealed Word of God, he'll say, "Absolutely." Is it authoritative for belief and practice? "Without question."

But guess what happens when Ken goes to work? He leaves the Word at home—not just physically but mentally. He doesn't mean to slight the Scriptures. But the truth is, it never occurs to him that they might have something to say about the way he conducts his business. Why? Because he perceives the Bible to be irrelevant in that context. "The business world is no Sunday school class," he told me. "You're up against things that aren't even mentioned in the Bible. So it doesn't exactly apply to your day-to-day situation."

Ken is hardly alone. Noted pollster George Gallup, Jr. has found that only 57 percent of Americans now believe that "religion can answer today's problems." That's a drop from 81 percent in 1957. At the same time, those who think religion is hopelessly out of date have grown from 7 percent to 20 percent. No wonder another Gallup poll concludes that there is "no significant difference" between the churched and the unchurched in their ethics and values on the job.

What about you? Do you feel like your faith is about as relevant as a hymnal when it comes to work and other matters of day-to-day life? Or are you among the many who would like to apply their faith to the issues of today but can't figure out how to go about it? After all, you don't find the burning topics of our society addressed in the ancient pages of Scripture. So how can you make the connection?

Let me suggest that the place to start is with context—both the original context of Scripture and the contemporary context in which we live. Context makes a profound difference in how a person applies biblical truth.

NEVER-CHANGING TRUTH IN AN EVER-CHANGING WORLD

Remember Genesis 2:24, where God set up the marriage institution?

> For this cause a man shall leave his father and his mother, and shall cleave to his wife; and they shall become one flesh.

What must Adam and Eve's marriage have looked like before the Fall? Imagine the level of communication, trust, partnership, and intimacy they must have experienced. But then they sinned. Now they have a new set of dynamics to contend with—mistrust, selfishness, pride, and lust. Yet God leaves intact the expectation to live as one flesh. That's a whole new context.

Jump ahead to Moses as he relates the Genesis account to the people of Israel. They are coming out of Egypt, where polygamy is common. For that matter, even Israel's own patriarchs had concubines. What does a one-flesh relationship look like, given that legacy? Again, a change in the context.

Later we find Jesus discussing marriage with the Pharisees (Matthew 19:1-9). By that time divorce had become common. The pressing question was how a man could get out of marriage, not stay in it. Yet Jesus cites Genesis 2 to reinforce the sanctity of the marriage bond. Apparently His words shocked His listeners. "If that's what marriage is all about, then why get married?" the disciples ask incredulously. The same biblical truth but a completely different context.

Later Paul writes to the Ephesians. Perhaps the wealthiest of all the Roman cities, Ephesus was the Orlando of its day, the tourist capital of the first-century world. By the time Paul arrived on the scene (Acts 19), marriage had fallen into a sorry state, particularly among the wealthy. Remarking on the women of his day, the Roman philosopher Seneca quipped, "They divorce in order to re-marry. They marry in order to divorce."[1] His equally cynical son defined a faithful married woman as one who only had two lovers.[2]

Paul had already caused one full-scale riot in Ephesus with his new and strange teachings (Acts 19:23-41). Now he astounds the young Ephesian believers with his letter. Like Jesus, he quotes Genesis 2:24 and then says, "[Husbands] each one of you also must love his wife as he loves himself, and the wife must respect her husband" (5:33, NIV). How does a couple pursue a one-flesh relationship in the context of first-century Ephesus?

For that matter, what does biblical marriage look like in the context of the twenty-first century? More than half of all new marriages are ending in divorce today. Sexual infidelity is on the rise, despite the ever-mounting incidence of AIDS and other sexually transmitted diseases. Two-thirds of married couples with children have a dual-income arrangement, with all of the demands that places on their time and emotional energies. More and more find themselves with blended families and the peculiar relational dynamics they create. How does a couple practice one-flesh marriage in today's cultural climate?

The point is that the Word of God is eternal and unchanging, but our world is not. Therefore, living out God's truth demands that we plug it into our particular set of circumstances. But please note: We do not change the truth to fit our cultural agenda. Rather, we change our application of the truth in light of our needs.

CONTEXT, CONTEXT, CONTEXT

How can that happen? How can we take a message that was written down in 100 A.D. or earlier and make use of it in 2100 A.D. and later? The key is the context. What was the context then? What is the context now?

We saw the importance of context to Interpretation. Now we discover its importance to Application. We've got to understand the ancient culture. The more we know about the culture in which a passage was written and to which it was originally applied, the more

1. Jérôme Carcopino, *Daily Life in Ancient Rome:The People and the City at the Height of the Empire* (New Haven: Yale, 1940) p. 100.
2. Will Durant, *Caesar and Christ: A History of Roman Civilization and of Christianity from Their Beginnings to A.D. 325* (New York: Simon & Schuster, 1944) p. 370.

accurate will be our understanding and the more we'll be able to make use of it in our own cultural setting.

But that's not all. We also must understand our own culture. Just as we seek insight into the ancient context, we need to seek insight into our own. Where are the pressure points? Where are we especially in need of biblical truth? What are the cultural dynamics that make the practice of truth difficult, and seemingly impossible at times? What influences our spiritual attitudes and behavior? What would the apostles be saying to us if they were writing to our churches today? Where would Christ be active if He walked among us now?

It's interesting that when David was putting together his army to establish a kingdom, he recruited the sons of Issachar. The text describes them as "men who understood the times, with knowledge of what Israel should do" (1 Chronicles 12:32). We could use a lot more sons of Issachar in the Body of Christ today—people who understand both the Word and the world, people who know what God wants them to do in their society, people who are not only biblical but contemporary as well.

STUDYING CULTURE

However, understanding our culture is not as easy as one might think. Just because we live in this society doesn't mean we're aware of how it operates. In fact, most of us go about our lives oblivious to the forces that influence us. We could stand to make a study of our culture, just as we study the cultures of the biblical world.

So I want to suggest a host of questions to ask as you evaluate today's cultural context. They are little more than the six keys to observation that we saw earlier: Who? What? Where? When? Why? Wherefore? We've seen how to use them to study societies in the ancient world. But they also apply to the modern situation.

Of course, the problem in asking those questions about our own setting is the tendency to settle for superficial answers. Remember, one of the killers in Bible study is the attitude, "I know that. I've already seen that. I've got that one under my belt." The same is true in studying one's own society. Never think that you completely understand the world in which you live.

There are many more issues to consider, but these will get you started.

Power

Where are the centers of power? Who is in charge? How do they gain control? How do they hold sway? How effective are they at maintaining control? Where are the challenges to their authority? Who makes decisions for our society as a whole? Who makes decisions at the local and individual level?

Communication

What are the means of communication? How is news and information distributed? Who has access to it? Who has access to the media? How does our society determine credibility and the reliability of information? How do the means of communication shape the messages that are communicated?

Money

What place does money have in our values? How do people earn a living? With whom does our society trade? What goods are exchanged? What are the means of transportation? How do people get from place to place? What resources do we have? What resources do we not have? What are the technological achievements of our society?

Ethnicity

What peoples make up our culture? Where did they come from? What history and values do they bring? How is our society organized socially? How is it stratified? How is status determined? Who is at the top? Who is at the bottom? Why? What racial barriers and problems do people contend with? How do they affect daily life? What traditions and values characterize the various subcultures?

Gender

What are the roles of men and women? How do the sexes relate? What problems confront either sex?

Generations

What value does our culture place on the family? How are families structured? Who are the key families? Where do they live? What are their histories? How do they maintain influence? How is power passed from generation to generation? How are young people educated and socialized? What are they taught? Who does the teaching? How does a person become an adult in this culture?

Religion and worldview

What are the dominant religions? Where did they come from? What condition are they in now? What are the trends? Which groups are growing the fastest? Why? What philosophical assumptions do people operate from? What outlook do they have as they look at the world and at life? What exposure to the gospel has this culture had? What has been its response?

The arts

What kind of art is our culture producing? What is the art telling us about ourselves? About our world? What place do we give to the artist in our society?

History and time

What legends and myths have been passed down? What stories are told and retold? Who writes our history? What stories have not been told? What is the pace of life in our society? How do people measure time? What place do we give to the elderly? What do children represent? For that matter, who represents children?

Place

Where is our culture situated geographically? What topographic and climatic factors influence day-to-day life? How mobile are we in comparison to other societies? How long do families live in one place? What land has passed down through the generations? What people have been displaced? What locations have featured prominently in our culture's history? Where have the wars been fought? Where are celebrations held? What monuments and memorials are there?

MAKING USE OF YOUR DATA

If you diligently answer questions such as these about the world around you, you'll develop some profound insights into how our society operates. But how do you marry that data with the truth of Scripture? How do you apply God's Word in the context of your own situation? After all, there is no one-to-one correspondence between verses in the Bible and day-to-day life. How can you make the connection? Let's find out in the next chapter.

You Try It

One of the pressing issues for Christians in the first century was whether they could eat meat sacrificed to idols (see pages 241-42). Paul devotes an entire chapter to this topic in Romans 14. But unless we understand the cultural context and why this issue was so controversial, we'll never understand or apply that portion of Scripture. So I want to give you a project to develop your skills in this regard. Once you understand what was going on in first-century Rome, you'll appreciate why Paul included this material and what significance it has for us today.

Start by reading and studying Romans 14. Use all of the observational tools outlined earlier. Don't jump into interpretation until you've bombarded the text with a barrage of observational questions.

When you're ready to start interpreting, the two most useful exercises will probably be comparison and consultation. Compare Romans 14 with other passages in the Bible dealing with this issue, such as 1 Corinthians 8. Use a concordance to find out as much as you can about the place that idols occupied in the minds of these first Christians.

For consultation, you'll want to find a good summary of Roman religion and the worship of gods and goddesses. Historian Will Durant gives a concise overview of life in the Roman Empire in *Caesar and Christ* (New York: Simon and Schuster, 1944). Your local library will be able to suggest additional sources.

As you work with the biblical text and the secondary sources, build a database of information on first-century Roman culture, using the kinds of questions listed in this chapter. If you do a thorough study, so that you could drop into Rome in about A.D. 60 and feel right at home, you'll see why the issue of meat sacrificed to idols caused so much trouble in the early church. You'll also be able to recognize the parallels to our own society and where Romans 14 might apply today.

43

THE PRINCIPLE OF
THE THING

What does the Bible have to say about genetic engineering, acid rain, and nuclear power? How about abortion, birth control, and euthanasia? What about leveraged buyouts, junk bonds, and managing for productivity? Is there anything about public education, prison reform, or universal health insurance? Would we turn to the Bible to help us solve problems in transportation, housing, or waste disposal? Can we find any verses on AIDS, arthritis, or Alzheimer's disease?

I'm not being foolish. If we're going to read the Bible in one hand and the newspaper in the other, we've got to face these kinds of issues. We've got to ask what connection there is between the revealed truth of the Word and the world as we find it. Otherwise, we're back to Ken's dilemma: The Bible has relevance only as a devotional guide; it has no bearing on the practical matters of life.

However, any sensible reader will immediately recognize a problem in this regard. There is no one-to-one correspondence between the verses in the Bible and the issues of contemporary life. We can't just "plug in" biblical texts in answer to the needs and problems we face. Life is far too complex for that.

Nor was the Bible written for that purpose. It is not a text on biology, psychology, business, economics, or even history. When it does speak to those areas, it speaks truthfully but not comprehensively. The Bible's primary subject is God and His relationship with humankind. And it is largely our responsibility to work out the implications of that for everyday life. We have to think them through and make choices—biblically informed choices.

THE IMPORTANCE OF PRINCIPLES

That brings us back to the dictum mentioned before: one interpretation, many applications. Without question, there are many specific matters that the Bible never mentions, things that weren't even issues in the days when it was written. But that doesn't mean it has nothing to say to those issues. On the contrary, it tells us the fundamental truths or principles that God wants us to apply across the entire range of human need.

What do I mean by a "principle"? A principle is a succinct statement of a universal truth. When we talk about principles, we move from the specific to the general. For instance, Proverbs 20:2 reads, "The terror of a king is like the growling of a lion; he who provokes him to anger forfeits his own life."

Technically speaking, one could argue that that verse doesn't apply to us who live in a democratic republic rather than a authoritarian monarchy. We don't have a king, so we don't have to worry about his anger. But that would be a narrow reading of the passage. It would also be a misreading of the genre, which is the proverb. Proverbs invariably state general truths through specific cases. Here, the issue is one's relationship to government. The principle is to respect the authority and power of government.

Does that cover every contingency with respect to government? Of course not. Nor should we expect it to. Not even legal libraries with miles of books can do that. But the principle does get us started in the right direction. It tells us the basic attitude that should characterize our relationship to government. Our specific behavior may vary from situation to situation, but in every case we're to show respect for the civil authorities that God places over us.

We saw another example of the need to see general principles in 1 Corinthians 8. The issue there is meat offered to idols. That's no longer a concern in our society. I suspect it is a concern for some Christians today in cultures where idolatry is prevalent. But for us, it is inconsequential. Does that make 1 Corinthians 8 irrelevant? No, because it gives us principles for some larger issues such as matters of conscience, tolerance, respect for other believers, and sensitivity to their backgrounds. Those certainly aren't irrelevant.

But suppose we're reading a biography, say the life of Daniel. Remember we said that one of the things to look for is that which is true to life. So what is it in Daniel's experience that resonates with real life? One of the most notable facts is that this godly man functioned in incredibly ungodly surroundings. In fact, a blue ribbon panel appointed to check out his dossier could not uncover one shred of damning evidence when they wanted to depose him (Daniel 6:1-5).

So what difference does Daniel make today? Well, what sort of work environment surrounds you? It's not as wicked as ancient Babylon, certainly. But maybe you know of deception and fraud at your company. Maybe you've been targeted politically by someone who wants your job. Maybe someone is making life hard for you because of your stand for Christ. Do you think the story of Daniel might hold some principles that apply to your situation? Do you think you might be able to learn from how he handled the challenge confronting him? Do you think there might be any lessons to learn about living as God's person in a secular, or even evil, system?

PRINCIPLES THAT GOVERN PRINCIPLES

If you can discern principles from your study of Scripture, you'll have some powerful tools to help you apply biblical truth. You'll bridge the gap between the ancient world and your own situation with the timeless truth of God's Word. But how can you determine whether your perception is accurate? What's to guard you from error and extremism as you generalize from the text? What's to ensure that you stay practical? There are no guarantees, but here are three guidelines to consider.

1. Principles should correlate with the general teaching of Scripture

This brings us back to the practice of comparing Scripture with Scripture. As you state a principle from a particular passage, think about other passages that reinforce that truth.

For instance, I generalized from Proverbs 20:2 that believers should show respect toward governmental authorities. If that were the only text in the Bible that spoke to that issue, I would need to be cautious about pressing the point too heavily. But a concordance tells me that many other passages reinforce that principle, such as Romans 13:1-7 and 1 Peter 2:13-17. So I feel confident in applying Proverbs 20:2 in that manner.

Likewise, Paul addresses the issue of meat sacrificed to idols in Romans 14. And Daniel has counterparts in Joseph, Esther, and Nehemiah, who also served pagan governments yet maintained their integrity and godly character. So I have plenty of backup as I seek to make application from those biblical texts.

People get into trouble finding a "principle" from a single verse and then trying to build a whole doctrine on the basis of that one reference.

For example, one young man insisted that God wants people to go barefoot. His rationale: Genesis 3:22 says that God used animal skins to make garments for Adam and Eve, but the text never mentions sandals or shoes; therefore, it's clear that God never intended people to wear shoes made from animal.skins. Not only is that an argument from silence and not only are there other texts that contradict that application (Mark 6:8-9; John 1:27; Acts 12:8), it sounds downright silly. It makes little doctrinal or practical sense.

Another error occurs when someone uses Scripture to justify what Scripture clearly condemns. One time a student was convinced that he should marry a certain woman. "God told me to marry her," he explained to me, and he quoted a particular verse.

I had a number of problems with that, not the least of which was the fact that the woman was an unbeliever. I said, "If you choose to marry her, that's your decision. But don't put words in God's mouth. He has clearly said, 'Do not be unequally yoked,' so it's highly unlikely that He would tell you something different."

We have to be very careful in generalizing from Scripture. It's not that we can't apply the Word broadly, but let's apply it sensibly and consistently.

2. Principles should speak to the needs, interests, questions, and problems of real life today

Checking a principle against the template of Scripture is only half the battle. As John Stott says, it's not difficult to be contemporary if you don't care about being biblical, and it's not difficult to be biblical if you don't care about being contemporary. But to be biblical and contemporary—that's an art.

It's where the study of our culture comes into play. If you've done your homework on society, you should have some idea of what matters. You should know where the flash points are, where the wounds are festering, where the breakdowns have come, where the pain is great. You should know who feels alienated from God, who is in doubt about Him, who is angry at Him, and who is deceived about Him. You should have a good idea of where God's people are active today, where they have stepped in to meet needs, and where they have dropped the ball.

In short, if you've become a perceptive student of your culture, you should know where the needs and problems are. And knowing that, you can begin looking for general truths from Scripture that might apply to the contemporary situation. They may have been used differently by people in the ancient world; but they are still true, and therefore still applicable to the issues people face today.

For example, one man initiated a study of Nehemiah. One of the first things he encountered was the prayer in chapter 1, the one that we looked at earlier. He noticed that Nehemiah was talking to God about the people in distress back in Jerusalem. And it dawned on him, "When was the last time I prayed for the people in my company?"

He was the owner of a small manufacturing plant. So he made a list of all of his employees. Then he listed his vendors. Then he listed his competitors. And then he began praying, talking to God about his relationship with each person, and mentioning his or her needs. That began a regular practice that continues to this day. But it began with this man's recognition of a simple principle from the Word—that God wants us to pray about the people and problems around us—and then his application of that principle to his own situation.

3. Principles should indicate a course of action

Management expert Peter Drucker points out that the best ideas in the world are useless until someone goes to work on them. Sooner or later they must produce action. That's certainly true of biblical principles. To be effective, they must produce action.

It's easy to remain hypothetical, to scrape the Milky Way with theological speculation. That was the problem Paul ran into in Athens (Acts 17:21). The people there loved to sit around and shoot the philosophical breeze. But God's Word was given not to tease our curiosity but to transform our lives. As we ferret out principles from Scripture, we constantly need to ask, *What am I going to do with this truth? When, where, and how am I going to apply it?*

I'm going to suggest a simple template for that in the next chapter. First let me tell you how this worked in one man's experience. I remember one of the Dallas Cowboys who was in a Bible study I was leading on the book of Ephesians. We came across the passage on marriage in chapter 5, the section I mentioned in the last chapter. I'll never forget the amazement of this huge, hulking fellow as he finally grasped the significance of what Paul was saying.

"You mean I've got to love my wife?" he asked incredulously. "You mean I've got to tell her?"

He was really getting a clear picture of how Paul's exhortation might look. I don't know what the men in Ephesus who first read the text made of it. But this guy was extracting a basic principle about marriage. And he was about to apply that principle in a very specific way to his own relationship.

He went home with a determination to tell his wife that he loved her. Not bad for a guy who hadn't said that since the day of his wedding. But all afternoon he hesitated, trying to work up the courage to tell her. And all through dinner he kept swallowing the words. Finally he decided to take the plunge. So he got up, came around the table, grabbed his wife, and literally lifted her off her chair. (She told me later that she thought he'd lost his mind.)

"Wife," he bellowed, "I just want to say one thing…I love you," and he gave her a big kiss.

That may not sound like much to you, but for this man it was a completely new experience. It represented significant life-change. He took a major step forward in his marriage by taking action in response to a biblical principle.

MULTIPLYING THE TRUTH

I once attended a lecture by former Secretary of State Henry Kissinger. In his remarks he talked about the explosive nature of events in the global arena. Everything operates in crisis, he said, which of course poses a severe challenge to leaders. How can they keep up? He explained that things happen so quickly, you don't have time to think, you only have time to react. Therefore, you have to operate on whatever reservoirs of knowledge and experience you bring to the job. You don't have the luxury of intensive, unhindered study.

I think there's a lesson in that for living the Christian life. Certainly we must take the time to study God's Word intensively. But often we face situations that don't afford us the luxury of reflection, only reaction. For instance, we find ourselves in a confrontation with a coworker. We're tempted to deceive a customer or a competitor. Our kids ask us a penetrating question just as we're dropping them off at school. We get a phone call from a friend who has to make a difficult decision and wants our input.

In situations like these, we have to rely on whatever reservoirs of knowledge and experience we bring to the moment. Sure, given enough time, we could probably come up with an elegant, refined response. But life frequently denies us time. So the question is, what familiarity with the Word, what biblical data base, do we bring to the situation? We don't have time for an intensive study. So what are we going to use in the moment?

If we stock up on principles from Scripture, we'll have a powerful set of resources to deal with the situations of life. You see, principles enable us to multiply truth. One interpretation; many applications. We may not have a specific verse to plug into the circumstances of the moment. But we can still navigate a godly path by extrapolating from the truth we already know.

You Try It

The ability to state principles from Scripture is one of the most powerful skills you can develop in terms of Application. It will enable you to relate the Word of God to nearly any situation you face. However, learning to do so takes a bit of practice. You can't just come up with something that makes sense to you and then bless it with the preface, "The Bible says...."

No, crafting useful and accurate principles requires accurate understanding of the text and perceptive insight into our own context. Here are several questions to help you develop and apply biblically sound principles.

1. What can you discover about the original context in which this passage was written and applied?
2. Given that original context, what does this text mean?
3. What fundamental, universal truths are presented in this passage?

4. Can you state that truth in a simple sentence or two, a statement that anyone could understand?
5. What issues in your own culture and your own situation does this truth address?
6. What are the implications of this principle when applied to your life and the world around you? What changes does it require? What values does it reinforce? What difference does it make?

Now use these questions to state applicational principles from three passages of Scripture: Proverbs 24:30-34; John 13:1-17; and Hebrews 10:19-25.

44

A PROCESS OF LIFE-CHANGE

The church retreat had come to an end. Participants were packing bags into cars and saying their good-byes. What an outstanding weekend they'd had, with lots of fun and good food and a rich time of study in the book of Philippians. Pastor Jones wore a wide smile as he received words of appreciation from grateful members.

Up came Larry, one of the congregation. "Pastor," he said, "this weekend has been...well, it's really changed my life. I'll never be the same."

"I'm glad to hear that, Larry," replied the minister. "Tell me, what was the most significant thing?"

"Well, I don't know. All of it, really." He laughed. "I've realized that I just have so much to learn. When I get home I'm going to start reading my Bible more. And I'm really going to change the way I treat people. And I think I may sign up to help out in Sunday school. And I think I need to take a look at my giving. I was really touched by your message on missions."

"It sounds like you got a lot out of this retreat," Pastor Jones said enthusiastically. "I'll be praying for you." The two men shook hands and parted.

On the surface, this exchange sounds wonderful. On the basis of Pastor Jones's teaching of Philippians, Larry identified a few specific areas for spiritual growth and action. That's great. But the bright picture dims a bit when we find out that Larry has been to at least a dozen retreats like this one over the years. He has made similar remarks after each one. But has he changed? Not one whit. He gets pumped up by the enthusiasm of the moment. But when he gets back home, his good intentions evaporate, and he never gets started on a process of change.

WHERE DO I BEGIN?

The problem for Larry is one from which countless people suffer—the problem of a plan. We could state it in the form of a question: Where do I begin? That may be the most determinative question to ask about application.

You see, anybody can come up with a grandiose scheme for change. One person says he wants to reach the world for Christ. Somebody else wants to study every book in the Bible over the next five years. Somebody else plans to memorize a hundred verses. Somebody else is going to become a Christlike spouse. Wonderful. Where are you going to begin?

Until you answer that, all you have is good intentions. Those have about as much value as a worthless check. After all, what good does it do to dream of reaching the world with the gospel if you can't share Christ with the person in the office next to you? How are you going to study the entire Bible when you don't even know what verse you're going to study tomorrow? How can you memorize a hundred verses when you've never even tried to memorize one? And rather than fantasize about a Christlike marriage, why not start with something simple, such as doing the dishes if you're a husband, or encouraging your husband if you're a wife?

Too much "application" stays at the level of good intentions because we talk about the end of the journey without specifying when, where, and how we're going to take the first step. As someone has well said, we don't plan to fail, we fail to plan.

So I want to give you a simple framework to use in planning your own process of life-change. In doing so, I don't mean to oversimplify things. Obviously, life is complex, and many elements of growth cannot be charted easily. But I also know that many Christians stall out in their spiritual development because they don't know how to get started. They know all about the glorious promises that are supposed to be theirs someday. But the real question is, what will they do today to start heading in that direction.

So here are three steps for translating good intentions into life-changing action.

1. Make a decision to change

In other words, make up your mind. Determine what sort of change you need to make, and then choose to pursue it. This is largely a matter of setting objectives. That is, how will you be different as a result of making this change? What will you look like at the end of the process?

Robert Mager, a specialist in learning and education, says that a well-stated objective describes what a person will be doing once he achieves the intended outcome. For example, the objective of this book is to help you ask observational questions of the biblical text, explain what a passage means, and then describe practical ways to use what you've learned in everyday life. This statement points to specific behaviors that we could measure if we wanted to know whether we had accomplished our objectives. For instance, we could listen to you probing the text with questions. We could read an interpretation that you might write. We could look at your schedule to see whether you were taking action.

So what objectives are you prepared to set in order to accomplish change? Describe what you'll be doing when you reach that objective. Do you want to become a better parent? What does that look like? Can you state it in terms of noticeable, measurable behaviors? For instance, "better parenting" might involve spending more time with your kids if you are a father. It might mean organizing and managing the family schedule if you are a mother. We can measure these behaviors, and we can use them to plan (see below).

The more clear and demonstrable your objectives are, the more likely it is that you will accomplish them. Fuzzy objectives lead to fuzzy results. If you say you are going to "evangelize more," you will have a hard time knowing when you've evangelized more. But if you say you're going to initiate conversations about Christ with your neighbors, John and Mary, you'll know exactly when and whether you've accomplished the task.

Does this seem too rigid, too confining? If so, may I suggest that you might be settling for a decaffeinated form of Christianity—one that promises not to keep you awake at night. You see, God gives us His Word not to make us comfortable but to conform us to the character of Christ. And that goes way beyond pious feelings and good intentions. It penetrates to the level of our schedules and checkbooks and friendships and jobs and families. If our faith makes no practical difference there, then what difference does it make?

Clearly defined objectives help us see truth as actions, not abstractions. Likewise, they keep our expectations on the ground, within reach. Is your aim to develop the compassion of a Mother Teresa? Wonderful. But don't make that your objective. A better place to start is with a soup kitchen in your own community. Determine some practical ways to meet their needs. That's achievable. That's something you can do right now. That's a realistic step in the right direction.

2. Come up with a plan

This is the step where you ask how. How am I going to accomplish the task? If you've done a good job of stating your objectives, this should be fairly easy to answer. If not, you may need to go back and revise your objectives, making them clearer and more doable.

A plan is a specific course of action for how you're going to reach your objectives—and I do mean specific. Think it through in terms of all that it's going to take to do what you say you intend to do. Who are the people involved? What resources will you need? When are you going to plan it in your schedule? What's the best timing?

For example, suppose your objective is to become a better father by spending more time with your children. How are you going to accomplish that? Maybe it means taking your son out for pizza and telling him about your own childhood. That could be an excellent plan. But what will it take to pull it off? When will you schedule it? Is your son agreeable to that? When would be the best timing? How long do you plan to take? Where will you go so that you can talk? What are you going to say?

Or suppose you're a mother for whom "better parenting" means organizing and managing the family schedule. How will you accomplish that? Maybe it means putting up a calendar in the kitchen. So when will you get a calendar? How big does it need to be? Where are you going to put it? How often are you going to update it? How will you know what to put on it?

Again, suppose you decide that you need to engage your neighbors John and Mary in conversation about Christ. You know that they have questions in that regard. How can you initiate that?

One way might be to give them a copy of C.S. Lewis's *Mere Christianity* as a way of stimulating discussion. If so, when will you get a copy to give them? When will you give it to them? How do you plan to follow up? Will you have them over for dessert some evening to talk about it? If so, when? Are they agreeable to that?

Planning a course of action means coming up with specific ways to achieve an objective and then thinking through what you need to do to run the plan. It assigns names, dates, times, and places to your intentions. The more specific your plan, the more likely it is that you'll succeed in it.

3. Follow through

In other words, get started. Does your plan begin with a phone call? Then pick up the phone. Does it start by having your secretary rearrange your schedule? Then ask her to rearrange it. Do you plan to evaluate your giving habits in light of your budget? Then sit down and update your budget so that you'll have the information you need.

The first step is always the hardest. But take it. Don't put it off. If you've come this far in the process, reward your efforts with solid follow-through. Pay yourself the respect of carrying out your commitments.

Three strategies can help you in this process. First, consider using a checklist, especially if your plan calls for repeated activity or a number of progressive steps. For instance, if you plan to memorize Scripture, you would be wise to list all of the verses you intend to memorize, and the dates by when you plan to memorize them. Then, as you commit the verses to memory, you can check them off the list. Over time, you'll be able to see and celebrate your progress, which will spur you on in your efforts.

A second strategy is to set up some relationships of accountability. These could be formal or informal. Informal accountability might involve telling your spouse or a close friend about what you plan to do. Then, as you work your way through the process, you can keep him or her aware of your progress, your struggles, and your victories.

However, for long-term spiritual growth, I recommend a formal accountability group. Jeanne and I have been part of such a group for years, and we wouldn't trade it for anything. A group of people committed to each other brings encouragement and wisdom to the growth process. And the dynamic of the group helps one follow through on the commitments he makes.

A third way of ensuring that you carry out your plans is to evaluate your progress. Keeping a journal is an ideal way to do that. As you set your objectives and accomplish them, write the process down. Record why you wanted to make changes, why you took the course of action that you did, and what you learned as you went about it. Later you can come back and review where you've been. You'll notice where you've made progress and where you still need to grow.

Another way to do this is to get away periodically for a time of personal reflection and evaluation. Take your journal, your Bible, your calendar, and any other records of what you've been up to during the past few months or so. Ask yourself questions such as: What have been the three greatest challenges to my walk with the Lord during this period? How did I respond? What victories do I have to celebrate? What failures do I need to consider? What specific answers to prayer can I recall? Have I changed for the better or for the worse? In what ways? Where have I spent my time? My money? What has happened in my relationships?

The point is, devise ways to measure your stride as you walk through life. Know yourself and how God has worked in your experience.

GOD IS AT WORK IN YOU

In a previous chapter, I mentioned the fear that the last part of Philippians 2:12 used to engender in me as a boy: "Work out your salvation with fear and trembling." The planning process that I've described in this chapter is a form of "working out your salvation." You have to take responsibility for making choices and taking action in order to grow as a believer.

But never forget the other side: "For it is God who is at work in you, both to will and to work for His good pleasure" (Philippians 2:13). As you set your objectives, make plans, and carry them out, God is right there with you. That's the encouraging thing about the spiritual life—you're never alone. God provides His resources to help you in the process. He won't make decisions for you or do what you are able to do. But He does work in ways known and unknown to help you become like Christ.

You Try It

Let me ask you the question I posed at the beginning of this chapter. Maybe you've identified an area of your life that needs substantial change. Perhaps you even know what steps you need to take. But the issue is, Where are you going to begin? How are you going to translate good intentions into life-changing action?

I want to challenge you to come up with one aspect of your life that needs to change, based on your study of God's Word. Then go through the three-step process outlined in this chapter to come up with an action plan for change.

As I say, this is my personal challenge to you. Remember that the aim of Bible study is to produce Christlike change in your life. Here's where that must happen. If you've come this far, follow through with the application of the Word to your life. Let it make a difference.

45

THREE SUGGESTIONS
TO GET STARTED

A. W. Tozer, for many years a spiritual gadfly to the Body of Christ, placed a burr in my mental saddle with these words:

A religious mentality, characterized by timidity and lack of moral courage has given us today a flabby Christianity, intellectually impoverished, dull, repetitious, and to a great many persons, just plain boresome. This is peddled as the very faith of our fathers in direct lineal decent from Christ and the apostles. We spoon-feed this insipid pabulum to our inquiring youth, and to make it palatable spice it up with carnal amusements snatched from the unbelieving world. It is easier to entertain than to instruct. It is easier to follow degenerate public taste than to think for oneself. So too many of our evangelical leaders let their minds atrophy while they keep their fingers nimble operating religious gimmicks to bring in the curious crowd.[1]

I'm afraid too many churchgoers today are listening but not learning. They are spectators, not students. They are passive, not participating. Why? Because we who teach often give them cut flowers that easily fade and wilt, rather than showing them how to

1. A.W. Tozer, "We Need Sanctified Thinkers," *Alliance Weekly*, November 9, 1955, p. ?.

grow plants for themselves—to discover firsthand the truth that God has revealed in His Word.

Of course, that's the purpose of this book, to introduce you to the joy of getting into the Bible for yourself. I can assure you that we have barely scratched the surface in this regard. We've only gotten our foot in the door of a very large house. The question now is, how can you conserve the gains? How can you make permanent what you've started to learn from this process? Let me offer three suggestions for building on the foundation that this book seeks to lay.

BEGIN A PERSONAL BIBLE STUDY PROGRAM.

I once saw a poster that fascinated me: "In twenty years, what will you wish you had done today?" Under that question, in large, bold letters, it said, "Do it now." I suspect that twenty years from now you will wish that you had started a personal Bible study program. So why not begin right now?

Determine your objectives

All you have to do is solve four problems. First, you have to determine your objectives. What do you want? Not just now, but at the end of life? Many people end up at the top of the pile in their field but at the bottom of life in terms of fulfillment. Ask yourself, *Do I want to have a personal Bible study program. Have I seen the crucial need for it from this book?*

Establish your priorities

Second, you have to establish your priorities. That is, how badly do you want it? What price are you willing to pay? There are plenty of things I'd like to do but not badly enough to pay the price required to do them. Ask yourself, *Do I want to develop a Bible study program on a personal basis? If so, what price am I willing to pay?*

Set a schedule

The third thing you need is a schedule. That involves asking, *What means can I employ to maintain my priorities and accomplish my objectives?* Unfortunately for most people schedules bring to mind a demon chaperon, somebody looking over your shoulder, ever ready to slap your hand and yell, "Hey, cut that out," or, "Now is the time to do this." But actually a schedule is just a tool to accomplish what you have decided you want to accomplish and are willing to pay the price to do.

Develop discipline

The fourth thing you need is discipline. Ultimately, that is a fruit of the Spirit. He can provide the dynamic whereby you maintain your schedule, keep your priorities, and accomplish your objectives. But often people tell me, "I'd sure like to study the Word, but I don't know if I've got the time." I answer that you've got all the time in the world to do what is essential. The question is, have you determined that Bible study is essential? Have you made it your objective? And are you willing to pay the price?

I recall a homemaker I spoke with once. She had five children—not exactly someone who was looking for something to do. She wanted to get started in her own Bible study program. "I'd give anything if I had some time," she told me.

I said, "See if you can carve out fifteen minutes a day."

"I don't know if I have that much time," she replied.

But she wouldn't let it rest. One day she came to me and said, "Guess what. I've discovered a time when all of my children are either at school or taking a nap—and I came up with twenty minutes."

I met a businessman who was the head of three international corporations. He obviously wasn't looking for something to do either. Like the housewife, he said to me, "Hendricks I'd love to have my own Bible study. But I just don't have time."

I said, "Let me give you a proposition. Would you be willing to pray that God give you some time? And if He does, will you use it to study His Word?"

"Well," he admitted, "I guess I can't turn that down."

So one day he was creeping along an expressway in Dallas, wasting his time along with everybody else in a bumper-to-bumper parking lot. All of sudden he said to himself, *What in the world am I doing here? I'm the president of this outfit. I ought to determine when I come and when I go home.* So he changed his schedule. He came in half an hour earlier in the morning, and he went home half an hour earlier in the afternoon.

As a result he gained twenty minutes in his morning commute, and twenty in the afternoon. So he called me up and said, "Hendricks, I got it." At first I thought he'd had some kind of a revelation. He was excited that he'd finally found some time. And he kept his word: he immediately began to read the Scriptures for himself, to his great benefit.

When I was a student in seminary, a choice man of God named Harry Ironside used to come and teach. I remember on one occasion somebody came up and said, "Dr. Ironside, I understand you get up early every morning to read and study your Bible."

"Oh," he said, "I've been doing that all my life."

"Well how do you manage to do it?" the inquirer asked. "Do you pray about it?"

"No," he replied, "I get up."

See, many of us are expecting God to do what God is expecting us to do. I can assure you that God is not going to roll you out of the sack. You have to decide whether you really want to get into the Word, and if so, when.

Ultimately, what matters is not when you have your Bible study, but the fact that you do, and that you do it regularly and consistently.

But one word of caution: Know that if you make this commitment, Satan will do anything to dislodge your schedule. He'll use every trick in the book. So your question has to be, Where is my heart? What is my objective? What is my priority? That way, if you should get off your routine, you won't be tempted to think you've lost your salvation. The next day you can get back on track.

Getting started

Now if you decide to start a regular Bible study program, you need to answer the question, Where do I begin? A good place to start is with a very small book. That way you can keep from getting bogged down. Sometimes a person will get carried away with enthusiasm. "I'm going to start in Jeremiah," they say. I wouldn't recommend it.

I suggest that you begin with a New Testament book, such as the book of Philippians. It has four chapters, 104 verses. Or perhaps the book of James; five chapters, 108 verses. You can plug little books such as these into your schedule, and in a relatively short period of time you will be making progress.

Then, if you want to take on something heftier, go to the Old Testament and try the book of Jonah. It's a beautiful narrative with an easy-to-follow story line with only four chapters. In this way you can gradually work your way up to tackle something that is longer and more difficult.

But suppose you say, "Man, I really want to go for broke." All right. Try the book of Nehemiah, especially if you're in business or interested in leadership. That book has more practical principles for organization and administration than any ten books on today's best-seller list. If you are just starting out, select a book that is reality-oriented like that.

And whatever you do, keep a notebook. "But what I come up with is not very impressive," you may reply. But the question is, did the Holy Spirit give you the insight? If so, don't despise it. We all start at the same place, at ground-zero. The most renowned expositor of all time had to start at the same place every one of the rest of us has to start—with the ABC's, with beginning material. It's a good habit to write down what God gives you. Record it, and seek an opportunity to share it with someone, because then you will retain it.

FORM A SMALL BIBLE STUDY GROUP

In our country we love to praise rugged individualism and self-initiative. But the fact is that most of us function more effectively as part of a team rather than on our own. That is certainly the case with Bible study.

Small group Bible study is a tremendous motivator. In fact, that may be its greatest value. You see, many of us are scared spitless to jump into the Word for ourselves. "I can't do it," people will say. Actually they can, but they need the encouragement that comes from others who are with them in the process.

Nothing motivates like the thrill of sharing a discovery with a group, and having someone cry, "Hey, that's fantastic. Did anybody else see that?" Pretty soon the person's back with more. He's out of his gourd with excitement and enthusiasm. He's also stimulating others to find things in the Word.

Another value of small group discussion is that it allows for participation and involvement. That's what excites me about small classes. I do teach seminary classes of a hundred or two hundred students. But frankly, I prefer to sit down at a table with about six or eight students and really get into a passage. That way, everybody can get into the act; everybody can profit from the process.

That kind of learning is less threatening. In a large group, some of the people who have the best things to contribute will never say anything because the size of the group intimidates them. But in a small group where they feel comfortable, they'll take off.

That brings us to the question, What is the ideal size for a study group? I think it works best at about six to eight. If you get six people, and you think that's too large, break it in half for part of the discussion. Then come together and pool your discoveries.

What happens if you can't find six participants? Then start with what you've got. Have you got one other person? Two people? Start with them. Are you married? Start a study with your spouse. Start one with your family. Some of the best times you'll ever have with your family will come from a joint study of the Bible.

That's been true for me. Without question, the best Bible study I ever have is the study I have with my wife, Jeanne. We select a passage. We study it separately. Then we come together to share the results. That gets rich. Sometimes she tells me what she's found, and I begin to think, Good night, I wonder if I've ever read that passage. She has profound insights.

Leadership is the key

So small group Bible study can be incredibly profitable. But the key is always the leader. As with any team setting, good Bible studies are the result of good leadership. If you are the leader, let me give you one suggestion: Don't be afraid of the hard question.

I was in a class studying Mark, and a lady suddenly asked, "How many gods are there?" You see, we had talked about God the Father, God the Son, and God the Holy Spirit, and she was confused.

Can you imagine what would happen in the average church if someone stood up and asked that question? I'll tell you what we did— we made a hero out of her. "Fantastic, Marge, run that question by us again." You see, here was a lady who was really coming to grips with the issues.

What happens when you can't answer a question like that? Simple: you tell the person, "I don't know." You'll never lose face that way.

The greatest professor I ever had, a man brilliant beyond words, was asked a very difficult question, one that he couldn't answer. So he said to the student, "Young man, that is one of the most perceptive

Start a Small Group

If you plan to start a Bible study group, here are a few suggestions:

1. Leadership is the key

If there is one determinative factor in small group Bible study, it's the leader. Bible study leaders should be people who enjoy getting others involved in a process, not dominating with their own ideas. They should be reliable, organized, able to keep a discussion on track, and willing to prepare for the group meeting. They need to be relaxed people, confident in their ability to handle Scripture. It helps if they can think on their feet, too. And of course they should be people who love God's Word.

2. Determine the purpose of the group

Bible studies meet for a variety of reasons: to focus on a deeper understanding of the text; to apply biblical truth to felt needs and current issues; to use the Word as launching point for prayer; to introduce unbelievers to Scripture. Whatever the purpose of your group, make sure that you state it clearly to anyone you recruit.

3. Recruit people who want to study the Bible

The goal of recruiting people is not to pack the group with bodies, but to produce life-change for the participants. Approach prospects who are genuinely interested in the Bible, not in a social club or a theological powwow. In general, the more homogeneous the group, the easier it will be for people to participate.

4. Make sure that everyone gets a chance to participate

The leader's goal is to get everyone involved with the Word and with each other. The danger to avoid is letting anyone dominate the process—including the leader.

5. Encourage discussion

The most effective format for small group study is discussion, not lecture. Everyone needs a chance to say something. The leader can facilitate that by preparing a simple, well organized discussion sheet. You might print the text at the top of the sheet (so that everyone uses the same translation), and then a few questions below. Develop the art of asking the open-ended question, the kind that has no particular "right" answer.

6. Stick to the Bible

This is partly a matter of keeping the discussion on track. Participants will have legitimate questions that require digression, but you should never get too far from the passage. If people have come expecting a Bible study, they should be rewarded with a rich time in Scripture, not a theological debate.

7. Show enthusiasm

One of the best ways to motivate people in personal Bible study is to celebrate their discoveries. Get excited over people's insights, no matter how simple.

8. Keep the group small

Six to eight in a group is ideal. If you have more, break the group into smaller groups. Remember, the goal is 100 percent participation, and it's hard to accomplish that if the group gets too big.

9. Divide the time between Observation, Interpretation, and Application

Group studies tend to suffer from the same problem as individual Bible study: they spend far too long on Interpretation, to the neglect of Observation and Application. Balance the time between all three. If you find yourself coming to the end of the meeting and having to say, "Well, folks, we'll have to talk about what difference this makes next time," that's a good sign that you've probably spent too long on Interpretation.

10. Keep your commitment...to the purpose and to the time

Make sure the group stays on course, that it carries out the objectives for which it was formed. As for time, pace the group meetings. Begin and end them when you say you'll begin and end them. And in setting up the group, determine an end-point, a date for terminating the group. People have a hard time making open-ended commitments, and you'll get a better response if you give people an opportunity to choose whether or not to continue.

questions I have ever been asked. My answer would be very superficial if I gave it to you now. So I will do some thinking and come back with an answer. Any other questions like that?"

I tell you, that man's stature soared in our opinion, because we had all had professors (just as you have) who replied to the hard question, "Well, inasmuch as...whereas...wherefore...consequently...." And we knew they didn't know the answer.

You never lose face by telling people, "I don't know. But I'll try to find out." Write it down and work on it later. And encourage the rest of the group to come up with more good questions.

SHARE YOUR RESULTS WITH OTHERS.

There are five words you can write over the process presented in this book: "Use me or lose me." The best way to keep what you've learned through this material is to give it away. If it has meant anything to you, then it's too good to keep. You're in debt. You've got to share it with someone else. And nothing is more exciting than getting others into the Word for themselves.

There are a couple of ways to share the fruit of your Bible study. First, you can share it by teaching. It may be a Sunday school class, a child-evangelism class, or a home Bible study.

Perhaps you should think in terms of a Bible study where you work. Maybe you're a lawyer or a doctor or in the business world. Why don't you get a group of lawyers or doctors or businesspeople together and tell them, "We're going to set up a little Bible study every Wednesday at noon. Bring your lunch, and we'll study the Bible. Just the text. We're not talking about religion, or controversial things, or politics. We're just going to talk about the Scriptures. What does the Bible say?"

Another way to share your results—really the ultimate way—is by living them. The greatest impact you will ever make on other people will come from a changed life. Impression without expression equals depression.

Walt Disney was one of the creative geniuses of this century. After he died, a cartoon appeared in the *Dallas Morning News*. It was quite simple: close-ups of Mickey Mouse and Donald Duck, crying. There was no caption. Words were unnecessary. The cartoon alone said everything.

Used by permission of *The Dallas Morning News.*

What about you? Does your life tell others everything they need to know about your commitment to Christ and your values and beliefs? I think the great need among God's people today is to get into Scripture for themselves. And because they are not doing so, they are losing the fizz in their spiritual life. They are flat and lukewarm. Nothing is more repulsive. People are weary of words, but they are starving for authenticity.

As Senate chaplain Richard Halverson has said, "People are not particularly interested in our ideas; they are interested in our experiences. They are not searching for theories but for convictions. They want to penetrate our rhetoric in order to discover the reality of our lives."

In Ezra 7:10 we have a model of the value of personal Bible study. The text reads, "For Ezra had set his heart [to do three things:] to study the law of the Lord, and to practice it, and to teach His statutes and ordinances in Israel." May his tribe increase.

Are You Ready to Make
the Commitment?

Good intentions will not get you started in personal Bible study. It takes a willful commitment on your part, followed by decisive action.

You might find it helpful to formalize your commitment, to make more than just a mental note of it. Here's a statement to help you think about what you are undertaking. If you agree to its terms, sign your name as a formal way of declaring your commitment. You might even want to pray this as a prayer to God, asking for His help to carry it out.

I, _____, have determined to start a
YOUR NAME

regular program of personal Bible study. I'm going to begin on

_____ at _____ at _____.
DATE   TIME   PLACE

The passage of Scripture that I'm going to study first is

_____, using _____.
NAME OF BIBLICAL BOOK OR SCRIPTURE REFERENCE   VERSION

In my study I'm going to go through the steps of Observation, Interpretation, and Application as outlined in this book. I realize that the goals of reading the Bible are a closer relationship with God and a life that is changing in accordance with His will and Word. To that end I commit myself to reading and obeying the Bible, with God's help.

_____
SIGNATURE

_____
DATE

Additional Resources

BIBLES

The Amplified Bible. Translated by Frances Siewert, this resource "amplifies" the message of the biblical texts by giving several synonyms for the major words, so that the various shades of meaning can be seen. (Zondervan, 1965)

The Bible in Pictures for Little Eyes. Ken Taylor's classic paraphrase puts Bible stories in language that young children can understand. It makes extensive use of a question-and-answer style of telling the story, so that children are engaged in the narrative. This colorful volume is a great way to get children started in the Word. (Moody, 1985)

The Cotton Patch Version of Luke and *Acts and The Cotton Patch Version of Paul's Epistles.* In the late 60s, Clarence Jordan of Koinonia Farm in Americus, Georgia produced these lively paraphrases because, he said, "we need to have the good news come to us not only in our own tongue but in our own time." By giving a "Southern drawl" to these New Testament texts, Jordan enables the reader to feel personally involved. Read these if you want a fresh perspective. (Association Press, 1969 and 1968 respectively)

The Good News Bible: Today's English Version. This translation of the United Bible Societies "seeks to state clearly and accurately the meaning of the original texts in words and forms that are widely accepted by people who use English as a means of communication." It's a good version to use for reading long passages of narrative, though not as useful for intensive analysis of individual verses and words. A good Bible for young people and those for whom English is a second language. (American Bible Society)

The King James Version (KJV). The classic translation of 1611, this is also known as The Authorized Version, though it was never formally authorized by any ecclesiastical body. The KJV has a richness of language that is hard to beat, especially in the psalms.

The Living Bible. This excellent and popular paraphrase came about when a man named Ken Taylor began rewriting portions of the Bible in a way that his children could understand. Like *The Good News Bible*, it uses simple, plain English and is good for overview and repeated reading. (Tyndale)

Nave's Topical Bible. Have you ever wished that you could read back-to-back all of the major passages on a topic? Orville Nave has reorganized the Bible in just that manner. He gives verses on more than 20,000 topics and subtopics, arranged alphabetically. This volume can be a timesaver.

The New American Standard Bible (NASB). This is one of my favorites for a study Bible. It is one of the most accurate English translations, though for that reason it sounds a bit wooden in places. Excellent for the steps of Observation and Interpretation.

The New International Version (NIV). The product of a broad-based coalition of translators, the NIV aims at a marriage between accuracy and clarity. It is one of the more readable translations.

The New King James Version (NKJV). The NKJV was produced "to preserve the original intended purity of the King James Version in its communication of God's Word to man." If you like the King James but struggle with its Elizabethan English, this is a very helpful translation. (Thomas Nelson)

The New Revised Standard Version (NRSV). The NRSV updates the RSV, based on linguistic and archaeological developments such as the discovery of the Dead Sea scrolls in the 1940s. Its English is clear and is noteworthy for its attempt at gender-neutral renderings.

The New Testament in Modern English (Revised Edition). This paraphrase by J. B. Phillips is one of my favorites. It is extremely readable and lively, excellent for getting a preliminary overview of a book. (Macmillan, 1972)

The Revised Standard Version (RSV). Published in 1952 by the National Council of Churches, the RSV gained its title from the fact that it revised *The American Standard Version* of 1901, which in turn was a revision of the King James. This translation will be familiar to many in the mainline denominations. It is not a bad piece of work, but there are now better translations available.

The Scofield Reference Bible. C. I. Scofield was a turn-of-the-century pastor, teacher, writer, and lecturer who wanted to "facilitate the study and intelligent use of the Bible." To that end, he packaged a comprehensive system of footnotes, cross-references, headings, and other helps with the biblical text. The result was an enormously popular volume that has become the grandfather of study Bibles. *The Scofield Bible* is synonymous with dispensational theology, the theological system he used to interpret Scripture. (Oxford)

Tommy dePaola's Book of Bible Stories. An internationally known illustrator of more than two hundred children's books, Tommy dePaola lends his inimitable style to this fine collection of Bible stories for children. The text is the NIV translation, and the illustrations are in color. This is an excellent way to help your children to start reading Scripture. (G. P. Putnam's Son/Zondervan, 1990)

BOOKS AND ARTICLES

Mortimer Adler and Mark Van Doren, *How to Read a Book.* This is a classic that you can't afford not to read (see pages 66-67). Adler covers the rules of reading various kinds of literature. You'll approach Bible study from an altogether different perspective after reading this guide. (Simon & Schuster, 1972)

E. W. Bullinger, *Figures of Speech Used in the Bible.* As I pointed out in chapter 36, figurative language can trip up the uninformed reader. Bullinger simplifies things by giving a comprehensive overview of the kinds of figures used in Scripture. Turn to this useful, 1,100-page guide if you find yourself mystified by biblical imagery. (Baker reprint, 1968)

Alfred Edersheim, *The Life and Times of Jesus the Messiah.* A nineteenth-century Oxford scholar, Edersheim devoted seven uninterrupted years to researching the Jewish culture of Jesus' day. Though this work is not light reading, it is accessible to the average person. If you are studying the gospels, his information and insights prove invaluable. Originally two volumes, Eerdman's has reprinted it in one. (Eerdmans, 1971)

Norman Lewis, *How to Read Better and Faster,* 4th edition. This is a superb workbook for upgrading your reading skills. Filled with exercises to improve reading speed and comprehension, it makes a good companion to Adler's *How to Read a Book.* (Harper & Row, 1978)

Leland Ryken, *The Literature of the Bible.* A professor of English at Wheaton College, Ryken has probably done more than anyone else to make modern-day Bible students aware of the literary dimensions of Scripture. This book will change the way you look at the Bible by introducing you to the crucial importance of genre. (Zondervan, 1974)

CONCORDANCES

Most major Bible translations (such as the RSV, NRSV, NIV, NAS, NKJV) have their own concordances. If you can't find one for the version you are using, check with the publisher. If no companion concordance exists, start using a different translation that has one.

Nelson Phrase Concordance of the Bible. This interesting volume from Thomas Nelson Publishers is a twist on the concordance genre. Rather than list individual words, it gives you Bible phrases keyed to five major translations. That can be a timesaver when you are searching for a phrase rather than an individual word. (Thomas Nelson, 1986)

The New Strong's Exhaustive Concordance of the Bible. The work of James Strong, this and Young's are the two concordances that Bible students have traditionally used. However, if you are using a modern translation, you need to find a concordance for that version. (Thomas Nelson, 1990)

Young's Analytical Concordance to the Bible. Robert Young's one-volume commentary is one of the classic reference works of Bible study. (Eerdmans, 1970)

Wordsearch Computer Bible. This is a "turbocharged" concordance that will appeal to you if you have a computer. It allows you to search for up to nine words and phrases simultaneously. *Wordsearch* can be a tremendous timesaver. It heralds a new generation of Bible study tools based on electronic technology. Available for both MS-DOS and Macintosh. (Navpress, 1990)

BIBLE DICTIONARIES

An Expository Dictionary of New Testament Words. The product of W. E. Vine's lifetime work, this dictionary is extremely valuable for word studies. Vine lists the English words (from the KJV and RSV), and gives the Greek words from which they are translated. He comments on the usages to explain their meanings in context. (Revell, 1940)

Nelson's Illustrated Bible Dictionary. This fine reference work was edited by Herbert Lockyer, known for his "all" studies, such as *All the Men of the Bible, All the Miracles of the Bible,* and *All the Occupations of the Bible.* Written in simple, readable English, the articles include four-color photographs. (Thomas Nelson, 1986)

The New Bible Dictionary (**Revised**). This excellent reference, originally edited by J. D. Douglas, was revised in 1980. It is really an encyclopedia of biblical studies, and includes illustrations, genealogical tables, maps, plans, and other information that brings the text alive. (Tyndale, 1980)

The Zondervan Pictorial Bible Dictionary (**Revised**). Edited by Wheaton scholar Merrill Tenney, this volume contains the expertise of more than sixty-five contributors. It offers information on the biographical, chronological, geographical, and historical context of the biblical subjects. (Zondervan, 1987)

BIBLE HANDBOOKS

The Book of Life. This twenty-four-volume set by Gil Beers is ideal for young people. Featuring color illustrations and photographs, it takes the reader through the entire Bible in a captivating, informative way. It includes the entire NIV translation in large print and a comprehensive index for quick reference. If you have children or grandchildren, I recommend this encyclopedic resource as an outstanding gift. (Zondervan, 1980)

Eerdman's Handbook to the Bible. Edited by David Alexander, this 680-page work is illustrated in color. It's an excellent one-volume reference work on the background of the biblical world. (Eerdmans, 1873)

Encyclopedia of Bible Difficulties. Gleason Archer deals with the apparent contradictions in Scripture. If you come across something that puzzles you, turn to this book for insight and background information. (Zondervan, 1982)

Halley's Bible Handbook. It was Henry Halley's conviction that everyone ought to read the Bible daily, and to that end he put together *Halley's Bible Handbook* as an introduction to the Scriptures. It's a useful, compact pocket guide to biblical studies. (Zondervan, 1927)

The Handbook of Life in Bible Times. This concise work by J. A. Thompson includes both color illustrations and maps. (InterVarsity, 1986)

Unger's Bible Handbook. Like *Halley's*, this is a concise introduction to the Bible. Unger takes you through every book and comments on subjects of historical, geographical, cultural, and theological significance. (Moody, 1966)

The World of the Bible. A. S. Van Der Woude and others have put together a fine encyclopedia on the history and culture of the biblical world. This makes a terrific background study for understanding the context of biblical passages. (Eerdmans, 1986)

ATLASES

An Introduction to Bible Geography (**Revised**). This little paperback is a brief primer on Bible lands by Howard Vos, offering a dozen articles on regions in the Near East. If you've never studied the geography of the Bible, this would be a good place to start. (Moody, 1983)

The Macmillan Bible Atlas. Two Jewish scholars put together this outstanding atlas, one of the most accurate in existence. It features 262 maps and commentary on the religious, military, and economic aspects of the biblical world. (Macmillan, 1977)

The Moody Atlas of Bible Lands. Barry Beitzel has created a beautiful presentation of the geography and terrain of biblical lands. He includes not only maps, but pictures and diagrams illustrating features of the Near Eastern world that affect our understanding of Scripture. (Moody, 1985)

The Zondervan Pictorial Bible Atlas. Edited by E. M. Blailock, this 491-page atlas is one of my favorites, because in the center are maps with overlays to do comparison studies of the changing geography. (Zondervan, 1969)

COMMENTARIES

The Bible Knowledge Commentary. Produced by a number of faculty at Dallas Theological Seminary, this two-volume set gives a sound introduction to the books of the Bible. Based on the NIV translation, it discusses matters such as authorship, recipients, date, theme, and purpose for each book. (Victor, OT, 1985; NT, 1983)

The Expositor's Bible Commentary. This twelve-volume series by Frank Gaebelein offers a fine commentary on the biblical passages. If you have access to a theological library, consult this resource as a guide to your interpretive studies. (Zondervan, 1976)

Galatians: The Charter of Christian Liberty. This is the only commentary on a single book of the Bible that I want to mention. Written by Merrill Tenney, this work is particularly instructive because it approaches Galatians using ten different methods of Bible study. If you want to learn from one of the masters, study the book of Galatians using this commentary as a guide. (Eerdmans, 1978)

The Interpreter's One-Volume Commentary on the Bible. This is a handy tool to have because editor Charles Laymon has packaged the articles into a single volume. (Abingdon, 1971)

OTHER RESOURCES

Biblical Archaeology Review. Published every other month by the nonprofit Biblical Archaeology Society, this periodical reports on archaeological findings and research that affect biblical studies. The articles are written at a level that anyone can understand. Back issues are especially helpful for researching subjects you are studying in Scripture. (Biblical Archaeology Society, 3000 Connecticut Ave., NW, Suite 300, Washington, D.C. 20008)

The Great Ages of Man Series. Time-Life Books has put together a series on the great civilizations in history, including *Ancient Egypt, Classical Greece,* and *Imperial Rome.* Although the editors take a thoroughly secular approach to their subjects, the material is presented extremely well and offers a general background to some of the cultural and historical aspects of the biblical account. The pictures are especially helpful.

The National Geographic Magazine. Don't forget this popular publication of the National Geographic Society. From time to time it features articles on places and topics related to Near Eastern and biblical studies. The photography alone is worth the price of a subscription. (For information call 1-800-638-4077.)

"The Topical Memory System." Produced by the Navigators, this set of flash cards will help you memorize portions of Scripture. It's a handy tool to carry with you and gives instruction on how to memorize. (The Navigators, P. O. Box 6000, Colorado Springs, Colorado 80934)

Walk Thru the Bible's "Keyword Learning System." A set of flash cards to help you memorize the names of the books of the Bible. Each card has the name of the book, a memory device called a "keyword," and a brief overview of the book's contents. (Walk Thru the Bible Ministries, Inc., P.O. Box 80587, Atlanta, Georgia 30366)

Moody Press, a ministry of the Moody Bible Institute,
is designed for education, evangelization, and edification.
If we may assist you in knowing more about Christ
and the Christian life, please write us without obligation:
Moody Press, c/o MLM, Chicago, Illinois 60610.

Let Howard Hendricks show you how to study the Bible on video

Now that you've read the book, why not further improve your Bible study skills through the

Living by the Book Video Series!

A master teacher, Dr. Hendricks presents his popular, practical method with creativity and humor in twenty fast-paced videos. A companion workbook guides you through each session to increase participation and help you apply his principles. Optional assignments allow you to tailor the material to your level of ability, whether beginner or experienced Bible student.

These twenty-five-minute videos are ideal for group study and discussion, such as Sunday school and Bible classes. A lesson-by-lesson leader's guide enables anyone to present Dr. Hendricks's material effectively.

> *The teaching of Howard Hendricks on how to study the Bible is beyond great! How do I know? During my days in seminary, I drank in each word as I absorbed every session he taught, which changed my life! Not a week passes without my using some technique or principle that I learned from this gifted man.*
>
> *Chuck Swindoll*

For more information on how you, your church, your school, or your Bible study can add this video series to your library, contact:

Video Ministries, Inc.
P.O. Box 280179
Dallas, TX 75228
1-800-825-8212
214-279-8200